KNOWING THAT WE DO THY WILL

KNOWING THAT WE DO THY WILL

By

D.B.Reed

First edition print

First published December 2012

First published in Great Britain in 2012 by the author's son James Reed using Lulu.com.

Additional help from Gina Gould to compile the index.

Read more about this book and the author at :

www.douglasreed.info

Revised first edition print – 001.2

ISBN 978-1-291-23955-3

To Dad,

it may have taken a while, but I happily present the first edition print of your book, published at last,

Merry Christmas and Happy New Year,

Love from James

The author's father Robert James Reed, on right, with an unknown friend, somewhere in the area of the Somme battle-front, Northern France during the period between August 1916 to December 1918, serving with the 18th Battalion of the Middlesex Regiment.

Acknowledgements

The author would like to thank the following special people for their unstinting support to him during the long years whilst this book was being researched and written:-

My wonderful wife Ellen, who indulged my passion with the Western Front, all 101.25 Miles from Steenstraat to Maricourt.

My son James, who put my draft writings in suitable order for printing.

My brother Raymond and fond neighbour David Nanson, who read my proofs and offered their useful and learned comments.

Finally, of course, I must extend my thanks to the Public Records Office at Kew, the National Army Museum in Chelsea and of course, The Middlesex Regimental Association, without which it would have been impossible to discover my Father's long and active army service in the Great War.

D.B.R.

Armistice Day Prayer

Teach us, good Lord, to serve thee as thou deservest;

To give and not to count the cost

To fight and not to heed the wounds;

To toil and not to seek for rest;

To labour and not to ask for any reward, save that of

Knowing that we do thy will,

Through Jesus Christ our Lord.

Amen.

Knowing That We Do Thy Will

Contents

Knowing That We Do Thy Will

Appendices

Finding The Proverbial Needle

Finding the Proverbial Needle when the Records are Lost :-

G/7458 L/Cpl Robert James Reed, Middx Regt.

1 of 16 in his Section

Note, An Infantry Regiment has a number of Battalions which form parts of an Infantry Brigade. The Middlesex Regt raised 40 Battalions in W.W.1.

1 of 4 Sections,

1 of 4 Platoons

1 of 4 Companies A. B. C. or D.

making 1 Battalion approx: 1000 men.

My Father saw service in 4:- The 5th, 3rd, 2nd & 18th.

The 3rd was part of the 85th I.B., the 2nd part of the 23rd.

4-5 Bns in 1 Brigade, approx: 5000 men.

His Divisions were:- The 28th, 8th, 33th, & 38th.

3 Brd's in 1 Division, approx 15000 men.

serving one Corps:- the Vth, parts of

4 Div's in 1 Corps, approx 60,000 men.

2 Armies:- first the 2nd, 4th. later.

4 Cor's in 1 Army approx 240,000 men.

5 Armies eventually

formed the British Expeditionary Force in France and Belgium approx 1,200,000 Infantry men.

28th.

8th.

33rd.

38th.

Infantry Order of Battle.

My Father's Divisional Signs worn as Arm or Shoulder Flashes.

Chapter 1

It was more than eight years into the last quarter of the twentieth century that I showed a proper interest in the part that my father had taken in The Great War of 1914-1918.

How I have come to regret this omission since then; and when a grateful ally such as France, not known for bestowing accolades on foreigners, awards its Legion of Honour on all surviving British veterans, eighty years on, it emphasises the nature of my neglect.

I had no idea I would discover such an epic story of service and fortitude that he and most of his generation acted out during that awful but necessary conflict. It is really the story of two world wars, shared by a fine generation that did not deserve that fate. The first war was absolutely necessary, the other should not have happened. Many history books, regarding the first, tend to concentrate on masses of infantry soldiers being used as cannon fodder charging blindly to their deaths under the orders of incompetent generals and all this being really to no avail. After my research I do not believe this to be the case. It is very far from the truth and distorts reality.

My father, Robert James Reed, like the majority of the men, who came back home in 1918/1919, were survivors of a horror and ordeal which they would not talk about for a number of reasons. A comparative few would wear their medals and awards on Armistice days. All genuinely remembered their friends and mates that they had had to leave behind in foreign fields. Their graves were truly scattered worldwide, in Southern Europe and Asia Minor, in the deserts and jungles of the Middle East and Africa, in the cold waters of the Atlantic and the seas off Jutland, but mostly in Northern France and Belgium. That was where the war had been won. Where they had really beaten a determined and professional enemy.

This is where my father served for nearly four years and the main reason why he and most of his contemporaries said little of these heroic times was because they felt their country had rapidly moved on and let them down after the fighting had finished. Their efforts had not been rewarded and politicians and historians were soon beginning to doubt the reasons and motives of those years of sheer savagery.

There were very few of "old" and "regular" soldiers who survived and therefore the men being demobilised from the great armies were civilian soldiers being speedily returned to their families and if they were lucky some sort of job. Very little or no back-up was provided. Counselling and after-care had yet to be invented except for a very few. Get them off the pay-roll was a high priority for the politicians. The great and the good received their bounties from a grateful state with honours and gratuities but most of the returning soldiers and sailors were lucky to receive their service back-pay in full. In fact there is still a sizeable fortune remaining in the Nation's coffers, which, if a greater effort had been made to trace the next of kin or heirs of dead and missing service-men, should have been dispersed.

These returning men had been promised a "land fit for heroes" but they were sold very short on that account. The Armistice and eventual Treaty Terms of their great victory were badly administered on their behalf. Reparations and pay-backs by the offending nations were mostly not exacted. The arch conspirator Kaiser Bill went to live quietly in Holland but continued to collect a fine income from his various estates in Germany. The defeat did not change his comfortable lifestyle. A respected historian has since written " It was absurd to expect that Germany and the other Central powers could be made to pay all the costs of the war, though the statesmen, from Lloyd George downwards,(the Prime Minister who had helped draft and had in fact signed the Treaty which imposed this condition amongst others) shrank from explaining how absurd it was". To this, I believe it needs to be mentioned, that the same belligerents were well able to afford and pay for a good second try less than twenty years later.

Probably for the first time in its long history the British nation was presented as being worse off after the supreme efforts of these demobilised service-men and their dead and missing comrades. Up to then the nation had benefitted from its exertions and to the British mind it fought wars for good causes which would not only put the enemy in its place but on the whole improve the status and well being of its own subjects. Losing did not feature in the nation's psyche. Inexorably and for this reason the nation had acquired its great empire and influence under its popular monarchs and progressive parliaments and the benefits were shared down to the men expected to fight the wars. The sharing may not have been very even but these men were educated to a standard where they knew the good reason for their leader's call to arms and, of course, their response had been overwhelming.

Accordingly, there was the picture of my father in khaki retained in one of my mother's many photograph albums. This picture prompted me in the nineteen eighties to find out more. My father had died in early March nineteen fifty two aged sixty two of heart disease and hard work before I had matured enough to ask him personally about his time in the army. He had not talked about it and at this late stage, although hardly a generation on, his family had no real or detailed information regarding the subject. His eldest son born in nineteen eleven could not remember his regiment but had a vague recollection of a German helmet and a couple of shell cases in the old family home. These I believe went missing when my father's first marriage ended and his new wife came onto the scene during the late nineteen twenties. His new family of three sons including myself and two daughters did not ask the questions that I now wanted to ask.

There were talks and jokes of putty medals, two Blighty wounds, the Die Hards, burgoo and the only good Germans being dead ones, but nothing about his time in France or the battles in which he had been involved. The period of the nineteen thirties and forties of my recollections are mainly of the build up to World War Two, a very happy childhood made more exciting after the age of eight by the freedom and independence the war gave to me during late childhood and adolescence. The period culminated in National Service for me and my brothers, and Dad dying whilst his youngest son Raymond was serving in Trieste

My father's death came as a great shock. He was the first to die of his own and my mother's generation. His two siblings and their spouses survived him as did my mother's five brothers and four sisters with their partners. My mother had his body brought home from St. George's Hospital, Hyde Park Corner where he died. He was laid out in his coffin in the best room with the blinds drawn and I remember the many friends, visitors and relations who came to pay their last respects. That custom, particularly for a young person, brings into very clear focus the significance of the passing of a loved one and a proper air of mourning pervades the family home. That my mother brought him home for those last few days before the funeral seemed to me to be appropriate for him. This practice, as with many things, rapidly changed in the post World War II years. Now it is normal for most deceased to repose in a chapel at the undertakers prior to their funeral.

Too many years later I was looking at his picture as a young soldier in uniform asking questions that would have been so easily answered had I addressed them to him in person. Where did you serve? You and your friend look as if you have been sleeping rough. Why did you join up? What was it like? Where and when were you wounded? What did you think of it? Was it worth it?

My research has answered many questions and in doing so has made me realise that the histories and facts, as recorded by professional writers and story-tellers, are not always as accurate as perhaps they should be. By careful attention to contemporary sources still available it is possible to build a very positive history of an individual's involvement during this now poignant time. It also helps to set many of the accepted beliefs and interpretations of the concurrent major events in a more true and proper understanding than is now common in the general public's view. A writer's spin on a particular event has often become the accepted version.

For instance it is not correct to believe that France was the weak link in the Alliance as is generally stated today here in Britain. The French bore the major part of the efforts of the Triple Entente on the Western Front in the Great War. They were more than an equal ally and their contributions should be appreciated and respected as they deserve. Her great armies fought along more than three-quarters of the Western Front with great elan and bravery and it is not without reason that the Peace Treaty was conducted and signed in the French capital. It is also incorrect to state that the United States of America won the Great War, in fact they played a relatively insignificant part in the events of it. Declaring war on Germany was done very reluctantly and when they did, in April, Nineteen Seventeen, they were not ready to participate until the final six months of a total fifty two month war, in Nineteen Eighteen. It is perhaps notable that the Americans were not signatories to the Armistice dictated by the French and British to the defeated Central Powers on the eleventh of November nineteen eighteen which ended the fighting and silenced the guns at eleven o'clock on that fateful day.

The army my father was destined to join was the original B.E.F. British Expeditionary Force which started fighting in late August, Nineteen Fourteen at a place called Mons . This average size Belgium town close to the French border Department of Nord and which is now forever associated with the "Old Contemptibles", the small British Army, so named by the German Kaiser, for having the effrontery to stand up against the overwhelming might of his armies. The Kaiser had put over four million men in arms against the West and at least two full armies heavily equipped with artillery were marching on through Belgium when the first exchanges between these protagonists took place. The B.E.F. at this time, some one hundred and sixty thousand men, was less than half the size of the later one, which was taken off the beaches at Dunkirk in May / June, Nineteen Forty . Over three hundred and thirty thousand men left the continent then, losing all their equipment and leaving Europe to its German masters for nearly five years. The contemptible little army in the late summer and autumn months of Nineteen Fourteen held the line again and again against superior numbers. They retreated and held, retreated and held again, until they and the French were able to push their enemy back and form a secure front, which they intended to keep. Indeed this front was held with minor revisions for nearly four years, first to deny the enemy access to the channel ports of Dunkirk, Calais and Boulogne and extra territory of France and Belgium, then to maintain a status-quo against an attacking enemy intent on destroying opposition and finally to make plans to defeat this powerful opponent.

Many battles were fought, of course, to achieve this result, some offensive and some defensive, but the ultimate objective was to stop German plans to dominate Europe by force of arms and to restore Belgium' integrity which had been violated. The fighting on the Western Front was confined to a comparative narrow strip of territory, mostly of farmland, across the continent from the Belgium coast at Nieuport through Flanders and parts of five French Regions namely Pas de Calais, Picardie, Champagne-Ardennes, Lorraine and Alsace, on the Swiss border. The type of warfare, developed on the Western Front, prevented serious casualties being inflicted on the civilian populations of the countries involved and grave damage being caused to a much wider areas, including large cities, towns and property, which, in future conflicts, did occur.

Such a lot was achieved by that initially small force which consisted of most of our standing army's best regular soldiers. Approximately two hundred and fifty thousand men were serving with the colours at the outbreak of this unexpected war. Eighty thousand of these were in India or Far Eastern stations and would require time to muster nearer to home. Nevertheless in an exercise, which would now be called rapid deployment, within a couple of weeks, just over one hundred and sixty thousand men from all branches of the land services, with their equipment and stores and commanded by an honoured Field Marshal crossed the English channel and were marching at a pace to confront the invading Boche in Belgium. The politicians had not planned the war they had declared on behalf of the nation, but I believe it can be reasonably stated, that the armed forces under a generalship used to protecting outposts of Empire rather than fighting massive continental land battles responded with credit. Field Marshal Sir John French's small army was in a telling action within eighteen days of Britain's declaration of war in that hot and summery August of Nineteen Fourteen.

The country had not fought any campaigns on the land mass of Europe since the Crimean War, and Ententes had been in place for a number of years, between various countries, designed to achieve balances of power and deterrents against aggression. Germany, ruled by their head of state Kaiser Wilhelm the Second, Emperor of Germany and King of Prussia, wanted a major war which he fully expected to win. The so called Central Powers of Germany and the Austro-Hungarian Empire used the assassination of Arch-Duke Ferdinand, the heir to the Austrian Imperial dynasty, at Sarajevo on the Twenty Eighth of June Nineteen Fourteen as the reason and declared war on its two largest neighbours France and Russia on the First of August with the intention of gaining territory from them.

To the west of Germany, their war plan, known from its author's name, the Schleiffen Plan, well scheduled and programmed over ten years earlier, required access to France through the small buffer state of Belgium. Many statesmen of the time believed the pledges of larger countries , including Great Britain and Germany, given to maintain the integrity of that small country would prevent action of this kind by any aggressor. However the Central Powers did not heed their own treaty obligations and consequently the British nation, having to honour their pledge, declared war for the first time in more than a thousand years against the country of their common Saxon ancestors.

Therefore, on the Fourth of August Nineteen Fourteen, like all the young men of his nation my father was at war, and if necessary, was expected to fight. He was aged twenty five, married with two young sons

George and Walter aged three and one respectively. He had married his wife Ellen on new years' day in Nineteen Ten. They had lived in rooms in a working class area of South Wimbledon since their marriage and he worked as a house-painter, journeyman, the trade in which he had followed his father.

Another painter, of similar social status, born two months earlier but in the same year as my father, then living in Munich, was also assessing the prospect of this war and the need to serve his adopted country, Kaiser Wilhelm II's Germany.

My father was a typical Englishman of his class and nation, reasonably educated leaving a state school near his home, having mastered reading, writing and arithmetic by the age of twelve or fourteen and was now working hard as the provider for his family. During his time at school he would have also gained a fair knowledge of history and the make up of the country and its associations around the world. Particularly he had lived through important events, the celebrations of Queen Victoria's diamond jubilee, Her Majesty becoming Empress of India, and her death in Nineteen Hundred and One when he was coming up to twelve. There was a reasonable economy, minimal taxes, stable prices and a greater emphasis of loyalty to the head of state than to the political parties. He had experienced a time when public transport had become available to all, electricity and gas was extensively used for light and power, the motor-car and road haulage systems were gradually taking over from horses, wireless technology was beginning and the Empire and Commonwealth were still expanding. Early aircraft were being designed and flown and great British ships were taking less fortunates from the neighbouring continent and Ireland across the Atlantic. There had been some far-off wars, fought and won by our regular forces, then celebrated, whilst his island home felt secure and well protected by the Royal Navy. Heavy industries provided wealth and the beginning of social welfare, taking the form of old age pensions, first came in Nineteen Hundred and Nine. National insurance was introduced a couple of years later and he may have jibbed when the State started to pay its M.P's at this time. However, for him and most of his kind, the late Victorian, total Edwardian and early years of the respected King George the Fifth's reigns gave a confidence in themselves and their country which was not to survive for very long after they had returned victoriously from the decisive defeat of their country's enemies.

It was given away and lost in a very short time by an inept government and the politicians from which it was formed. It is little wonder these veterans did not want to talk about this war, the war that they had been assured during the fighting, by these same leaders, was going to end all wars and leave them with homes fit for heroes.

It is indeed sad and ironic that these blunders and ineptitudes, also "did for" nearly three hundred thousand more Harrys and Jacks, in the Germans' second attempt a brief twenty years after my father took off his khaki for the last time. And today that other painter is most blamed, even before the Generals, rather than the real culprits.

Extract from Siegfried Sassoon's war poem[*]

"The General"

"He's a cheery old card", grunted Harry to Jack

As they slogged up to Arras with rifle and pack.

But he did for them both by his plan of attack.

---

[*] *Copyright Siegfried Sassoon by kind permission of the Estate of George Sassoon.*

Chapter 2

The war was not going at all well when my father volunteered to join the army on the 15th January 1915. It was on a Friday and he had only Saturday to go to complete his normal work for that week. By an agreement reached earlier with his wife Ellen, they had decided to forego his pay for Saturday, and he called at the army recruiting office established in the town centre in Wimbledon to attest to serve his King and Country for the duration of the war or for three years, whichever was longer.

He and his wife had hoped that the optimists would be proved right and the war would be all over by Christmas 1914.It had been said by the pundits that the war would be finished well before even all those eager patriots, who had flocked to the colours back in the warm summer days of the previous August and September, had had a chance to show "what they were made of"."Before the leaves had fallen" they had said with all confidence. Alas, it was not to be, and for a generation of young married men, including my father, with heavy responsibilities towards their wives, children and homes, five months on, they had to make the heart-rending decision to put all they held good and dear at risk by enlisting to fight a difficult enemy.

In the past Britain had fought its wars with rather small well equipped armies, supplied with effective weapons and well trained. Recruiting, for a great many years, since the press-gangs and similar methods had been abolished, was voluntary and its size was fairly strictly controlled by establishment quotas approved by Parliament. The country's powerful navy kept the peace and protected the global interests of the Empire. Ordinary folk like my father were not expected to join the forces in large numbers during times of crisis and military service by conscription was not a national policy.

There was little or no social welfare available to the main working population and families relied on work for their well-being. Property was owned by landlords which the working classes rented or if the accommodation was tied to the job as in agriculture and some heavy industries this benefit was reflected in a smaller wage. They had very little savings to fall back on, bank or saving accounts were virtually non-existent. Most wages for the working classes were paid and used up on a weekly basis. For those living in the towns and cities the rented rooms, in which they lived, were paid for weekly, in advance, to a landlord. He usually used an agent, who would call at the home on a set day each week, to collect the few shillings rent. This would be about five shillings (perhaps 20p in today's money) approximately a quarter of their weekly income of £1.00 to £1.50. Having paid the rent, it left less than a £1.00 for food, clothing, heating, lighting and all the other items needed to sustain them. These were a self supporting and independent people, expecting to work for what they got, and it was not for money these men were joining the army. The army paid even less.

A trained infantry soldier received less than a shilling a day (5p) on top of his keep and uniform which was significantly lower pay than that offered to a live-in cook advertised in "The Times" on the day my father enlisted

.That position, amongst many others, was for a vacancy in the Copse Hill area of Wimbledon, the employer being willing to pay £24.00 per year plus laundry to the successful applicant. In the same paper a quality hotel in Hastings ,where they were proud to employ no Germans or Austrians, was offering "En pension" for 3.5 guineas or £3.675 per week. Another advert aimed at officers on leave in France would welcome them at the "Carlton Hotel" in Biarritz for 12 French Francs a day inclusive, about 30p.

It is difficult to imagine now, over fifty years into the welfare state, when even beggars on the street, or in squats, collect their regular entitlement from their nearest Benefits Office, that the likely place a destitute widow and her children would have to go, in 1915, was to the workhouse and face the stigma these proud people attached to that place. Even so, with those sorts of risks, these men, supported by their wives, were prepared to go to fight what had developed into a deadly war. One asks the question "why?" and I have come to believe, they did this for a genuine faith and love of their country and way of life. Knowing my father as I did, I cannot accept any other explanation. During the twenty years I knew him he was a very contented man, happy with his family life, hard working and always ready for a laugh or joke and getting a lot of enjoyment out of the modest things that he had. He had no great ambitions or cravings for greater wealth when I knew him and I know of nothing that would have made him any different, back in the days of his first marriage, when he was much younger.

My father, at that time, had a brother, Percy, who had joined the army as a peace time soldier in 1911.He had been serving with the King's Own Yorkshire Light Infantry in Dublin, as a member of the 2nd Battalion when the war had been declared. By early 1915 he had become one of The Kaiser's "Old Contemptibles" as his battalion had been rapidly deployed in the previous August to Belgium and France. He had seen lots of action, at Mons, Le Cateau, on the Aisne and the Flanders area around Ypres, all before the end of November 1914 when the Western Front became an almost static line of trenches stretching across Europe from the North Sea coast of Belgium through France, to the Swiss Border..

No doubt Percy's letters home would have had an influence on his brother that Christmas in 1914 when the rest of the family met for the festivities. There would have been much talk about the war and what the papers both national and local were reporting. The newspapers were the only means of learning about the awesome events now taking place less than one hundred and fifty miles away in Belgium and France. I have been unable to ascertain if Percy had been given any leave during this period but, if he had been, no doubt his experiences would have been related with chilling realism to my father and the rest of his family. The B.E.F. as he knew it, sent out in those heady days of August 1914 under Field Marshal Sir John French, had hardly survived. More than two thirds of the one hundred and sixty thousand men of this army had become casualties by the start of the New Year of 1915. That is something over one hundred thousand men. Percy, or Raleigh as he was sometimes called, had come through it, but my wife and I have seen many of the graves of his comrades along the famous line of retreat from Mons, south-west to Le Cateau and the Aisne, and back again northwards towards Ypres after the

French and British armies had put a stop to the Schleiffen Plan. He would have been able to tell my father from first hand experience, reiterating that earlier almost lone prediction of Lord Kitchener of Khartoum, serving as Secretary of State for War, that the conflict would be long and bloody and would involve the need for great armies. Britain's favourite soldier and a Field Marshal at that, not the so called experts or pundits, was indeed being proved tragically correct.

The lengthy and detailed casualty lists for the previous October- November's heavy fighting around Ypres were being published in the daily newspapers through-out the week when my father chose to join up. Over sixty thousand casualties were suffered by the British in these battles which were subsequently officially named by the Battles Nomenclature Committee approved by the Army Council as Operations in Flanders,(1st Battles of Ypres),Battle of Langemark, Battle of Gheluvelt, Battle of Nonne Bosschen. According to certain records the German army suffered even worse casualties, losing more than a hundred and thirty thousand men in these same battles. In Germany the Battle at Langemark is remembered as "The Massacre of the Innocents at Ypres -(Kindermord von Ypern)". Here rows of untried, but brave young volunteers were mowed down by the awesome rapid rifle fire of the remnants of the British battalions determined to hold their lines. With the French and Belgian losses added to these figures the antagonists were really beginning to bathe in a sea of blood.

In the mid-nineteen eighties, when I started my research, I quickly ascertained that the Ministry of

Defence had custody of all soldiers records from 1914 onwards, if they existed. These records had not been placed into archives to which the public has reasonable access. Unfortunately Lance Corporal Robert James Reed's personal records were destroyed by fire and water during the German Luffwaffe's blitz of London in 1940-41 when parts of the then War Office, Records Section in Walworth S.E.17., were hit by high explosive and incendiary bombs. The loss of these documents, together with nearly three-quarters of the other soldiers' records for the Great War period, has made research of these times extremely difficult as far as my father's individual activities are concerned. It has also taken much longer to do than I had expected, beginning with the several months before the M.O.D. were able to confirm that my father's records had not survived.

I believe that this delay was mainly caused by the military method of filing personal matters concerning an individual soldier under their service number, the folder for which is then filed and stored with others in chronological numerical order. If the person making enquiries did not have the correct service number the search for that soldier's particulars became very difficult under this type of filing system. Of course, as every old soldier will confirm, you never forget the number which is issued to you personally, it stays in your latent memory forever after, always ready to be retrieved and stated parrot fashion. 22182536 springs to my mind as I write this account more than fifty years since I was using it for real but that was my number and unfortunately I did not know my father's. However, since I made that initial enquiry, the Public Records Office at Kew have taken over quite a lot of the available service-men's records and have made public access more easy by providing indexes to available documents in alphabetical surname order rather than by the men's service numbers. Their medal records in this form are particularly useful for research purposes.

The lack of my father's personal records forced me to become a sort of archive detective, having to glean information from many sources and establishments and I hope I acknowledge faithfully all the help and kindnesses I have received over a very long period at the end of my story.

Part of the attestation my father made and signed on Army Form B.2512 Short Service. (For the Duration of the War, with the Colours and in the Army Reserve.) was the oath set out as follows:" I Robert James Reed swear by Almighty God that I will be faithful and bear true Allegiance to His Majesty King George the Fifth, His Heirs, and Successors, and that I will, as in duty bound, honestly and faithfully defend His Majesty, His Heirs, and Successors, in Person, Crown, and Dignity, against all enemies, and will observe and obey all orders of His Majesty, His Heirs, and Successors, and of the Generals and Officers set over me. So help me God." The next four years service was to prove how faithful he and millions of his comrades were to that undertaking, and, after it was over, how unfaithful to their word his and their Government turned out to be.

On the same form would have been recorded my father's chosen regiment i.e. The Middlesex Regiment. Why he made this choice I have been unable to ascertain. It was not his local county regiment, this would have been the East Surrey Regiment or The Queens and his brother, if he had wanted to serve with him, was then with the "Koyli's", the vernacular for the King's Own Yorkshire Light Infantry. I believe there are two possible explanations (i) he had found out that this unit's depot was quite near his home-town of Wimbledon and he would be able to travel back to his family easily when leave became due or (ii) this unit had need of recruits urgently, to make up strengths due to heavy losses in action, and when he volunteered there was no real option.

Whatever the reason may have been, his local newspaper, "The Wimbledon Boro' News", which is still published weekly, the same as in those long gone days, duly recorded the fact. In their issue dated Friday, 23rd January 1915, they published under its "Great War" columns, additional names included in their on-going Wimbledon Roll of Honour of local men who had enlisted in the services to fight in the war. They reported that eight hundred and twenty three men had enlisted to date, and that Mr R.J.Reed had joined as volunteer number seven hundred and eighty five. My father had been amongst another sixty one Wimbledon men who had answered the nation's continuing call to arms that week. A few weeks later, on the 27th March 1915, the same newspaper recorded that a total of six hundred and fifteen Old Boys from my Father's school, Haydons Road Boy's, had enlisted to the cause. Their Roll of Honour was increased with another thirty six names since the previous list was published and included my Father's name telling how he had joined the 5th Middlesex. For the times, what a credit that modest urban district school was to the nation and empire and so indicative of the feelings of the great majority of the King's subjects of this time.

The Middlesex Regiment or to give it its full title Duke of Cambridge's Own (Middlesex Regiment) was usually known by its glorious nick-name "The Die-Hards". It was a front line infantry regiment formed, under this title, from the 57th and 77th of Foot during the army reforms of the eighteen eighties when most of the county regiments were established. The Die-Hards earned their name during the Peninsular Wars against Napoleon at the Battle of Albuhera and, of all their battle honours, this name is scrolled across their regimental badges just below the Prince of Wales feathers and emblem from which the badge is formed. Their Commanding Officer, Colonel Inglis was heard to use the words "Die hard 57th, die hard" as his regiment of "fighting villains" stubbornly held their ground during that rain soaked battle in Spain on the 16th May 1811. Even now Albuhera Day, 16th May, is still remembered every year by today's regimental descendants of "The Die Hards" by a service held in St Paul's Cathedral. The service is held in the Regimental Memorial Chapel there, where their historic colours, decorated with battle honours from "Mysore" and "Seringapatam" through to various Peninsula, Crimean and South African honours, are laid up with the others for forty six battalions who fought in the Great War (over ninety honours won),seven battalions in World War Two (nearly fifty honours won) and last but not least, the seven honours won in Korea when the regiment fought as part of the United Nations army gaining and then protecting the freedom of the South Koreans.

At the out-break of the Great War the Middlesex Regiment had a strength of ten battalions, each made up of approximately one thousand officers and other ranks when at full strength for service in the field. Officers were the men with a King's commission, the remainder being non-commissioned officers (NCO's) or privates (having no other rank). Order and discipline were maintained through a command structure, via the highest to lowest ranks of officer or NCO. In an order of battle infantry units fought as Battalions, which in turn were part of a Brigade generally consisting of four or five infantry battalions, and there were three Brigades to form a Division. A Division with support or divisional troops of artillery, engineers, transport units and supplies, pioneers and medical units would consist of between fifteen and eighteen thousand men. A Corps was made up from four Divisions and an army was established with four Corps, totalling a strength of more than 260,000 men.

Eventually there were five armies in the field in Belgium and France consisting of over 1.25 million infantry soldiers. One of these soldiers was my father, regimental number 7458 Private, later Lance Corporal, Robert James Reed of the Middlesex Regiment, serving in a unit or a number of units at various times. When and where is what I had set out to discover. Like his regimental number, which I had eventually found on a copy of his discharge certificate, sent to him in letter form in November 1938 by "The War Office", I was gradually filling in the blanks of his epic service. To do this in detail it was essential to know which battalion or battalions he joined and when, and then discover where they had spent the war.

The ten battalions which made up the Middlesex Regiment at the start of the war, were in service as follows: there were four regular battalions(1st to 4th), two reserve battalions (5th and 6th) billetted and in training at

Mill Hill Barracks in North London, and the remainder (7th to 10th) were Territorial battalions, part of the British Army's part-time volunteer civilian reserve, who met in depots at Hornsey, Hounslow, Willesden Green and Ravencourt Park, all in the old county of Middlesex. The 1st regular battalion formed the garrison at Woolwich Barracks, the 2nd was part of the Mediterranean garrison in Malta, the 3rd was in India, part of the 8th Lucknow Division and the 4th was stationed at Devonport as part of the Eighth Infantry Brigade of the 3rd Division.

This 4th battalion had embarked for France on the second day of the war on the 5th August 1914 and, as part of II Corps under General Sir Horace Smith-Dorrien, were amongst the first units to see action against the German army on the 21st August. One of their men, a Private J.Parr, holds the unfortunate distinction of being the first man of the B.E.F. to be killed in action on the Western Front. His grave can be seen in one of the earliest war cemeteries, originally given to the Germans by a local landowner during their occupation, for their war dead from these early encounters.

The beautiful cemetery is at St.Symphorien, a couple of kilometres east of Mons, where the British army had its first action against a strong force from Colonel-General Alexander von Kluck's First Army. In this poignant setting, for all the world like an English garden, German and British soldiers, casualties of the first and very last clashes on the Western Front, have their well kept resting places. The very last man to die lies beneath the standard British Headstone made from Portland stone, Private G.E.Ellison who was killed on the 11th November 1918. The Commonwealth War Graves Commission now manage this war cemetery and all the many others, but it is interesting to comment, when the Germans decided to mark this place for their own men, they decided to honour both sides with appropriate memorials. One such memorial, near which "The Die Hards" lie, takes the form of a dignified column of stone erected by their enemies, not long after these first battles, in-scribed there-on to "The Royal Middlesex Regiment". These Germans obviously believed, such a formidable regiment as they had encountered, had to be "Royal". However, like the prophet in his own country the regiment was not so honoured, although the monument remains for all to see, to this day.

It was to this regiment my father went on that Friday afternoon, travelling less than fifteen miles due north across London, to their barracks at Mill Hill where the 5th Battalion were training new recruits to become infantry-men.

The basic infantry training programme has not changed significantly over the years. For the new recruit the twelve weeks to passing out day, viewed from induction into the military, feels like an aeon away. Generally one is introduced very early to a number of aspects which now apply to one's every day (and night's) experience, not previously encountered as a civilian. Routine, discipline and training take on new meanings. One could say one learns to sleep by numbers, dress by numbers, eat by numbers, parade, march, run and get fit by numbers, load and shoot guns by numbers and even keep smart and tidy by numbers--often at all times!!!

This fairly tough training and discipline is frequently loathed at the time but never forgotten, ask any old soldier to carry out a present arms (general salute), even if using a broom stick, he will be able to slap out the seven distinct drill movements from the "at ease" position to "present arms" without having to think. He would most likely get the timing and smartness right as well. My father's training would have followed this strict but usually fair pattern and when he went on leave for a few days after his passing out, he would have carried his swagger stick with a certain pride no doubt.

At home his wife and family would have been so pleased to see him, to make the most of the precious time before what they all knew was fast approaching, when he would be sent off for what he had been trained to do.

My father landed in France and was in the front line trenches in a field in Belgium, at the tip of the most easterly salient of the whole of the Western Front exactly fifteen weeks and a day after he volunteered. He had picked up the torch and did not intend to break the faith of John McCrae's elegy.

Extract from "In Flanders Fields"

From failing hands we throw

The torch; be yours to hold it high.

If ye break faith with us who die

We shall not sleep, though poppies grow

In Flanders fields.

Chapter 3

That field in Belgium was growing a crop of cabbage and sweet-corn when my wife, my two young sons and I located it just over seventy three years after my father was there. All those years had not made much difference to the flat and not too scenic landscape. Agriculture and light industry still dominate, as it did previously, this part of Flanders, just east of the city known either as Ypern, Ieper, Ypres or Wipers. I believe there may have been more than twenty five ways used to spell its name over its long history going back beyond the year 1000, but I shall use the last two versions I have mentioned, to be like the ones used by the British in the Great War. The rich soil of the area is extensively cultivated and there is a rather large population living in the city and in the many small towns, villages and farms scattered amongst the fields and plots of the area, all of which are linked by numerous small roads and tracks. These places have unfortunately acquired sanguinary names like, Passchendaele, Zonnebecke, Broodseinde, St Julien, Gravenstafel, la Belle Alliance Farm, Berlin and Turco Farm and now the whole area has far too many cemeteries and memorials for brave young men.

Only the low railway embankment, which ran along one side of the particular field I wanted to visit, enabled me to pin-point its precise location. The light railway tracks had been removed, but the raised embankments of the line that used to run from Ypres eastwards to Roulers remained, where it had been required to keep the tracks level or to a very easy gradient. For reasons unknown to me, the embankments, over their considerable lengths, remained uncultivated and not made level with the adjoining land on either side of them. Of course, this significant feature, in a fairly flat landscape, was a great help to me in finding the actual field which had contained the trenches indicated on the sketch maps I had located in the War Diaries for the period when my father was there. These sketch maps also showed the railway line and various roads and tracks to the nearby towns and villages relative to the trenches. It was to these trenches that my father had been sent after he had finished his military training in the late spring of nineteen fifteen.

However, the visit by two later generations of the Reed family to that field could not have been more different than when my father found it. Dad shared part of the field with his enemy who were using every endeavour to blast him and his comrades in arms out of it. The front line trenches of the opposing armies ran parallel in the field less than thirty meters apart! Behind the British front line fire trench, which faced east towards the enemy, were other trenches running back to link or support or communicate with another, second, defensive line of trenches and dug-outs about seventy five meters behind the front one. One of these communication trenches had been dug close to and parallel with the embankment using the extra height for slightly more protection from the rifle, machine-gun and artillery shelling that the Germans were constantly using against the British dug in there. The British at this place comprised the 3rd Battalion Middlesex Regiment to which my father had been posted. His new Battalion was occupying and vigorously defending a short length of the front, not much more than a hundred meters, when he joined them on that Sunday of the 2nd May 1915. He had no time for a church parade on that day.

A major battle was in progress. It had been going on for ten days and nights when my Father arrived, and history records it as the battle in which the Germans had started to use poisonous chlorine gas for the first time in warfare. Their offensive had started in the late afternoon of the 22nd April. For a few days the line around the bulge of the Ypres salient looked as if it would collapse and the enemy would roll up this part of the front and go on to capture the channel ports of Dunkirk, Calais and Boulogne. Capturing these ports was an important feature of the strategy of General Duke Albrecht of Wurttemberg, Commander of the German Fourth Army. It would not only cut off essential supply and communication routes from England, it would turn the whole left flank of the Triple Ententes' Western Front defences to the Swiss frontier near Basel. At the Swiss end, for about fifty miles, the trenches were actually dug in German soil where the French army had encroached and occupied about three hundred square miles of Germany between the frontier at Basel northward towards Colmar. This land in Alsace-Lorraine however, had been French until Bismarck had made it German by the treaty signed and agreed after the Franco-Prussian war of 1870/71. The remainder of this line of trenches over four hundred and fifty miles long dividing rivers and streams, roads and tracks, villages and hills, but mostly through farmland had been dug in captured and occupied territory of Belgium and France. In Belgium the line was about thirty miles long, with less than three per-cent of that country still free and sovereign, whilst in France there was about three hundred and eighty miles of front with over 6,600 square miles of La Belle France occupied by the Boche, which is about three per-cent of the French landmass.

If this attack was successful it could re-instate the German High Command's Schleiffen Plan. This plan, which had failed earlier during the previous August and September, was to drive several massive armies through Belgium and Northern France and to turn south and westward to encircle the French capital of Paris. This war winning manoeuvre had failed because their armies had turned too soon and were checked on the River Marne to the east of Paris. The German armies were then out-flanked and made to retreat by a series of fine French moves, using their superior forces, that were quickly put in place under the orders of their Commander in Chief General Joseph J.C. Joffre later to become a Marshal of France. The German commander Colonel-General Count Helmuth von Moltke was dismissed by the Kaiser for this debacle and never recovered from this history changing mistake. It was, despite all their other attempts, the closest the German nation ever came to permanently and fully conquering and controlling the continent of Europe by force of arms and subsequently exercising that power into an indefinite future. Great Britain, even had her Navy managed to keep her free, which was most likely, did not have the clout to mount an invasion of mainland Europe against the consolidated and superior land forces of the Kaiser. He, for the German people, had a positive plan for the long term political future of mainland Europe, which would have been difficult to alter. This could have been the Thousand Year Reich, the Austrian Corporal, less than twenty years later, felt his people should have, nearly achieved and perhaps would have, had he kept to fascism and well away from racism and anti-Semitism, which caused his undoing.

At the time my father arrived, as a member of a draft of one officer and thirty men, specifically mentioned in the Battalion's war diary for the 2nd May, this part of the British line was still holding out despite enormous pressures and casualties. Less than a half mile to the left of their position, the German XXVI Reserve Corps, under General von Hugel, had broken through and taken by force over a third of the salient to the north east of Ypres since the battle had started. Their use of poison gas had, at first, caused panic in the French ranks defending the northern sector. Hastily, primitive types of gas masks were devised and a new line stretching back to the Yser Canal, near Ypres, a distance a little less than seven miles, had been formed after a series of violent battles. For the moment, this line was being tenuously maintained by several battle weary Divisions of British, Canadian, French and Belgium troops. To the right of the 3rd Middlesex, bearing in mind their position was at the easterly apex of the battle lines when my father joined them, the front had held, maintaining the positions established after the earlier battles, named as 1st Battles of Ypres, which had ended the previous November. There was no tactical advantage to holding this particular field, it just happened to be where the troops and their officers of the opposing sides had decided to stop and glare at each other and dig in as the rest of the western front solidified and the war of movement ended towards the end of 1914.The landscape is without major features, nearly flat but with a gentle and even slope going up towards the village of Passchendaele perched on the rounded top at less than eighty feet above sea level and less than a mile away. In fact the ground is so flat that, if my father had known the geography of the area and had been able to put his head above the parapets to look around; if the day had been clear and he had looked slightly towards his rear and to the north west, he could have made out the light-house for the port at Dunkirk and the English Channel beyond, a little under 30 miles away. Of course, there was no way he could have been so aware of his location, but his son could, over seventy years later, whilst standing near the Cross of Sacrifice in the near-by cemetery of Tyne Cot, now situated just yards or metres from this other long forgotten field of battle.

Tyne Cot, how succinctly the Geordies of the 50th Northumbrian Division, named their pals' and fellow Tyne-siders' last resting place. They share it with many others who fought and left their dead here during the cruel battles of 1917 commonly known as "Passchendaele". The official title for these battles is Battles of Ypres 1917 (3rd Ypres) and it has seven individual named engagements starting with the Battle of Pilckem and ending with 1st and 2nd Battles of Passchendaele. The whole series of hard-fought engagements started on 31st July and went on continuously until 10th November, and many say it rained every dreadful day of that period. Tyne Cot cemetery is the largest of all British and Commonwealth War Cemeteries worldwide, containing nearly twelve thousand graves. There is also a "roll call" on the rear perimeter wall, built of flint and Portland stone panels, listing 34,888 names of men who went missing in the mud and shell torn horror and whose bodies have never been recovered. Three of the most troublesome German machine-gun posts, constructed of massively thick and shell splintered concrete, that had to be captured during the last phase of the battles, remain as part of the memorials of this awesome but inspiring burial ground. His Majesty King George V suggested that these old German pill-boxes were kept as part of the design whilst on his own pilgrimage to this hallowed place, and hence they remain, as an appropriate royal reminder of what had occurred here. However, this part of my story is ahead of itself, and for now I must go back to May 1915.

"The Die-Hards" and the other units each side of them were doggedly defending their positions. To their immediate left, on the other side of the railway embankment, was a company of the 2nd East Surreys. Next to the East Surrey's stood two full battalions, one the 3rd Royal Fusiliers, the other the 2nd Buffs. The Buffs held the line to Berlin Wood, a small copse so named by the Tommies, where it turned sharply to the west and continued as the tenuously held line mentioned previously. All these men were part of the 85th Brigade, commanded by Brigadier General A.J.Chapman, units of which had manned this part of the front since before the battle started in April. It was at Berlin Wood that the front remained intact, on its left the defending troops had been overrun. To the right of the 85th was the 84th Brigade, next came the 80th whose men were defending Polygon Wood, a place where men and horses used to rest and relax under its shading trees, but now of more ill repute as those fine trees were torn and splintered by much artillery fire. All these units, parts of the 28th and 27th Divisions, were in difficulties. Due to the failure on their left, their positions could now be attacked from three sides at very short range by the 51st, 53rd and 54th Reserve Divisions of the German XXVI and XXVII

Reserve Corps who had been ordered to advance towards Ypres in unison with the forces on their right.

The freshly trained infantry-man 7458 Private R.J.Reed had had quite a journey to this daunting corner of hell. Leaving his beloved family on Wimbledon Station had been bad enough. He and his wife would not have known much about his likely destination, except that it was likely to be France. The farthest the pair had ever been away from Wimbledon was to Brighton and Margate on enjoyable but rare day trips to the sea-side during the summer Bank Holidays. The young couple would not have known when or where they would see each other again. He would not have been told the prospect of future leave. They both thought his embarkation leave had gone too quickly as they walked from their rooms in South Wimbledon to Merton High Street, then caught the fairly new electric powered tram which ran along this road to the railway station, about a mile away. He would have been loaded down with his full field service kit, his complete soldierly belongings, weighing over sixty pounds, whilst she looked after their three year old son. Their younger child had been left with his Grandparents. Dad's Short Magazine Lee-Enfield rifle (SMLE) included in that kit gave a vivid recognition of the business in which he was shortly going to be engaged.

As all men tell their wives when going off to war, he would have told her that she had no need to worry about him and that he would let her know as soon as he could that he was O.K. His wife Ellen would have felt that apprehension, tenseness and anxiety for her dear and loving husband, only known so vividly to women in these circumstances, when their men leave. All three shared a final hug and kiss as he suggested he could be back before they had missed him, especially now "he" was off to put matters right.

He would have kept the dark side of his thoughts from his wife, but he would have known that it was possible for a soldier to be saying his goodbyes to loved ones on a railway station anywhere in the United Kingdom and less than twelve hours later to be in the thick of battle. It followed, that it was also possible for the same soldier to be hit immediately in that battle and begin the same short journey back, depending on the seriousness of the injuries or wounds he had sustained. A similar situation, but not quite the same, involved aircrew during World War Two. These men had to make their dreadful journeys into enemy territory far more frequently during the course of their particular tour of operations and come back whether wounded or not, if their bomber could still fly, knowing that if they were still fit, they would probably have to do a similar journey a few nights later.

All too soon, and whilst they were still embracing, the light steam train would have come into the railway station to take my father to his rendezvous with the rest of his draft. He had been ordered to go to Victoria Station in Central London on Friday evening on the last day of April 1915. The R.T.O. (Railway Transport Officer),to whom he had been told to report, had the task of mustering and instructing various men for the numerous large and small drafts of soldiers assembling on this busiest of London main line termini. My father like most soldiers off to war, although from different walks of life and ranks, would be now having different feelings than when he was saying goodbye to his family. Apprehension and anxiety for the journey and the future would be his concern. What is it going to be like and can I do it? The constant hub-bub and noise and comings and goings on the busy station adds to his angst and he is glad to find the R.T.O. and begin taking orders again. Your group is to catch the train on platform X he is told, and whilst the sorry looking casualties being taken from the train on the adjacent platform, does not improve his confidence, he is glad to be with his pals again. Of average height, slim, trim and very fit after his training he was typical of his race and although a degree fearful and tense ready to be put to the test.

The crowded troop train he and his group had been directed to join was soon steaming out of Victoria Station on its journey to Folkestone to become another of the many connections feeding troop-ships berthed in the harbour. Efficient troop moments has long been a feature of the British Forces and they still are. Only the means of travelling have varied. From the seeming chaos of individuals, groups, and battalions of men milling around and arriving at the station or muster point, over a period of time there comes a gradual and positive sorting out which began by a series of orders issued, usually, at the General Staff level of the army command structure and gradually filtering down, ultimately, to an order to an individual soldier. To fill a troop-train and then a troop-ship would require literally hundreds of written orders to achieve the proper co-ordination of the event, and of course, the secret of all this is efficient Staff work. Similar efforts are then needed to get the men with all their necessary equipment and supplies to their ultimate destination, which, in my Father's case, was the battle front.

The sea voyage across the English Channel at night would have had its worries whether Dad had been ordered for guard duty or not. German "E" and "U" boats had managed to sink a number of troop transports on this busy sea route despite Royal Navy protection. It was a dangerous crossing. If he had been ordered a duty as deck look-out he would have classed it as fairly "cushy" bearing in mind, if there was a possibility of being sunk, that the deck is not a bad place to be. But, knowing my father, he would have much preferred playing crown and anchor with his pals, even if there was not much space in the troops' quarters below decks. One thing is certain, there would not have been much time for rest and very quickly his first sea voyage would have been over. The darkened vessel would have nudged along the quayside at Boulogne for a quick dis-embarkation of the men and supplies on board. No custom or passport formalities for these men, fully loaded with their arms and kit. They would have filed down the gang-planks, been ordered to line up in their appropriate groups and marched to the awaiting train and away to make space for the next batch in this constant turn round of soldiers and supplies being fed into the battle areas. The homeward or return journeys would have been pain-filled ones for most of the wounded or "can't get back quick enough ones" for those lucky to have "clicked" for a spot of Blighty leave. Three other French ports were kept very busy day and night to service the British effort at the front, Calais with Boulogne, with their short sea crossings from England, being used for most of the needs for the northern areas near to Ypres in Belgium and Armentieres and Loos in France. Dieppe and

Le Havre served the main needs of the sectors at Arras and the Somme, although the sea crossing from Southampton was much longer. All these ports had good railway connections and facilities to the hinterland, the roads being used in those days mainly for local horse transport, pedestrians and the occasional motorised truck or automobile.

Today, French railways, particularly the SNCF and Eurostar trains, give services of excellent comfort, high speed and keep to good time. The local trains are modern, comfortable and efficient. Except for a couple of specialist routes and certain privileged passengers this was not so in 1915. No Wagons-Lit for my Dad and his soldier friends. Every piece of old and dilapidated rolling stock had been called back into service with the French railways, and the stock offered to the British Army were very often goods-wagons rather than passenger coaches for the transportation of troops..Trucks that offered to take between 30 and 40 hommes or 8 chevaux were much used and caused a wry humour amongst the Tommies, especially as they interpreted the comparative value of men to beasts. It is now hard to imagine that our soldiers often shared their transport to the front with horses and mules. Nevertheless, it happened and it is perhaps harder to imagine that more than a quarter of a million of these animals were killed in action whilst serving with our armies. Harder still to justify, less than thirty years on, that these and similar wagons had even more tragic occupants of all ages and sexes as they trundled, locked, across Europe to places with names like Belsen and Dachau. The other painter, the same age as my Father, at this time a Corporal in the 16th Bavarian Reserve Infantry Regiment, and perhaps, mostly responsible for those journeys, had recently won his first Iron Cross on the same front to which my Father's train was heading. So there it was a fair number horses travelling with my father's company on the short journey from the port of Boulogne to the French-Belgium border and then on four to five miles into Belgium to the military rail-head at Poperinghe. Still, not much comfort for these tired men on their first trip abroad. The train having given a bone- shaking ride with the virtually spring-less rolling stock and the fifty odd mile journey taking just less than an interminable five hours including the odd stop for a bite of bully and a drink of char. This would be brewed in a dixie at some remote and unpronounceable station courtesy of the train's quarter-master and his small catering staff and would have been gratefully received. It could and did get worse.

As the men de-trained they could hear the sound of shell-fire. It had been going on all the time as they approached the war zone but now that the rattling of the train had stopped it was very distinct and foreboding. The front was now just over six miles distant at its nearest point in the south-east between the villages of Vierstraat and Wytschaete and the most easterly tip of the Ypres salient was about twelve miles march away. That was where my father and his group of reinforcements were heading. The time was getting late on Saturday evening when the train had pulled into Poperinghe and a hot meal was served to the men after they arrived. It was dished out to them in the open in the town's square, a short distance from the station. The officer in charge of Dad's group told them that they would not be going into billets as they were required to join their new battalion in the trenches as quickly as possible. There was going to be no gradual initiation into the battle area for these travel weary and inexperienced soldiers. They were told that they would be marching the last part of their journey in battle order which they were required to organise after they had eaten. Battle order meant the men would be carrying only essential infantry equipment consisting of most of their webbing kit and contents on a belt with two sets of ammunition pouches, long bayonet, water bottle, trenching tool and case, small haversack and ground sheet. The standard issue SMLE rifle would be carried with a loose sling. Steel helmets were not part of their kit at this time, and the characteristic gas mask case worn on the chest had yet to be designed. Their kit bags and main packs holding their spare sets of clothes, boots and heavy great coats etc would be carried part of the way by a horse drawn wagon allocated by the 3rd Battalion's quarter-master and his assistants who had met the new intake. He and his men would accompany them most of the way until they got to Battalion Headquarters which had been established about three miles behind their front line position. Because it was hoped that most of this dangerous journey would be undertaken at night, in the dark, battalion guides would be on hand advising on the authorised routes these men were required to take. The killing zone they were about to enter had to be carefully controlled. The occupants' guns were loaded and shoot to kill was the order of the day there. Unrecognised or unauthorised movements would bring down heavy fire which could belong to friend or foe alike. This mind focussing state of affairs did not take into account another awesome peril, the round the clock, intermittent and periodic artillery and machine gun fire being directed into the salient's core centre, the unfortunate city of Ypres, through which all British Army traffic had to pass, or skirt around, on its way to the front line it was holding.

The first part of the march, over twelve miles in all, was a little like the many these men had previously undertaken back in England whilst in training. Lined up in fours, the small group, headed by the officer in charge, would have stepped out accompanied by other units heading in the same direction and initially marched to attention to keep the discipline going. However, the first shock was almost immediate; the streets in Poperinghe were surfaced with cobbles, the infamous pave, and not much liked by the British soldier used to marching on metalled roads or un-surfaced tracks. The uneven pave was very hard and quite slippery to the standard nine studded army boot and foot there-in and caused hardship to men during prolonged marches. Foot inspections, during these long marches, were just one of the onerous regular duties of a young subaltern on active service with the King's infantry at this time. The remedy, to avoid problems, was good fitting boots and feet clad in snug clean woollen socks and where-ever possible reasonable breaks along the march route. These essential rules were very important to an army whose principal method of mobility was by the march, particularly in the war zones.

Poperinghe, the town through which they were marching, was the last town before the places and landscape began to become badly affected by the conflict to its East. It was soon to become known affectionately as "Pop" to the many thousands of British veterans who fought in the salient, a place where nice and normal things began to happen again after a stint with the unspeakable horrors "up the line", the then army-speak for the trenches. Despite the occasional shell or bomb that landed on the town over a period of near to four years, it kept an air of friendliness and normality, if one ignored the regiments of men and their arms and equipment that literally filled the whole town and its surroundings. As a principle forward base it also had the atmosphere of a garrison town and despite its nearness to the front provided cafes and lodgings and recreational activities for men and officers alike. Troops' billets provided by the civilian population that had stayed on were much appreciated by the soldiers, when they were lucky enough to get allocated to them, during their periods out of the line and not in reserve, waiting to be called back into the trenches. When the town billets were not available, the men were allocated accommodation either in out-lying villages near the town, or they would have to occupy hutted or tented areas set up as rest camps. Of course these places were run much more as military establishments and the men much preferred the homeliness of a civvy billet.

That respected, though now less known, worldwide organisation, Toc H, still had several months to go before its inception on Gassthuistraat, Poperinghe, when my father first passed through the town and its founder the Reverend P.B.Clayton, C.H.,M.C. had not yet got his well deserved honour. However my family and I, when we first went to the town, visited the house where, "Tubby", as his friends knew him, had founded the unique "everyman club" late in 1915, and where a scroll over the door stated "All Rank Abandon Ye Who Enter Here". I believe this establishment epitomised what many of higher rank attempted to create for the fighting men, which was in such direct contrast to the harshness of life generally on the Western Front. Here men could come and relax, write a letter home, have a cup of tea, even make it for oneself and share a man's company without having to think about the priority of rank. Clayton's stories of this place are legend and I particularly like the one which tells about him having a conversation with a young subaltern undergraduate from St.John's interrupted by a rather scruffy middle aged Royal Field Artillery driver. Asking the man what he wanted, he replied, saying that he wondered if the library contained something less elementary on Palaeolithic man than he had been able to find. "Tubby"'s astonishment went off the scale even more when his friend from St.John's asked the older man "Excuse me ,Sir, didn't I used to come to your lectures at ???? College?" and the driver replied "Possibly, and mules are still my speciality".

This house is only one of many positive aids that the Generals helped to initiate, but for which they have since received little credit from those writers out to blame them for the agonies of the Western Front. Clearly the Commanders had to fight the war that had been imposed on them by the politicians, and it took nearly three years for them to be provided with the means to end the stalemate and then go for the ultimate victory. In the interim there were many shortages. Shortages of men, of guns and of equipment and there was to be much suffering, ameliorated, I believe by the likes of Talbot House. My wife, another Ellen and I, during our first visit added our prayers to the many that had been offered in the small chapel still in the Upper Room in this unassuming house where the first Toc H lamp was lit and which had so many stories to tell.

Earlier Dad and his small group had crossed the Grand Place or Groot Markt to take the exit road towards Wipers. The town centre would have seemed quite impressive to him and his friends. The well built stone and brick high gabled buildings, surrounding the square, were old but well kept and there were quite a lot of red tabs and brass hats about as they passed the Brigade Headquarters building next to the elegant Gothic Stadhuis at the end of the square. Most of these features were still in place, as I tried to recreate, in my mind, so many years later, my father's first journey into his war. Of the vast dumps of supplies and stores, ammunition areas, horse lines, fodder heaps, hutted and tented camps filled with troops and artillery, there was no evidence, when we passed along the same road out of "Pop" as he did. We were travelling in a comfortable car, as we thought the twelve mile walk or march might be a bit much, and we could not see the flashes of the guns on the 180 degree sweep of the horizon all around and ahead, as he had done. The late evening gloom emphasised the constant flashing and rumble of the guns, and as they marched towards the enemy, the noise got louder.

The straight road lined then with poplar trees, now nearly all removed for road widening, marked out their route ahead and offered a sense of protection to the units of men and horses marching beneath their regularly spaced and stout columns. Two miles out of the town they reached the hamlet of Brandhoek and being still in a relatively safe area with its neighbouring village Vlamertinge on the same straight road less than two miles on, they got their first look at one of the many Casualty Clearing Stations (C.C.S.) that had been established in this part . Sorry looking soldiers, very pale and strained, roughly bandaged, with bloody dressings, the walking wounded, were queuing for treatment at the C.C.S. set up by the Royal Army Medical Corps in and around these two small villages. Stretcher cases lay on the verges of the road patiently waiting their turn. These never ending queues, day and night, returning from the front had to be quickly assessed by the medical teams for their next, if any , phase of treatment. The new men's thoughts are not hard to imagine as they passed by, getting ever nearer to the cause of all this agony.

For us the evidence was gone, except of those who got no further in any direction. Their permanent resting place is that corner of a foreign field set close to one of those C.C.S.. What stories those simple headstones can tell the modern traveller who wants to know and is prepared to find out. Along that road, another but un-named "Voie Sacree" similar to the one between Bar le Duc and Verdun that the French were pleased to honour and give that name, tracks lead off to the graves of the bravest of the brave. One of England's only two men to be awarded the Victoria Cross twice, Captain N.G.Chavasse, V.C.and Bar, M.C., R.A.M.C. lies in Brandhoek New British Cemetery, whilst CSM John Skinner, V.C., D.C.M., K.O.S.B. was buried in Vlamertinge British Cemetery on the 19th March 1918 after being killed on the 17th. The shot that finished this exceptional soldier was the ninth wound he had sustained whilst on active service. He had received his Victoria Cross from the King at Buckingham Palace a short while before and he had returned to the front to be with his men earlier than was strictly necessary. An example perhaps of "the brotherhood of the trenches" encapsulated by the Christian Toc H movement when the fighting was over. The 29th Division paid him the full honours he deserved. The padre of the South Wales Borderers, the Reverend Kenelm Swallow conducted the internment in a teeming rainstorm, in the presence of many men from his own and other regiments and his coffin bearers consisted of six fellow V.C.s from the 29th Division, an event unprecedented before or since.

As one stands and reflects on these events and sees the other headstones, some with names inscribed, unlikely to have been visited by their kin since they were erected, and many un-named, marked as " A Soldier of The Great War Known Unto God", I could not help thinking, in the circumstances of those times how many more deserved the same honour. I concluded, many more than we shall ever know and perhaps that over-sight should be remedied one day. The French awarded the Croix de Guerre to each of their soldiers killed in action, the award being given to their nearest kin. They took the view, rightly I believe, that a soldier giving his life for his country could not be more heroic. Recently on the 80th Anniversary of the Armistice they honoured all surviving British veterans of all ranks with the Legion D' Honneur, another "beau geste".

There is one building still standing as it did when my father passed by, that my family and I were able to share. It is the old hop store, a tall red brick building not far from Vlamertinge that was used in his time as a Field Hospital. The near-by pump, from which the passing troops and horses slaked their thirst, had gone but the atmosphere of that age still lingers. Built close to the road it was to this building that the very first British gas victims were brought.

After their brief stop, Dad's column resumed their march and not very much further on they could make out the beginnings of the city of Ypres. The city was dying, being shelled out of existence by a bombardment from virtually every point of the compass except due east. There was an eerie moonlight as the column approached the city limits, and the men were ordered to proceed through the town in extended single file. The going became horrific for these new soldiers. There were dead men and horses littering the rubble strewn streets, lit into grotesque fantasies, with their broken equipment and limbers, by the orange and red flames licking out from the burning buildings. The sights were bad enough as they filed through two kilometres of savaged streets to the city centre but the smell of war was probably worse. The reeking stench of dead horses and corpses pervaded their route in that hot airless night. It was even worse than the roar of the really heavy shells that felt like express trains passing within yards and with nowhere to go to avoid them.

So it was that not all from the original column of more than a thousand men, that started on the western outskirts, made it, even though the brass considered it was relatively safe to go, via the city-centre route, to the exit at the Menin Gate and into the salient beyond. The alternative was to go the northern scenic route around the city's edge. That route was obviously reserved for the times when Fritz was really cross and was not using his unending supply of shells on other unfortunates and really concentrating on dear old Wipers. Such would my father and his friends have been thinking as war became a reality to them.

As Woodbine Willy, another forces padre, wrote in his poem "The Spirit":--

....

When the world is red and reeking,

And the shrapnel shells are shrieking,

And your blood is slowly leaking,

Carry on.

....

Chapter 4

Much time had elapsed since the war in which my father had fought had ended and my family and I listened to the Last Post Ceremony played under the great arch of the Menin Gate Memorial at Ypres on the 26th August 1988. It has been played in this same place at 8 o'clock every evening since 11th November 1929, except when the city was occupied by the Germans for nearly four and a half years of the Second World War. It was the 16,061st time this moving ceremony had been played out since that emotional Saturday, 6th September 1944, when, the German army having retreated from the city, its faithful and caring citizens, that same evening, reintroduced it. It will take until 27th April 2085 to have been played for each of the 54,896 men listed on this memorial, and who lie in unmarked graves in the nearby battlegrounds. It will take, in our terms, forever, to honour in this way, each individual British, Empire and Commonwealth soldier killed in action in the Great War and yet lies unrecognised in that rich earth.

Dad had not lingered either at this old exit gate or, earlier, at the shell torn and burning ruins of the magnificent Gothic Cloth Hall and St: Martin's Cathedral in the smoke palled Grote Markt, or Grand Place, just opposite from where my wife, two sons and I were now staying. He had had to continue on his march with the draft of reinforcements he was with towards those never silent guns about six or seven miles beyond the city. The mission he was on required his urgent attention, to hold the line as part of the British army and stop this city and what lay beyond it from falling to the same enemy that took it all in the later war. Our forces of 1939/1940 were not strong enough or adequately equipped to withstand the Corporal's armies this time, particularly with their overwhelming armoured forces and air power. There were still many senior officers and old soldier veterans from the lost Kaiser's war, in this ex-regimental runner's almost invincible, although, illegal and treaty breaking forces. They had been made all the more powerful by a younger generation, equally intent on world domination for their substitute and certainly lower class Kaiser. Everyone of these ardent followers had certainly paid no heed to their leader's social background when averring their fealty to him in the true medieval sense. The weak and poorly armed Allied forces could not succeed in the uneven contest and lost the battle their political leaders had managed to inflict upon them for a second time. Once was probably excusable, in the concept of the 1914 period, but for it to happen twice in a generation's lifetime, is beyond justification. The safeguards were there, as I was to discover from the terms and conditions accepted by this enemy during the meetings and conferences of 1918 and 1919 and which had originated from their pleadings to stop the war that they had started. Some of the same politicians who had imposed the terms were still in our Parliament and in power when the benefits of those conditions had been allowed to lapse, decline and dissipate and cause this dreadful state of affairs to take place.

My father and his kind, fortunately for Europe, did stop the enemy taking the city in 1915, although they were outnumbered and outgunned, particularly as far as artillery and its supplies of ammunition were concerned. For these pressing deficiencies, he had no time, like his son had, when he arrived in the city, to rest and freshen up; his date was with an inhospitable trench, under that heavy fire a few miles away.

Three years into my research, which I had started in 1985 by looking at the only photograph the family had of him in uniform, I had discovered where he had been sent to fight after his infantry training with the 5th Battalion Middlesex Regiment at Millhill Barracks in London. Having researched the information from contemporary documents and diaries of the period, I was anxious to see for myself what sort of place it was. In a busy professional and family life, research for me was a slow process, as so many other matters had a lien on my time. Nevertheless in the centennial year of his birth I decided to spend a few days looking at the places along the old front line he had frequented all those years ago.

Unlike Dad, my family and I thought we would approach the infamous salient in daylight. We therefore booked into our hotel in the Grand Place on the opposite side of the square to the restored Cloth Hall and Cathedral early in the afternoon. It had taken us just over the hour to get to Wipers since leaving the Dunkirk ferry terminal and getting round the congested motorways and onto the original smaller roads used before mass car travel. The whole of the city had been reduced to rubble and mud by the time the last and 4th Battle of Ypres was over, but now most of the city had been painstakingly rebuilt as it used to be using the old Flemish plans and photographic records that had somehow survived.

We found our accommodation to be very reasonable except in one important aspect. In Flanders many towns and cities boast of their clock towers and intricate sets of clarion bells. Ypres is no exception and the massive clock tower of the Cloth Hall, which happened to be exactly opposite our bedroom windows, contained a clarion of no less than 49 bells! They struck every quarter with a variety of changes and certainly avoided the possibility of oversleeping. Except that our comforts were better seen to generally, than those provided to the owners of "Genevieve" during their stopover in Brighton in that classic film, our sleeping arrangements were very similar. Intermittent to say the least, but we did have plenty of hot water.

Notwithstanding this, I felt the city had a certain ambience and "je ne sais quoi" that appealed to me . The streets were clean, the shops smart and well stocked, the architecture attractive, the people friendly, the restaurants served good food and wine and, of course, my Dad had been there. The cobbles in the Grand Place had felt his boots as he marched towards the Menin Gate and out of the city towards the edge of the salient on the left of the Broodeseinde-Passchendaele Road.

We planned our evening stroll that night after dinner, to coincide with the short nightly ceremony at eight o'clock at Sir Reginald Blomfield's magnificent archway. This was built in the original opening of the city's ramparts through which the road passed as an exit to Menin and other important towns to the east. The archway had been erected to honour men like my father who held the line and to remember nearly 55,000 of his fellow soldiers, by name, who lie in graves, known only to

God, in the ground mostly to the east of the city where so many actions were fought. The memorial was inaugurated in July 1927 by the General who took over command of the Second Army on the 27th April 1915, briefly to be known as Plumer's Force. It was to this Force that my father had been posted as a member of the 28th Division, arriving as a newly trained infantryman just a few days later. General Plumer, now promoted to Field Marshal and then known as Viscount Herbert Plumer of Messines, was still a much loved and respected soldier. This title he had taken in commemoration of an important British victory of 1917, which had taken place a few miles from this city gate. It is interesting to record that the same place, Messines, from which the Field Marshal took his title, was still being honoured and remembered as late into the 20th century as November 1998. A new and important memorial to both sides of the Irish divide who had fought there in the common cause was inaugurated by our Queen, the Irish President and the King of the Belgians on the 80th anniversary of the Armistice. My wife and I, who were on a later visit to this area which coincided with this event, were allowed to visit the site which overlooks the old battle lines, just before the V.I.P's arrived.

The British imperial lion which now peers out from atop the Menin Arch across the salient was not the one my father saw. As he passed the opening in Vauban's 17th century city defences, he would have seen two smaller stone lions sitting on their haunches, one each side of the opening. These lions were moved for safe keeping during 1915 and are now in Canberra, Australia, given by the citizens of Wipers in recognition of the many sacrifices made by that Commonwealth Country. I am also fairly

53

certain he was probably too anxious at this, his first time filing through the gap, to say to the chap behind him to pass the message on that the last man through should make sure he closed and bolted the Menin gate! It has been said that many a more battle experienced wag had been heard to utter this quip at some raw and gullible mate, who, in truth, did pass the message on!

It only took us a few minutes to walk over those, perhaps, same cobbles of the Grand Place which my father's boots had felt and along the Meninstraat to arrive just before eight o'clock at this special place. The unique tribute had been endowed in the late 1920's by the Surrey County Branches of the British Legion and the six silver bugles provided by the Queen's Royal (West Surrey) Regiment, the first infantry regiment in order of precedence. The endowment arranged that every night at least two buglers from the city's fire department would sound the Last Post at 8 o'clock beneath the Memorial Gate in remembrance of the British, Empire and Commonwealth War Dead. Accordingly, even on that inauspicious Friday evening, we were not alone when the traffic was stopped, a small group had gathered and stood reverently as those evocative strains were played for those distance Tommies. Lawrence Binon's "........at the going down of the sun and in the morning..........." were in my thoughts.

Moving as this was, however, we had not come only to visit cemeteries and remember the fallen. Dad had somehow managed, in Robert Graves words, to survive "all that" and I wanted to walk the fields where he had first been in action and glimpse, if possible, parts of the route he had taken to get there. The War Diaries that I had read often described the way units came to and left the front line trenches during their periods in and out of the line, and in my mind's eye I had a very good idea of the areas I wanted to see from these descriptions and the maps and sketches I had studied and copied. We, that is my family and I, intended to do this on the day following our arrival in Ypres and despite the "bells", we were all up and ready to go reasonably early that Saturday morning.

At breakfast I was provided with an added bonus. Amongst the other guests in the hotel restaurant, there was an English group with obvious similar interests in the old battlefields. Being, I suppose, rather rude, I managed to overhear their conversations and saw the maps that they were referring to regarding their proposed excursions for the day. The large scale and quality of these maps exceeded any I had seen previously. The owner of these maps, when I approached him, was only too pleased to help me and did not hesitate to loan me for the day his map of the area around Zonnebeke which indicated in much greater detail fields, paths and minor roads not shown on my Michelin. He informed me that such maps as his were now quite difficult to find. The burgeoning interest in all matters connected with the old front line had stripped the specialist shops of the earlier dated maps and now they were very hard to come by. He told me that his group had a general interest in the Great War and, during the course of their visits, they would trace and follow every aspect of troops journeys to the various fronts, including ports of embarkation, disembarkation, train and road routes and walks up to the front and back into the rest areas. In this way, one became familiar with the various locations of the General Staff Headquarters, supply dumps, reserve areas, field hospitals, training areas and virtually all the matters it took to fight this war.

I was not quite into this type of activity. My interests revolved around my father and we were staying in Ypres for only a few days to visit the places where he had fought during his first few weeks on the Western Front. Nevertheless, the map so kindly loaned to me would be of great assistance. The map matched my sketches and was similar to the trench map I had inspected at the Imperial War Museum in London of the front line area which had been held by the 28th Division up to the 3rd May 1915. It also showed the Frezenberg area in detail around which my father's battalion had seen so much action between 8th to 13th May 1915. It did not take in the third area I wished to visit which was at Bellewaerde where his battalion had played a significant part in stabilising the front during the final phase of the Second Battle of Ypres between the 21st and 29th May. All these places were within less than four miles of each other and were sited along the old single track railway line that used to run from Ypres to Roulers now called Roeselare. The line, being no longer used, is not shown on modern maps and I was delighted to see that the map I had borrowed indicated the embankments on which the tracks had been built. This would certainly assist in my orientation attempts.

We visited the Saturday market, which is held in the Grand Place, before setting off to try to locate these old battlefields. My sons, James and John, were fascinated by the livestock on offer. Fowls, geese, ducks, rabbits etc had been brought in from the surrounding farms together with all types of diary and vegetable products. There was also a good choice of clothing, sweets, cheeses, cooked meats and chickens on offer. After a good look round we stocked up with a fine looking cooked chicken, some cheese, freshly baked bread and pastries and a decent bottle of wine for a picnic to be taken, in the old jargon, "up the line". The children's soft drinks were already in the cool box.

My father carried his drink in a service issue water bottle fixed to his belt. It probably contained the water he got from the stand pipe by that field hospital in the old hop store near to Vlamertinge just before getting to Wipers. Night had settled as he and his group filed out of the city and their silhouettes stood out from time to time, emphasised by the gun flashes and star shells, to the now classic images much favoured by war artists and photograghers of the time. A 20th Century version of a marble frieze depicting the warriors of ancient Greece or Rome. The darkened way of their twelve mile trek, which had started in Poperinge earlier had still several hours to go. Once outside the city into the open country roads they remained in extended order to march towards the guns in front of them and away from Ypres. In fact the noise and flashes were all around them, and one eye witness account of this actual night recorded that the shape of the salient was now like an acute isosceles triangle which was being attacked all along the two longest sides with Ypres being the short base. The man who wrote this also mentions a cynic in his party expounding, that the only part of a soldier's body moving up the line which was not in any real danger from a direct hit was the centre line traced down his spine.

The new and untried reinforcements passed many reserve units along their route who had been there maybe two or three days. They had come out of the line as survivors of this ongoing battle and were sheltering as best they could in the fields and along the verges until they were needed again. Some were in shallow trenches and pits that they had dug to give some protection from the intermittent shell and long range mortar fire being targeted on all parts of the salient. Some were also using shell holes, any "ole" as Bruce Bairnsfather's Old Bill would have said, to tuck their heads down as the whizz-bangs and moaning minnies kept exploding and spraying out their lethal shards of white hot death. Most popular of all the Great War cartoonists, Bairnsfather was wounded during the battle here whilst serving with the 1st Battalion of the Royal Warwickshire Regiment. This unit was fighting alongside "The Die-Hards" between the 8th and 10th May a week or so after Dad arrived, and during the second time my father was in action. The wounds Bairnsfather received did not keep him away from the Western Front for long, and fortunate for our heritage and the many who appreciated his work at the time, he was sent back as an official cartoonist and his work was given a wide circulation. The drawings he produced became prime examples of how humour and clever caricature can boost morale and give a more realistic although sometimes irreverent view of dreadful situations. Laughter of all sorts, be it cynical, innocent, or funny ha ha, was needed and much used to temper the on-going everyday horrors which had become such menacing spectres for the men and women involved in most aspects of this war

The first village on their way to the edge of the salient was a small place named Potijze, where the 2nd Battalion of The Queen's Own Cameron Highlanders, part of the 81st Brigade, were located, resting and in reserve. They were with dismounted elements of the 5th Cavalry Division, spread out in the surrounding fields and copses astride the road to Zonnebeke. The Divisional Headquarters of the 28th Division had been established in and around a small Chateau on the edge of the village and as my father passed would have been the scene of much activity and comings and goings as the battle was reaching a crisis point. The Chateau was also used for some time as an advanced dressing station but it was eventually all but destroyed by shellfire and never rebuilt. Today three military cemeteries take its place, and it is one of many examples that belies the libel and slander that staff and senior officers did not share, relatively speaking, the same dangers as their troops.

A short distance on from the village, my father's draft would have seen some of the preparations for an effective fall-back line being laid out to consolidate the front should the worse happen and the existing front be overwhelmed or made completely indefensible.

It should be appreciated and understood in the overall concept of this conflict, that the Allies were not fighting to maintain the status quo that had existed since the activities along the Western Front had become a type of siege warfare. They were charged to recover land and property that had been taken by force and remove the violators and restore independence to the lawful owners. Their raison d'etre, therefore, was quite different to their enemy's. The Germans wanted to keep and hold the territory they had conquered and they were prepared to build massive defensive barriers to do so. This was not in the Allied Commanders' remit. They had been ordered by their political masters not to give up any more land, and to defend every last centimetre that was in danger of being taken. They also had to design their tactics primarily to recover lost territory even at this early stage of the war, and so repeated attacks and counterattacks with brave infantry were necessary as the only means available to regain ground. This policy largely accounts for the oft asked question "why so much blood for such vile, stinking and often waterlogged stretches of mud and trench?" These Commanders, also, needed to defend effectively these abominations when under severe pressure and the only effective element they had to do this with were the infantry battalions, lightly armed with rifles and bayonets and nothing much else except a lot of guts and courage. They had limited artillery support which had acquitted themselves with great distinction in a number of actions but as yet did not have the great fire power of the enemy. The only other significant force available to them was the cavalry, but this could be only used effectively in their intended form, if a major breakthrough could first be achieved by the P.B.I.(Poor Bloody Infantry). If the Triple Entente forces were not to withdraw and concede the war to the enemy the previously heavy losses would have to continue. There was no other way, "c'est la vie, c'est la guerre." Great Britain was committed to assist France and Belgium in their efforts to get back their lost territory and until the balance of force and power had swung in their favour, by more time, more production and more civilian effort, the Generals would have to fight the war against an enemy better equipped than they especially as far as machine guns, large calibre guns and mortars and supplies of shells were concerned. The quality of the men of the various armies was probably set equal, numbers were important, in so far that it was vital to quickly fill the slightest gaps, but the war could only be resolved by knocking the enemy out of the way and taking territory from him continuously by being significantly better and more powerful in all aspects of waging war.

It was certainly not anywhere near that state of affairs as my father was going forward and he would have seen the efforts being made to strengthen the older positions from a previous battle that had taken place when the French had been occupying this zone. These defences had become known as the G.H.Q. Line and lay on an axis along this road about midway between Potijze and the next small town or village of Verlorenhoek in the easterly direction he was going. The trenches, dugouts and earth redoubts extended, basically, across the salient from this axis for just under four miles until each end turned back westward to cover the north and south flanks outside Ypres. As well as strengthening the barricades and trenches, the barbed wire entanglements in front of them were being extended and repaired where damaged and, of course, it was necessary when laying out these very hazardous obstacles to allow access for any movements needed by ones own forces for ingress or exit.

An important and much respected General had been sacked a few days earlier for what was going on along this line, just as Dad was enjoying his last two days of leave. This General, Sir Horace Smith-Dorrien, the Commander of the Second Army had been fighting this battle, mainly with V Corps, a force of just over 60,000 men defending a line about 10 miles long.

He had been out in France and Belgium as the Commander of II Corps since the start of the war, just as my father's brother Percy had been, serving in one of this General's infantry battalions. A very distinguished soldier with service dating back nearly forty years, Smith-Dorrien had soldiered in most outposts of the Empire and fought in most of its wars during that time. In 1879, as a subaltern, he had survived against all the odds as one of the only five officers to escape the massacre of a British red coated column, of nearly fifteen hundred men, by Zulu warriors at the Battle of Isandlwana in what is now South Africa. At the start of the Boer War in 1899 he was a Lieutenant-Colonel in charge of a Battalion and ended that war commanding the equivalent of a Division as a Major-General. Those promotions were earned by merit in serious commands.

In France, now one rank higher, a Lieutenant-General and a KCB, his record was second to none. Under his leadership the stronger German field armies had been twice checked and sent reeling back on their heels by the much smaller forces under his command. These events happened first at Mons, where even the German Commanders praised his troop dispositions, and later at Le Cateau, where his tactics successfully gained essential time for the B.E.F.'s other Corps under General Douglas Haig and turned a potentially disorderly rout into a properly controlled and planned withdrawal. The old B.E.F. who had done so much retreating, loved him for this and gained much confidence from these comparative minor successes in a war that was not going all that well. During September and October 1914 when the major engagements were the Battle of the Marne, an important Allied victory, the swift movements north of the opposing armies in the tactical manoeuvres known as the Race to the Sea and finally First Ypres, he showed equal prowess. Considering the limited resources at his disposal, especially at First Ypres, he had contributed much to prevent a major catastrophe. The official history of military operations in France and Belgium after First Ypres sums up the remarkable and awesome achievements of both the men and their commanders, which includes much of the leadership of Smith Dorrien, as (paraphrased by the author) "... only the rifles and bayonets of the remnants of the British Empire's standing army, made up from unwashed, unshaven men, covered in mud and dressed more in rags than uniforms, saved that proud empire from utter ruin."

It is such a pity that so much that is expressed by the mass media today fails to emphasise the credit due to our country's soldiers and their Generals of this far off war and much more should be done to make the modern generation aware and understand what actually happened. An instance, there were units of Pathans, Gurkha, Baluchis, Sikhs and many other groups from the Indian Sub-Continent playing a significant part in these battles for which they are not often acknowledged, and it is fairly certain that their cooking smells of curry wafted in the air, as my father and his group proceeded up the line. He commonly acknowledged their bravery and I never heard him speak disparagingly of them when their efforts came up in conversation mainly during WWII, and so it was that I was well pleased on a more recent visit to the Menin Gate, to see more than one party of Sikhs and Hindus paying their respects to their countrymen and kin named on those honoured stones. It is not often that these people, now a great part of our Commonwealth of

Nations, get a mention in connection with this European war, but they were certainly there, and there early, with more of their brave kind paying the supreme sacrifice than each of the earlier Commonwealth members of which so much is written and retold.

After the impasse of these bloody battles and particularly First Ypres, both sides settled down to spend an uncomfortable and very cold winter punctuated by daily periods of hate, still regularly killing and maiming each other, but restricted by the supply of the means to do so. The British factories were still sorting out production problems with the trade unions and our troops suffered many shortages in their trenches and camps. The Germans and other Central Powers were building up ever larger and more sinister stocks of nasties to hopefully deliver the coup de grace in the spring.

There was one brief and short lived relief from all this, which started on Christmas Eve. An old soldier I was privileged to meet during my research, took part in the 1914 Christmas truce and told me that he sincerely believed that there had been an even chance for peace at this time. A member of my father's regiment, he had heard his enemy singing "Silent night" in their own trenches and seen their candle lit Christmas trees on the parapets. He had also witnessed the first Germans to leave their trenches and walk into no-man's land, along the small British sector, unarmed, calling for our men to join them. He did venture out and vividly recalled to me how he had met a ex-tram conductor who had worked on the London trams until he had been called back to Germany in the previous July to rejoin his regiment. Like all men of military age on the continent he had been

trained during his national service and was subject to
recall by his country when required and ordered to do so.
Another conversation, this over ninety year old veteran
was able to recall with complete clarity, a factor I found
very normal with the old soldiers I had met from this war,
was regarding the common ancestry of the men meeting
in this bizarre fashion. It had stuck in the mind of
Corporal R. Weedon of the 2nd Middlesex down the years
and he recalled to me of one enemy soldier he spoke to,
on that briefly quiet but shell torn and snowy wilderness,
on the eve of both their God's birthday "I am Saxon, you
are Anglo-Saxon, why do we need to kill each other?"

The answer to that question was not theirs to give.
"It was orders". The Generals could not allow this and it
never happened again. Smith-Dorrien and all the other
commanders, when they began to realise that the
incredulous facts of this event were true, issued strict
orders, that conformed with their own, that fraternisation
would not be tolerated. Only the political masters had the
privilege to decide a return to peace. The killing was to go
on and an improvement in the means available had
occurred.

By the end of the pre-Christmas lull, more trained
volunteers had become available. The Territorial Army
had been mobilised by an agreement with their members
to serve abroad and enough essential supplies had been
sent into France and what was left of Belgium to enable
the B.E.F. to form two armies where previously there had
been only one. In fact there were enough men now on the
ration strength to also have a small reserve. Promoted to
full General, Sir Horace Smith-Dorrien became
commander of the Second Army and General Sir Douglas

Haig became responsible for the First Army. Both these men were answerable to the B.E.F.'s G.O.C., Field Marshal Sir John French who kept control of the reserve force. He in turn was answerable to the politicians and they had made it very clear they expected the British armies in the field to act and fit in generally with the strategy of the much larger armies of France.

It was for this reason that General Smith-Dorrien lost his command. His Second Army's V Corps was doing its best to defend what was left of the salient in front of Ypres after the enemy's initial successes with their offensive supported by the surprise use of poison gas. He knew full well the line had to be straightened and shortened to produce a much less pronounced shape from which the enemy was able to bear down his fire on the same defenders from three distinct directions. Contrariwise the French High Command wanted another try to regain the losses using their own reinforcements and Smith-Dorrien was just three days premature in suggesting a controlled withdrawal to a more defendable position. Field-Marshal Sir John French backed the French, ordering his Army Commander to handover the command of V Corps direct to General Plumer effective from 7.50am 28th April 1915, thus removing the former's authority without dismissing him outright.

The French efforts failed, even as the British and Canadian counter attacks had done a few days earlier with such tragic losses. The enemy was too strong, particularly insofar as his artillery and well sited machine gun emplacements were concerned, to enable the infantry to succeed. Just as the British and Empire troops had paid the awful price so too the French left their gallant dead and dying in the same fields without improving the situation. Thus it was that my father and his small group were playing out the very last phases of the attempts to recover the territorial losses caused initially by the chlorine gas attack. He was still going forward just before his new commander would issue the necessary orders to retire. Having passed through the controversial preparations of the new defensive line, which had cost the career of a gallant soldier, the facts of which would have been the topic of a lot of speculation by the men in the salient now known as "Plumer's Force", it was time for Dad's group to have another break and a smoke. The Woodbines would have come out as the men took their rest but there was still no point in trying to get a little sleep. It was here that an extra item of equipment was to be issued and explained to them for the first time.

The young officer in charge was handed a packet by an N.C.O. from the 8th Middlesex Battalion who were in the area of Verlorenhoek with others members of the 85th Brigade, when Dad's draft had stopped. The parcel was marked "Gas Masks Type I" and, when opened, contained oblong patches of flannel and cotton wool with bandage type tapes fixed to both sides. When the items were handed out to each man I have read that the men were not a little sceptical about their use and efficacy. The instructions that came with these very first official gas masks stated that the pads should be placed to cover as much of the mouth and nose as possible and tied tightly behind the head when the greenish yellow vapour of the gas being used was detected. Until a proper gas helmet, which also protected the eyes, became standard issue much later and long after this battle, many soldiers preferred to use a folded face towel, dampened with their own urine which served to palliate the effects of this obscene weapon on the eyes and lungs.

The half hour "rest" was soon over, the last sedative drag inhaled from the pipe or fag and the marching resumed. What a war to be marching towards. Nothing similar in content or scale had occurred before and to the noise of the guns, and crumps of the shells, that kept demanding more and more attention, the deadly sound and pings of small arms fire was becoming distinctive and threatening. Along the Zonnebeke Road their way continued almost due east, until it crossed the single track railway which used to go to Roulers and which two opposing armies had now cut in half a short distance on. At this crossing, the party now down to thirty men, turned off left and the last two miles, again in single file, was tramped along the edge of the railway embankment and into the area of front occupied by what was left of the battalion to which my father had been posted. Even the battalion's Commanding Officer (C.O.), Major G.H.Neale was in the trenches when these thirty men and one officer arrived just as it was getting lighter in the eastern sky. The journey my father had started from his home in those rented rooms in South Wimbledon ended in this unpretentious cabbage plot in Flanders, which had so far cost the 3rd Middlesex, in denying the Germans possession, over 300 casualties from its original strength of just under 900 men when it joined the battle just over a week ago.

The young officer would have reported his own and his draft's arrival to the C.O. who had established himself in the dugouts built along the edge of the road to Gravenstafel and which ran parallel behind the front fire trenches. A series of these dugouts formed his command post from which Major Neale would issue and receive his orders. A field telephone had been installed, connected by land lines to Brigade and Divisional Headquarters. These early forms of mobile telephone communications were much affected by shellfire which cut the wires, no matter how deep in the ground they had been installed, and wireless equipment was not yet available to this type of Command. What would a Field Commander have given for a few of the mobile phones that now are used by all and sundry for everyday business and social purposes as well as emergencies. An instrument weighing a few ounces can now be used to let ones spouse know the 6.15 is running 5 minutes late out of Waterloo, when on the actual train; whilst on the international level, for example, it was simple for a neighbour's daughter to let her parents know, with that now ubiquitous bleep, that their house in Wimbledon had been burgled, just as they were about to enjoy the delights of Italian opera in Florence or Verona. What indeed, would any General have given for such easy links up and down his chains of commands. Their equipment was extremely cumbersome and even worse often unreliable. Therefore, at this time, if the lines were out, orders and instructions had to be conveyed by messenger or runner, in the same way as the first marathon came about, or the news travelled from Aix to Ghent. Not much had changed over the long years between these events and the Great War, although the tip of communication technology was just peeping through. Accordingly, as in all conflicts before and now, there had to be a body of men based at this and every command organisation waiting to deliver messages and orders. These men, like their forebears, spent their precarious lives dashing around the battle fronts and rear locations on foot, bicycle, motor-cycle and even horse, delivering all types of updates and orders. On either side of the battle line this type of organisation was necessary and the enemy's Fuhrer in the second round twenty years on had already won the first of his six awards for bravery doing this dangerous job.

Another five men had been killed and twenty eight wounded in the last two days. The incessant artillery and machine gun fire was whittling down the Battalion's strength. My father and the other twenty nine new men were needed and there was not much time for long introductions. They would have been quickly allocated to one of four companies A.B.C and D into which the battalion was divided. D company was usually allocated to the Battalion H.Q. some of whose men carried out administrative duties under the control of the C.O., and provided amongst many other services, those of Battalion runners. Each company, in ideal circumstances, consisted of about 250 men, commanded by a captain who had at least four subalterns and four sergeants to take charge of the next sub-division of four platoons. Sixty was the ideal number for a platoon which was finally split into four sections at the base of the pyramid structure of an infantry battalion at war. Accordingly an infantry battalion at full strength consisted of sixty four small well controlled units at the cutting edge of battle. Junior N.C.O.s, corporals or lance corporals looked after the sixteen or so men of each section under the command of a sergeant and a subaltern where possible.

Unfortunately I cannot distinguish to which company, platoon or section my father was attached from the diary entries of the time. I suspect he went to the company that had lost some of its men most recently, although the whole battalion was in a pretty sorry state. I do know, however, there was plenty for the new men to do and rest was not yet on the agenda. Fortunately the diary does describe in some detail the events and activities played out during the valiant days of my Father's initial arrival at the front, which in turn has given to me an almost first hand authentic version that I feared I had missed. There are two sets of entries covering the period of my father's real baptism of fire. Getting there was now just a dreadful preliminary. One of the entries is a type of summary by the C.O. and the other a rather matter of fact low key daily record of the period. For the P.B.I. it was a time of very hard work and anxiety. The whole 3rd Battalion, or what was left of it, was in the fire trenches. If you were not on sentry or look-out duty you were repairing the trenches from the damage being constantly inflicted by close range artillery and mortar fire. The front and rear heaps of sandbags or earth each side of the trenches, known to the military as parapets and parados respectively, had to be constantly reformed and strengthened as they were flattened or blasted by enemy fire. This work had to be carried out day and night despite the risks, as the mounds provided essential protection and it was very heavy work keeping them intact. Until 1916 steel helmets were not issued to protect the heads of our soldiers and of course the officers and men knew only too well from the shocking facial and brain injuries how important the parapets and parados were.

In these early days of trench warfare the Allies' lines were not very elaborate and there were token rows of barbed-wire entanglements for a dozen yards or so in front of the parapets, supported on wooden pickets, to deter Fritz from getting too close, particularly at night. Where the wire had become displaced or damaged by shell fire, it was another job to be carried out in darkness, when the "lucky" detail had to crawl over the top into, I suppose, the most exposed position along the front, carrying heavy and spiteful rolls of barbed-wire and pickets to do their task of reinstatement.

I imagine the horror in the minds of my father and his contemporaries as they were first silhouetted by the frequent star shell or Very lights whilst out in no-mans land on these details; knowing full well that the enemy' machine guns they had been hearing all day, were now zero-ed in on the very edge of the trenches just behind them. They would have been ordered or advised by their more experienced mates to remain still and quiet to avoid detection in the bright light, but their instinct to drop to the ground must have been hard to resist until their continuing survival proved the point.

The diary records that many reconnaissance patrols were sent during this period. The Battalion needed to know what the Germans were doing and often a patrol across the wire was the only means to find out this information. It was done at night and, whilst I cannot be sure, I believe the Company Commanders charged with this duty would have used a mix of the experienced and new men to do it. It needed great nerve and care to crawl towards your enemy in silence and undetected. These two or three man patrols would listen for movement and try to assess if more men were being assembled under the cover of darkness for a likely dawn attack. They were often expected to take a prisoner from their opponent's patrols or silently kill any unsuspecting or vulnerable individual they came across.

If Dad missed out on these tasks due to his initial naivety, the records show that he and the whole Battalion were standing to arms for long periods of time, defending their ground with rifles and bayonets or returning fire against the enemy who had even dug a sap across part of their front line positions. In this sap, which bisected the Middlesex's foremost trench, and infiltrated their ground, the Germans had managed to install one of their many machine guns and this was providing harrowing reverse fire across the Battalion's positions. The Battalion diarist gives emphasis to this problem and the fact that mining activity by the enemy was also causing much harassment and concern. The German army in their attack mode were constantly beavering away at tunnels and saps to infiltrate the British lines and there was a continual need to be ready to repel an enemy at close quarters every time he made his move above the ground. My father with all the others would be standing on the fire steps with loaded rifle and fixed bayonet peering through the smoke and noise of the battlefield waiting to kill any German soldier who came within his range or body zone.

The men previously killed, friend or foe alike, still littered the shell scarred ground of no-man's land where they had been hit, hung up on the barbed wire or crumpled on the ground. A dead man's body was usually not worth the risk of recovering when out in the disputed areas. But there were still many men from the Bavarian Regiments of the 6th German Army to take the places of these dead soldiers and to try to occupy that which Private Robert James Reed was charged to defend.

How many attacks my father and his mates fought off is not recorded in detail but a message received from their Brigade's H.Q.(85th) at 7.30 p.m. on 2nd May 1915, give the flavour of what was occurring all the time. "Enemy's attack repulsed up to date with heavy losses-- pinned down by rifle and artillery fire. Buffs report enemy moving south in small parties in square D11A- confidently rely on you to smash up any attacks, but will send up East Surreys if you want more men".

It is one thing to be taught to fire a gun or use a bayonet in training, it is another great leap to do it in earnest against your fellow beings for real. Killing your first man, especially by rifle fire, is a step that is hard to envisage unless it is experienced. It is premeditated, the rifle is a single shot weapon that is aimed and fired, unlike the automatic weapons in the form of various sub- machine guns, which came into use much later and is now the standard weapon for infantry. These automatic arms are generally fired indiscriminately with great sweeping cones of bullets pointed but not aimed at groups of the enemy and designed to send them to ground. The Lewis Light Machine Gun was the first principal automatic for the British Army, but that was still nearly two years away from being in general use. One knows instantly if your aim is true when using a .303 rifle, the man in your sights will fall over before you reload. Reloading is done by drawing back the bolt to discharge the bullet case and then sliding the bolt forward again to push another round into the breach, or in the jargon, "up the spout". This takes all of a half a second or less and you are ready to kill the next man if the man you have just shot stumbles, or you try again if he comes on.

The descriptions in the 3rd Battalion's War Diary convince me and I have no doubt my father added to the daily toll of the Kaiser's men shot, killed, maimed or crippled on his very first day on the Western Front. He was doing what he had been trained to do, it is one of the infantry's main jobs. These unknown enemies appear on some casualty list and this would be the start of the agony many a mother, wife, or sweetheart would suffer as a result of those who fell at his hand during this continuing nightmare.

According to the records the Germans alone suffered 7,142,558 casualties killed, wounded or missing in the course of this war's 1561 days. I calculate that this means nearly 4,600 men in the German forces alone became victims of the conflict as a daily average and a minimum of 1,136 of these men were killed or died of their wounds every day. On this awesome Sunday, 2nd May 1915, I shall never know my father's true contribution to these lists as these details have never been kept and he certainly did not keep a tally. Perhaps it is just as well there are no such records, not many soldiers wanted to know the actual identity of the victims they shot, killed or mutilated; although the attitudes of these men varied relative to their feelings at any particular time. The enemy was always the enemy, but if one had just seen your best mate blown in half, your hate and callousness exceeded the normal by very much. I have heard men tell of instances, when, after German machine gunners, who had been chained to their guns to stop them running away, had been finally overcome they would be trodden face down into the mud and slime regardless as to whether they were still alive, wounded or dead. No quarter was given generally in those types of circumstance.

The real pity is, although my father and his kind did not want the war, they believed by the end of it, they had done enough for it not to happen again; but no, it all re-started with even greater terror for both sides whilst their personal memories were still so vivid. Put in today's terms these casualty figures of German dead alone are the equivalent of having at least three full Jumbo Jets crashing without survivors every day continuously for more than four years. At least ten more full Jumbos would be needed to crash daily to account for the victims from the other states involved, including the British, and the politicians did not think once was enough. If these victims had really been Jumbo passengers, would Boeing have been given the orders to continue building and supplying this Armageddon fleet, after say, the first month, yet alone an additional six years?

The diary stated that it was not considered necessary to mention all the incidents that occurred during these first two days of May as most were known to the senior command already; but another note mentioning a great shortage of water sets the scene for more trauma for those involved.

That dryness and tightening in the throat and mouth suffered by my father, as he first stood to arms in a kill or be killed mode, could not be slaked properly. The canteens of fresh water despatched full by the battalion's Quartermaster from the water point three, four or maybe six miles in the rear, arrived mostly half empty. Elevenses were out, and the men had to go thirsty for long periods during most parts the day.

With a little thought and analysis, it is not hard to work out the cause of this. A full battalion of say 900 men would conservatively need 250 gallons of clean water every day, (two pints per man for drinking, cooking, washing and shaving). Today's water companies are expected to service each individual with at least 30 gallons daily (240 pints) to meet our sophisticated needs, so it can be seen that that ration is not exactly excessive, especially if you are trying to clean a wound. Water weighs 10lbs per gallon, and even this meagre allowance, involves moving more than an imperial ton (2240 lbs) up the line at least once a night to keep just one battalion minimally supplied with this essential commodity. More than 40 men (usually from the resting infantry!) each carrying a 60lb burden of 6 precious gallons would be needed to hump this awkward load, by hand, ducking and diving along the shelled and torturous route if each man in Major G.H.Neale's trenches was to receive an enamelled mug or mess tin of tea may-be twice a day. Not a lot of relief or sustenance for men continually on some sort of heavy or throat tightening activity.

The C.O.'s diary note on the shortage of water due to receiving half empty tins, however, seems to me more a "cri de coeur" for his men than a probable criticism for an impossible supply problem. Such uncaring men these officers. He well knew he needed every possible round of SAA (small arms ammunition), trench tool, tin of bully, iron ration, field dressing and any other store that could survive that difficult journey. Everything needed to fight this prolonged battle had to be manhandled over impossible terrain, night after night for as long as he and his men remained there.

Much the same was happening on a larger scale along the whole war zone. There would be over 50,000 men defending the approximate ten miles of this critical front, and these would need, at a minimum, over fifty tons of fresh water every day. They too would be lucky if they got their full quota all the time. It all depended on the fatigue parties coming and returning every night all along this battle front and it is certain that as many men were carrying supplies as were actually manning the line, another good example of the quality of the staff work needed. It is also well to be aware of the ever loaded tramp back for these parties, with amongst other burdens, the badly wounded, who often had to experience much the same spills and jolts on their stretchers that the water had on the way up but with much more pain.

So the first two days of my father's fighting war merged into a period of continuing Gothic horror; did he and his kind really volunteer for this primitive barbarism? The County Battalions were having to merge as their losses continued. Two companies of East Surreys were sent as reinforcements whilst there was an urgent request from Brigade H.Q. to have back anyone from the Durham Light Infantry that had strayed into "The Die-Hards" zone. These men were not in the same Brigade and were needed elsewhere to hold the ring. Another C.O.'s message to all trenches during this time stated "Warn all to keep good lookout, Germans are attacking "near Fortuin" (a small village on the Battalion's left rear flank). The British were being shot at from all angles and directions. Later he records that the barricade on the actual railway was being heavily bombed and this had to be reinforced by a party of 1 sergeant and 12 men who helped fight off the attackers.

Day merged into sleepless night, followed by another dawn and still the tension did not ease. At 8.00 a.m. the C.O. tried to contact the R.A. (Royal Artillery) but his direct line to them was out. Oh for a mobile phone. The Battalion was being heavily mortared by what turned out to be a weapon sited in a ruined house near the railway embankment only about 50 yards from their own forward barricade. The British guns were too busy to blast this menace according to the 85th Brigade H.Q. people when Major Neale eventually got through to them but at last the better news was given that the impossible line they had been holding for more than a week was going to be shortened. My father and his comrades still had another full day to last out, hampered by much German troop activity and the continuing bombardment. Snipers were also causing casualties and they had to be dealt with by ground patrols sent out across the wire; whilst the replacement supplies arrived too late for distribution before daylight added to their burdens.

Reading my copy of the diary entries as I sat with my family on a grass bank at the side of these small fields (they were still innocuous cabbage patches) there was so little within the scene to recall the events I had ascertained had occurred there. But we were there because my father had taken the trouble to come here. We were enjoying the chicken, the fine wine and cakes out of the back of a luxury car, al freso but in complete comfort, because he had been prepared to fight against impossible odds to provide a proper future. We were out of sight of any memorial or graveyard and the only things to remind any traveller stopping at that spot of its true history was that pile of rusty unexploded shell and bomb cases the farmer had left on the verge on the other side of the

79

Passchendaele Road, just opposite from me and my family. I wondered, had those duds been aimed at my Dad all those years ago, and had they only come to light earlier that morning or the day before when the farmer had been working in the near-by fields. That is another thing about this war that I will be unable to trace; the Belgian army do not leave the continuing iron harvest by the side of the roads for long before they are dealt with and destroyed. There are now no official bodies interested to discover the dates when these rounds were made, who fired them or plot the accurate location from which they came or resurfaced. They do know, however, that it will be well into the 21st century before the last relics expose themselves again; and I am certain I am very grateful, that my dear father must have learnt rather quickly to heed the advice given by **Anon to a New Army Soldier**:-

"I learned to wash in shell holes, and shave myself in tea,

While the fragments of a mirror did balance on my knee.

I learned to dodge the whizz bangs and the flying lumps of lead,

And to keep a foot of earth between the snipers and my head.

I learned...................................

I never told the sergeant just exactly what I thought,

I never did a pack drill, for I never quite got caught.

I never stopped a whizz bang, though I've stopped a lot of mud,

But the one that Fritz sent over with my name on was a dud."

———————————————————

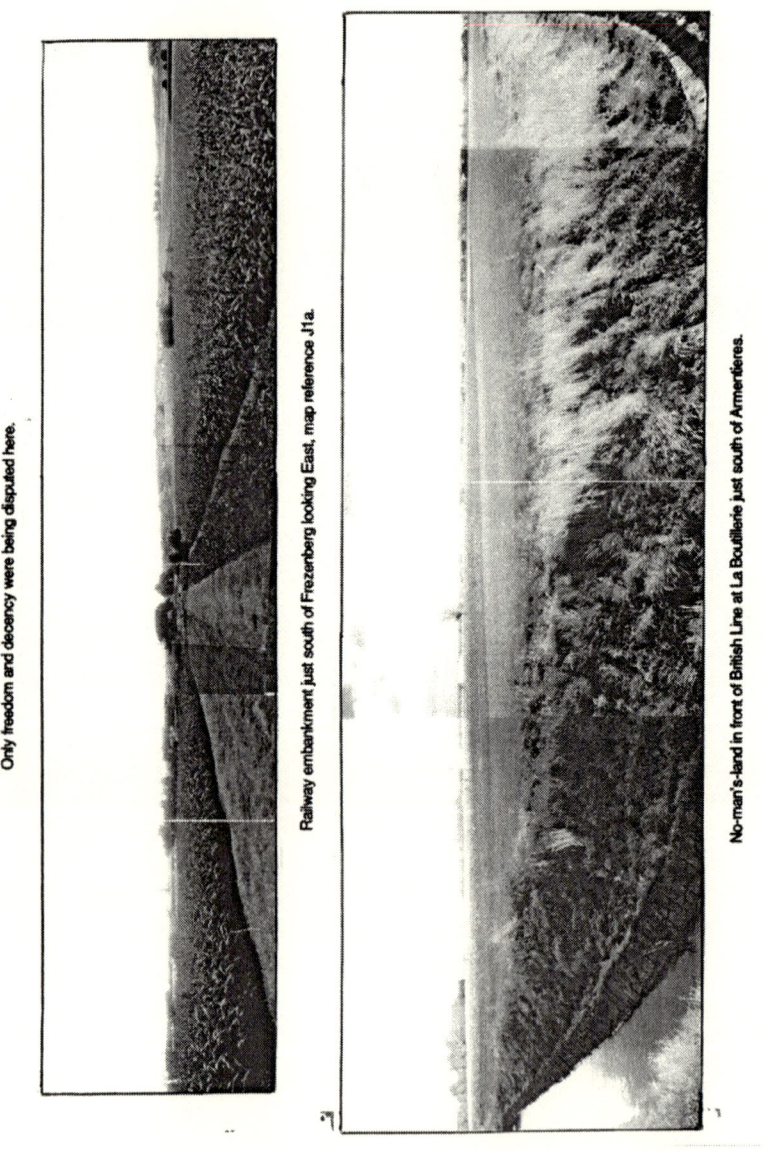

Only freedom and decency were being disputed here.

Railway embankment just south of Frezenberg looking East, map reference J1a.

No-man's-land in front of British Line at La Boutillerie just south of Armentières.

Chapter 5

The orders, received by the defending infantry battalions on the 3rd May 1915, to shorten the line across the Ypres Salient were extremely detailed and precise. They were given to units of V Corps, known since 28th April 1915, just six days ago, as "Plumer's Force". Until the 27th April they had been part of the B.E.F.'s 2nd Army commanded by General Sir Horace Smith-Dorrien; and now they were commanded by General Sir Herbert Plumer; hence the name "Plumer's Force". The B.E.F.'s Commander, Field Marshal Sir John French, had not sacked Smith-Dorrien completely, he had relieved him of command of V Corps whose men were heavily engaged fighting a major battle for the city of Ypres, which is now known as 2nd Ypres. Smith-Dorrien as Army Commander, and Plumer as Commander of his V Corps, before the 28th April, had worked together on the plans for a tactical withdrawal to shorten the line, which they both agreed was necessary. Now the former was about to lose his career through those same plans and the latter was awarded with promotion. Such can be politics in High Command and for men who cannot read the niceties from a political angle, it can be catastrophic. Sir John French was bending to the French Armies Commander's wishes to have another attempt to recover lost ground and re-establish the old positions, and backed by his British political seniors, he dismissed Smith-Dorrien's recommendations for a planned and orderly retirement, out of hand, with much personal criticism and harsh unjustified demerit. In politics somebody has to be blamed, and very often it is not the culprit. The very same orders were issued just six days after Smith-Dorrien had been relieved of his command.

The British military command knew that the salient could not be returned to its original state at that time, the enemy was too strong to be pushed back to their old lines. Even the French army, under General Joseph Joffre, really knew it was impossible to recover this small area of Belgium captured by the Germans, but a further attempt had to be made to satisfy the politics of the matter. When the French army's attempt failed as the other efforts by the British, Indian and Canadian forces had done, the orders were given to shorten the line, even though more than half of the original line was still being doggedly held.

The Generals also knew, of course, that the previous salient, before it had been weaken, was a much better shape to defend than that which was being proposed, but given that their remit was that Ypres should be held at all costs, due to its strategic importance and the likely affect on Belgium morale if it were lost, this new option, in the present circumstances, became their best effort, and a good General's career destroyed because of it. Smith-Dorrien's command of the whole of the 2nd Army ended on the 6th May 1915 and he returned to England, not to hold a significant position thereafter.

My father who had only a couple of nights before passed the new line on his march to the top of the hill would be marching down again quite shortly, because of these orders. A song or nursery rhyme was not written for this event, indeed, until my research, even his family knew nothing of it. It is very probable that his draft, consisting of thirty men and one officer were the last reinforcements to arrive for this phase of the battle. His part of the front had withstood all the German efforts to force them off; the area at the very eastern extreme of the salient had not been taken, but it was now decided that it would be abandoned in favour of a more defensible line a few miles back.

The first battle, in which my father took part and made his contribution, was over by the 4th May. It had taken just over three months for him to get his baptism of fire as a newly trained infantryman from being the unassuming painter tradesman with a nice wife and two young boys leading a very normal and domesticated life in a peaceful suburb of South West London. He had not taken long to provide a vital service to his Nation, King and country and he was destined to provide a lot more during the valiant days and years ahead. The Battle of St. Julien, so named by the Battles Nomenclature Committee as part of 2nd Ypres ended with this tactical retreat, without giving up the land by force of arms. It became the first battle honour on my father's flag of service that I had set out to discover. In addition the end of battle became another good example of how the British Generals were managing to control the course of these complicated struggles rather than let it become some piecemeal, un-coordinated retreat of a disordered army.

The battalion diary for 3rd May sets down verbatim, using three pages to list the eleven conditions ordered by G.H.Q. of how the changes would be achieved. No one, with a modicum of sense could mistake the intentions of the orders or confuse their clarity. In today's jargon they were idiot proof. I have pondered the reason why these written orders had been entered so meticulously in the diary in this way and I believe the following to be the most likely reason. The Battalion C.O. did not want to be accused of coming out of the line without specific orders if matters some-how went awry. If the withdrawal became a debacle, say, by the Germans getting wind of the British Army's intention, then Major G.H. Neale wanted it fully understood that he was following orders. A short while ago, he had been involved in a small ad-hoc retreat for which there was much to pay. Whilst researching the H.Q. Diaries of the 85th Brigade, I had noted some very interesting records of an enquiry that had taken place during the middle of February. It concerned the lost of a single trench by a company of the 3rd Middlesex without them being given any apparent or appropriate orders to retire. This very searching enquiry went up from Battalion H.Q. to Brigade, then to Division, on to Corps and then right up to 2nd Army level before it was finished. It was obvious from these notes that the powers that be took great exception to troops retreating or behaving unilaterally and held the participants in these circumstances to full account. The investigation finally concluded that members of the Battalion had not acted badly but it served to let everyone know, particularly those in command at the front, no matter the rank, be it Colonel, Captain or Sergeant, that withdrawal from defended positions could not be carried out without much authority from very senior staff, and fully co-ordinated by them with all the other units likely to be affected. Discipline and a respect for orders are essential parts of an effective and well run military force and any lack soon reduces such a force to a common rabble. The British army never degenerated to that in this war despite all its traumas and hardships. There were many reasons for this. The two major ones were a respect for the men in charge and the cause for which they were fighting. I believe a number of historians and some media story-tellers should take these facts on board before rewriting real history. These people often purport to know better and present difficult campaigns as awful blunders and badly run events. Blaming the Generals with the benefits of hindsight and the absence and urgency of decision making makes this a fairly easy option. In most wars there are ebbs and flows for the victors as well as the defeated and I do not believe, from the evidence that I have read and seen that the soldiers, lions though they were, were led by donkeys.

My father's Battalion was to be relieved together with the rest of the 85th Brigade into billets prepared west of Ypres and located in areas denoted by specific map references, along the Poperinge to Ypres road. These billets had been allotted to the Quartermaster by a Staff Captain and billetting parties would meet the various units and direct them to their new quarters. The 85th Brigade under Brigadier General A.J. Chapman consisted of five battalions, 3rd and 8th Middlesex, 2nd East Surreys, 3rd Royal Fusiliers (City of London Regiment) and 2nd Buffs (East Kent Regiment). Probably at less than half full strength by now, due to the casualties from the heavy fighting, there was still a need to provide accommodation for over two thousand officers and men who had not slept or eaten properly for the last eight days. Today, this very small part of the overall exercise, would be like accommodating more than two thousand football fans at an away game in Belgium or France. Four or five complete Holiday Inns would be needed and how often do these privileged excursions end in a complete uncontrolled shambles of bad behaviour caused by a comparative few? It did not happen when these troops came out of the line and their accommodation was certainly not to "Holiday Inn" standards.

The new defensive positions Dad had passed on his way up the line were to be manned by the 83th and 84th Brigades taken out of reserve for this purpose. The only gaps in the new line were where existing roads and the railway passed through it. Elsewhere, along the remainder of the front, extensive barbed wire entanglements had been put into place in front of the continuous trench lines and firing positions. It would be along these roads that the gradual withdrawal would occur. The landscape offered no natural defences and the trenches and dug-outs needed to be protected by good barbed wire defences to stop the enemy who would not be long in following the retirement even if they were not on its very heels.

It was because the roads and railway were used that my family and I were able to follow the same route taken by my father on this tactical withdrawal. Although time did not allow us to tackle the whole of his heroic return journey, it enabled me to glimpse at his own and his fellows efforts and partly imagine this on-going drama at the very locations where they had taken place. Only by doing parts of these journeys can one really appreciate perhaps what it is like to trudge long distances (often up to ten miles) fully laden with kit and rifle as well as, for instance, a clutch of trench stores packed in two or three heavy sand bags or even your best friend tied to a stretcher and in agony. The common and flat geography of Flanders and Northern France which I had often passed through before on holiday journeys to the south where it is sunnier and more picturesque, take on a different aspect. For me at these times the land becomes the essence of Hesperides and need of much reverence.

As soon as it became dark enough on that evening of the 3rd May 1915 the wounded remaining in the trenches were evacuated. The orders explicitly required this to happen and they with their escorts were the first to leave. They were not to be left to be taken prisoner, or worse, when the Germans had found out what was happening. The remaining stocks of ammunition and trench stores were divided into loads to be carried by the men as they left. No transport was made available so these soldier's burdens were far from easy, but at least they were not abandoning their equipment to Fritz.

The first groups left their positions at 9 p.m. and were instructed to be quiet and careful. They consisted of half the men from each of the four companies of each battalion. Led by an officer or N.C.O. who had been explained their particular route, each group as it departed spread the Brigade's defensive screen up front ever thinner. Notwithstanding the thirty key men picked from each company who would act as the final rear guards, twenty different groups in all, made up from the Brigade's five battalions, started the complicated manoeuvre from various parts along their front which would go on for several hours during a particularly dark evening and it had begun to rain. Three or four miles to the rear where a subsidiary line had been established, a Staff officer had been posted, with a telephone, to tell off each group as it came in. Dad would have had a short break here had he been with the first group or last. The first group arrived there at 10 p.m. stayed until 10.30 p.m. before moving on, the second group of the other half companies arrived at

11.30p.m. staying until midnight before moving off. At midnight the back stops or rear guards, consisting of the especially picked men from each company under selected officers, the very last to leave, also left their trenches. My father may well have been one of these men, they did not stop at the subsidiary line, but went directly to the new one on the Frezenberg ridge which they reached by 1.45 a.m. on the morning of the 4th May. After reporting to the Staff officers they then proceeded to their allotted billets situated on the western side of Ypres. Another eight or nine miles on top of the four they had already done.

Thanks to some fine planning and great care and discipline from the troops concerned and I would add, a lot of credit to providence, their enemies did not discover or appreciate the significance of all these activities and the complete withdrawal of 3rd Middlesex and probably the whole front was carried out without loss, my father included. The men did not have to carry out the fighting retreat ordered by their Generals should they be discovered whilst on the move and in the open. The congested roads would have been such rich targets for the German artillery until the troops had managed to disperse and, even then, the ground would have offered little protection or assistance in fighting off an attacking enemy. Finally Brigade Headquarters was eventually successfully moved back from their establishment near to the village of Verlorenhoek. They were the last to leave having been ordered to wait until the very last man from the battle front had been counted through and listed on the tallies they were keeping. The records indicate this was finally achieved between 2 and 3 o'clock that morning, the whole complex manoeuvre lasting more than eight anxious hours.

My younger brother Raymond, fed on a diet of incompetent Generals, was surprised when I told him stories like this and that there were many casualties amongst the Generals and higher staff ranks throughout the war. Over 200 serving Generals were killed or wounded, which relative to their total numbers is serious wastage. They certainly shared quite a few of the ordinary soldier's everyday risks. He had been told so often that the Commanders stayed in their fancy quarters well out of harm's way planning battles to use up the men under their command and sending them to their deaths in millions. That is patently wrong, and the troops who served under "Inky Bill" and his like knew better; but I am not sure I convinced Raymond, the myths and broad libels go deep. Major-General E.C. Ingouville-Williams, C.B., D.S.O., to give "Inky Bill" as his soldiers knew him, his proper respect, was one of six senior officers killed on the Somme in 1916. He was aged 54 and lies buried under a standard British headstone in Warloy-Baillon Communal Cemetery between Amiens and Albert, sharing a similar space permanently amongst and alongside all ranks, many of whom must have been under his command.

The Generals, who had commands during this conflict, were some of the most valiant and able soldiers of their time. Many had won awards for gallant acts in battle and compared very favourably with our national heroes from campaigns further back in our long history. Just one instance, Sir William Robertson, eventually to be Chief of the Imperial General Staff (C.I.G.S.), had a Field Marshal's baton in his kit bag on his way up from the ranks in which he had originally served as a private as well as every other rank and his courage did not diminish as he achieved promotion. There are so many more and the list of these full time soldiers who spent a lifetime studying and carrying out their profession is endless. They knew their trade well and accusations against them by less skilled writers and programmers is unfair and often inaccurate. Fighting wars is not easy, winning them requires enormous skill and the record of the British Army and its Commanders for winning its wars is second to none.

Unfortunately this war was not yet in its winning mode when my father marched off his first battlefield and he had only his legs to carry him all those long and uncomfortable miles. A twelve mile footslog, carrying up to a eighty pound burden was his next hurdle before he could settle down to half a night's sleep at the billet in a field just outside Poperinge. He had survived his first real test and I can imagine his thoughts were of home in this hostile and God forsaken place. Did he really leave his beloved family only five days ago? He was much too tired to ponder the question for long and sleep no matter how uncomfortable was a welcome relief.

The battalion diarist records Tuesday 4th May in two words "In billets."; and I have no doubt he was still very tired like the rest of them when reveille was sounded. The army does not sleep in, and when on active service there is often even more to be done. The men were told that first parade after breakfast would be at 9 o'clock and they were expected to tidy up before this time. A wash and shave was essential followed by the first reasonable hot meal Dad and his mates had eaten for several days.

The hot bacon and fresh bread tasted good when there was plenty of hot tea made with condensed milk to go with it. A ration of jam with butter on the bread started to build up the energy and willpower to put one's kit straight before falling in for a roll call to be taken. Being late for this first parade was not an option and whilst the uniforms were not exactly well pressed their turnout was acceptable. There was not an answer to every man's name as it was called, these were the battalion's final bout of casualties before leaving the front but my Dad would have answered "Sir" or "Sergeant" when the company sergeant shouted out "Private Reed", depending whether an officer had been present or not. His company and the others were still very much fighting units although not at full strength and replacement men would be joining them during the next few days to stiffen up their numbers. Brigade H.Q. would want to know the battalion's total strength urgently in order to allocate fresh drafts which were arriving all the time. The men parading were told that the Divisional Commander, Major-General E.S.Bulfin, would inspect the battalion the next day and most of their first day in billets would be used getting prepared of this. It does the morale good to get the attention of their senior commanders and all the veterans I have met have put great store on the thanks they receive when eventually they came out of the line. Great efforts were made to look their best on these parades and although the turnouts would not be quite the standard of the Guards when on duty at Buckingham Palace the men would show the same swagger and style. Besides there were not any metalled surfaces to stamp out the drill movements, only the open grassed fields in which to assemble and parade close to the billets the men were using.

93

Many of the battalions of the old county regiments had their corps of drums to accompany them when they went overseas. These were a source of much pride and provided special esprit to men just out of battle with their familiar and often stirring repertoires whilst on special parades or just relaxing. These were the times when people from all walks, knew and sang popular and favourite songs which covered all the mood swings in a special way. There was not much other music available, except perhaps the odd wind up gramophone and these mostly belonged to officers. A gramophone was quite heavy on top of all the other kit the average soldier had to carry and his normal accommodation space was not very suitable for such an item. I have not been able to confirm whether 3rd Middlesex had their drums with them in France or Belgium but I expect they did. 2nd Middlesex certainly had theirs and they played for the King when he inspected them on one of his many visits to the Western Front.

A winsome veteran from 2nd Battalion recalled to me, nearly eighty years after, how he and his battalion had paraded for King George Vth in similar circumstances to those my Father was expecting on his return from the trenches. He expressed, in his telling, the deep pride he still had regarding the event that had taken place just before the Battle of Neuve Chapelle in March 1915. They, that is his Battalion, had just come out of the trenches having completed their normal stint and they were literally smothered in mud and dirt. Their Colonel benignly informed them he wanted one more effort from them as they were to be inspected by the King the next day and he knew he could rely on them to not let him down. Accordingly, and despite their fatigue, in his words the whole battalion got "stuck in" cleaned themselves up and presented a parade worthy of a King's inspection. In fact the King and his Commander in Chief were so impressed by their turnout that both sent their compliments the next day expressing their pride in the efforts shown by these soldiers. "Soldiers of the King" in the real old fashioned sense; and although now perhaps not so politically correct, I believe the Sovereign, still has a very good edge as far as the forces are concerned, when compared to their feelings for their political representatives.

Dad and all the battalion survivors fit for duty were duly and properly thanked for their efforts by the Divisional Commander on their first full day out of the line. They were also told that the new Army Commander wanted to see them. Obviously, General Sir Herbert Plumer, the recently appointed Commander of the 2nd Army, needed to get to know the calibre and state of the infantry that were the mainstay of his army. He knew there was still a lot more to be done merely to hold the new salient he had planned after the losses on the French flank. Personal contact was good for morale and much deserved by these men. Accordingly, the battalion would be paraded the next day and inspected and addressed by him. My father had not seen so much brass since he had joined the army. Now that he had been in battle he was seeing them every day, or so it seemed. Up to then the C.O. of the battalion was the highest rank he had encountered but he at Half Colonel (Lt-Col) did not even justify the red tabs that identified all staff officer ranks. Now he was parading for Army Commanders and the like and being thanked for his efforts. It was not all bad; or so it seemed for a brief few days.

It was not to last, the luxury of being in billets in safety and removed from a constant threat of violent death or injury, came to an end much sooner than was expected. Not satisfied yet with his territorial gains the Hun wanted more and was continuing the fight to achieve it. The Kaiser's forces were pushing on and my Father's expected respite was reduced to only three days before he was urgently ordered back into action.

Another muster of tired men during the retreat from Mons, comes to my mind. A cavalry officer, who achieved high rank, was much decorated, three times wounded and seven times mentioned in dispatches during his Great War service, rallied flagging troops at St.Quentin, in the very early days of the fighting, with a tin trumpet and toy drum, an event which one of our National poets turned into rousing verse part of which I believe is appropriate here:-

Wake up and take the road again,

Wheedle-deedle-deedle-dee, Come, boys, come!

You that mean to fight it out, wake and take your load again,

Fall in ! Fall in ! Follow the fife and drum!

Extract from
"The Toy Band--A Song of The Great Retreat."

By Sir Henry Newbolt.

Chapter 6

"Fight it out again", 3rd Middlesex certainly did. On the 8th May 1915 the battalion's strength was down to just 289 men when the roll was called early the following morning with the battle still raging. They had gone into the line with just over 600 men. It was even more tragic the day after and these startling figures prompted me to look again at the casualty lists for my Father's name. My research notes had high-lighted the losses as I was carrying out my initial read of the original documents at the Public Records Office. I had recorded then, several years before I started to write this account; "----- interesting extract from 28th Division papers:- Feeding strength of 3rd Middlesex on 9th May 1915---7 Officers, 130 men !!, with those sort of figures it seems very likely Dad was wounded during his first few days at the front."

However my painstaking second search of the available casualty lists, despite much extra care, confirmed that his name was not listed and Dad was therefore still very much in action in this battle.

This look, also, stressed again the powerful shocks and fortitude my Father and his like were to bear from their very first days at the front. At least half of his draft of thirty men who had joined the battalion six days ago were now dead or seriously wounded. This second look put names to some of these men who shared a regimental number close to my Father's. Men with whom he had trained for three months and become friends on the great adventure were gone, wiped out, with numerous others, by the enemy's punishing onslaught with such superior artillery and machine gun fire. To name just one, a young volunteer from the same school and whose home was two streets from where my Dad lived, was now missing without trace. He still is. His name, William Jupp, Private, G/7456, 3rd Battalion, Middlesex Regiment is carved on the great Menin Gate memorial in Ypres in Belgium, Panel 49, his passing noted as 8th May 1915. The young man had gone west, as they would say at the time, in less than a week from arriving at the front. My Father's regimental number, as I have mentioned before in an earlier chapter, was G/7458. What decree of fortune determined that fifteen, of the twenty young soldiers, whose allotted regimental numbers spanned chronologically either side of my Father's, were to be killed in action before the conflict ceased, I make no attempt to assess. It does, however, emphasise the awesome risks men like my Father were prepared to take to serve their country and what they believed to be right.

It took some time to verify these facts regarding my Father, as the information regarding individual named injured or wounded men, except officers, is now virtually unobtainable. Wounded soldiers or O.R's (other ranks) were very seldom mentioned by name in the battle returns and diaries kept by Battalion, Brigade or Division, although these are available in the public archives. These records mainly give the location and activities of the particular units. After making serious enquiry, I have come to the conclusion, there are no official records giving this information in a form that can be used to trace an individual soldier's history of being wounded. I am convinced there were such records. For example, according to a very knowledgeable and esteemed senior officer and military writer, the British Army required all units to report in detail every individual killed, missing or wounded by name, rank and number on a daily basis. Such casualties would have been first reported when the roll was called at least once a day either in the trenches or some other parade and a list compiled. Lists and Status reports such as these and the ones recorded at the Casualty Clearing Stations, where each wounded man was listed, labelled and assessed, are not in the available archives. When linked with the destruction of most of The Great War's soldiers' personal regimental records during the London blitz of 1940/1941, the search for a positive and accurate detail of our Nation's heroes of these gallant years becomes a painstaking and often difficult business.

Fortunately, I have found one source that is available with information regarding casualties, other than those who died. It is "The Times" newspapers of the period but reference to which demands intense care and concentration, as it is so easy to miss the name you are seeking. I will explain the reason for this.

At that time "The Times" newspaper took to publishing the daily casualty lists issued by the military authorities in the various theatres of operations. The activities in France and Belgium caused the longest lists to be issued and the form in which they were published makes it quite difficult to trace any individual soldier now. I do not state this as a form of criticism, as I believe at the time these lists went out they were used to serve quite a different purpose. The lists, headed "Roll of Honour" were published daily for virtually the entire war period and contain the names of several million men. In their present form they are not very helpful for research on individuals, as the names are not in a convenient alphabetical order for easy reference. They are there though, and the back copies of "The Times" are available on micro-film in most public reference libraries.

The daily casualty tolls as issued by the British, Commonwealth and Empire Expeditionary Forces have a Base Date usually at least two weeks before they had been made available to the press. The casualties listed there-in, mostly had been inflicted at least a month earlier. Obviously, for security reasons, these lists had to be quite late and out of time to ensure they could not be of use to the enemy. The lists, especially after major engagements, indicate the almost complete wipe out of particular units. These "Rolls of Honour" as published then take the military form of order or chronology. Officers first, Other Ranks next, the rolls then give headings of the types of casualty, e.g. Killed, Died of Wounds, Accidentally Killed, Missing, Wounded, Prisoner of War, and finally Various Corrections of previous lists. Each one of these headings are further sub-divided before getting to the actual person. Each casualty is listed under his regiment and battalion and the regiments occur in their customary order of precedence. There were over one hundred and twenty regiments active during The Great War, many with five or more battalions in service. To add to the excitement or frustration of finding or not finding a name "The Times" often decided to publish two lists in the same newspaper making it necessary to study the index efficiently before looking at the paper.

At the time this information was published, the relatives knew their men's details. They knew his number, rank and name, they knew his regiment and battalion, and very often the information published was confirmatory. The next of kin had already received the telegram and the publishing of these lists were truly a Roll of Honour and graphic illustration of the enormous cost the Nation was paying each and every day for its own freedom and well-being and helping to secure or restore the same in many other countries.

It was to these lists I referred again before continuing my story. His name was not there for this period. Dad was not a casualty, he had come through what history would call "The Battles of Ypres, 1915", although a lot of his friends and comrades had not. Their names had appeared. They had survived only days in the violence of the German Army's onslaught to try to capture Ypres and ultimately win the war.

Consequently, my father quickly added two more battle honours to his list; "Battle of Frezenberg" May 8th-13th and "Battle of Bellewarde" May 24th-25th; making the total three for his first month on active service. I, subsequently, visited and walked the ground of these actions and followed the points of reference from the battalion's diary and other official histories.

It took the Germans more than a full day to realise the old salient trenches had been left by the British and Plumer's Force had withdrawn to a new defensive line about three miles (4-5 Kilometres)in front of and to the east of Ypres making the salient on plan now look more like a minor pimple than the serious boil it had been. Contemporary accounts including Field Marshal Sir John French's battle report to his Prime Minister mentions the time it took and the wastage of the enemy's heavy and small arms fire before they became conscious that the birds had flown and they were attacking empty trenches and emplacements.

Gingerly they regrouped and advanced westwards across the open countryside, through the wrecked Belgium towns or villages of Zonnebeke, Broodseinde, St Julien and Gravenstafel before clashing against the new British defences centred on the small village of Frezenberg each side of the road from Ypres to Zonnebeke. The German army, however, once it knew how its foe had deployed, did not take long to re-exert pressure by bringing up their heavy guns and much of their massed infantry onto this point immediately east of Ypres.

The 28th Division of Plumer's Force, which by this time, 7th May, had reverted back to its original designation of Second Army, was fighting to defend and hold the centre axis of this important front from the attacking forces of two German Reserve Corps . Heavily outgunned and out-numbered, the 83rd Brigade, part of the 28th Division, immediately in front of these forces, needed help.

Initially, a Brigade from the 27th Division was planned to relief the pressure on the 83rd on the 7th May, and my Father's unit, part of the 85th Brigade, was still thankfully expecting to enjoy a few more days rest before returning to the fighting zone. They were getting their breathe back in the comparative safety of the 85th Brigades billetting area midway between the rail-head town of Poperinghe and the straggling village of

Vlamertinghe. In fact, they had been ordered by their Brigade masters to report their trench strength by 10am the next day (8th May) and to be ready to move on the night 9th/10th May. Every man, it was emphasised, must be included to make the requisite numbers. There were also further orders and advice included in Brigade's instructions to 3rd Middlesex that day. The enemy had dug in, setting his new positions much further back from the British lines than at the previous front, no doubt intending to make far greater use of his superior artillery and Brigade told its battalions, approaching these new lines for the first time, to use Very lights sparingly at night. They explained that the use of Very lights tended to give away the position of the trenches and assisted the German artillery in pin-pointing their targets. To make up for this lack of vision it would be necessary to keep constant and regular patrols in No-man's land at night and, to this end, a regular system was to be arranged. The higher command expected these patrols also to lay ambushes for the enemy's patrols so as to provide intelligence regarding the identification of the German forces on this front which was urgently required by the staff controlling these defensive battles.

Although not privy to all matters that pass between the various levels of command, I expect my Dad, in common with most of the other soldiers in the lower ranks, soon got to know that the orders to move had been issued. This kind of information travels fast, especially in the close knit military environment of which they were a part. To them, it meant that, although they could hear the conflict, the guns never stopped, they had a measurable time before they became part of it again. Thankfully it would be another three good days before they were. Dad and the 3rd Middlesex had had three good days of relief and could expect three more. Days when you eat regularly, drink properly, wash and keep clean, parade and train as soldiers, sleep or dream of home and wish the war was over. He did not have that tight feeling in the throat, the dread of killing or being killed. The jokes, the laughs, the games of cards, house or crown and anchor, the parades with shouting N.C.O.'s, the pep-talks and training together with the spirit of men sharing adversities keeping you going, still had a while to run. The pity was, it all ended quicker than he and the rest expected.

Just after reveille on the morning of the 8th May the battalion was told and it is recorded in its diary for that day, " due to heavy bombardment along our whole front, 85th Brigade will stand-by ready to move at once if required." All, but a few, would have pondered that onerous call without an anxious trepidation about the immediate future. It was not long afterwards that another more urgent message was received from Brigade H.Q. It read "All units will fall in at once with 175 rounds of ammunition, respirators, emergency rations and fully equipped in every respect. One mounted officer per unit will come to Brigade H.Q., Battalions will be down on their parade grounds. 3rd Middlesex will move at once and will halt at some convenient spot between Vlamertinghe and Ypres." My Dad was going back into action. The rush was on. Now there was no time to think; the platoons' corporals bark their orders to their men to get lined up outside their billets "now!" in battle order, rifles, webbing, packs, kits and bedding, such as it was. Vacated billets were totally cleared every time the men occupying them received orders to go elsewhere. The same accommodation would soon be filled again with another battalion or unit, either just arrived in Belgium or being regrouped from elsewhere. Lined up in less than ten minutes and brought to attention the platoons are marched to the Quartermaster's stores were they hand in their kit bags, bedding and most personal belongings and are then issued with the .303 small arms ammunition etc necessary for fighting the war, items which are kept in the Q.M. stores when the battalion is out of the line.

Orderly, the whole Battalion of six hundred and thirty four men, two thirds its proper strength, now assembled into four companies, fully equipped for the fight in less than two hours, marches off eastwards, towards the guns, down the familiar road to "Wipers" and the carnage beyond. Whilst they were preparing, their orders had been further updated. Time had become of the essence, there would be no stopping at that convenient spot before Ypres. The new orders make it clear and precise, "Move at once to reinforce 83rd Infantry Bde. moving to G.H.Q. line about Potijze moving via N.of Ypres by route along which you returned on night 3/4 May. Send an officer on to report at 83rd Infry Bde H.Q. in 1.3c 2.8 in dug-outs". (map references applying to 1:20000 sheets of the general area which had become the standard issue to H.Q. companies.)

It took 3rd Middlesex marching four abreast about one and a half hours to reach the battle zone which was nearly eight miles from their billets just east of Poperinghe. Artillery and small arms gun fire was incessant with the smoke and noise from the tortured city of Ypres the worse and most horrific spectacle. They recognised again the red brick old hop store at Vlamertinghe with its never ending stream of pale and drawn walking wounded queuing patiently to see a hard pressed doctor. There were not many other prominent buildings or features in the country landscape through which they were marching. It was a little early in the war for the well known signs and names Tommy gave to points of important reference that became so necessary in a barren landscapes to enable units to orientate themselves on their way up the line. .

They passed Ypres on their right, by way of its northern outskirts, and with their ground being just slightly higher than the city's, they could see and hear the explosions and fires destroying, stone by stone, that unlucky place. They could see but they had no time to stop, even taking their smokes and drinks on the move, at the infantry rate of ninety paces a minute. The place may be being destroyed but it was not to be taken by the enemy. My Father and his kind had been charged with that, and for a brief but important few hours the fate of the British effort on the Western Front would be determined by these men and their fighting prowess.

At 12.55 p.m. 3rd Middlesex were ordered into action to retake trenches lost by 83rd Brigade in the latest German infantry assault which had been accompanied by much artillery back up. These trenches stretched from the village of Arret south of Frezenberg to a wood in J.1 c. south of the railway line. This was the same railway line which flanked 3rd Middlesex' positions in Dad's earlier and first engagement with the enemy a few long days ago. It was further back towards Ypres than that place; between three and four miles of Belgium ground had been given up; but the single tracks, or what was left of them, were still constructed on a narrow embankment that was prominent across the flat polder-like landscape.

The C.O., Major G.H.Neale, had been informed that a gap in the defences, about 800 yards long, had developed in which no troops appeared to be in place and that the enemy were filtering forward unopposed. The enemy were to be expelled and the gap needed to be filled and properly manned. At the extreme left of the breach the positions were held by 83th Brigades' 3rd Monmouthshires and 2nd King's Own (Royal Lancasters) and 800 yards (700 meters) to the right by 80th Brigade's troops. There may have been the odd unit still holding out but with the German assault continuing the situation had become critical. The whole centre of the new salient protecting Ypres was in danger of collapsing should the enemy be able to turn the British flanks at the extremes of this breach. Accordingly, three other battalions of the 83th Brigade, the 1st Yorks and Lancs:, 2nd East Yorks and 5th King's Own, were moving to fill the gap north of the railway and joining 3rd Monmouth and 2nd King's Own to repel German infantry and regain the trenches lost along just over a half of this front. These battalions were also picking up any remnants of British troops they found on their way who had been overrun and separated from their units of command. 3rd Middlesex were ordered to attack and retake any of the original 83rd Brigades trenches which were in possession of the enemy south of the railway.

The battalion sustained heavy casualties re-securing these lines and by about 6pm were reporting back to their Brigade H.Q. that they needed more artillery support directed against the enemy's guns before they would be able to advance any further. The fields and hedges were littered with their dead and wounded but they had recovered a lot of the lost ground and the British front line was once more continuously defended. What trenches and pits there were that had survived the terrifying bombardments were dangerously overcrowded with men. In fact a number of units were sheltering from the shelling in shallow pits or by any sort of a mound that offered some cover from the enemy's superior and continuous fire power.

They still needed to recover more of the original line and push any German troops from their ground or kill them in the process. There was scant help to be had from their own heavy guns and my Father and his like had to shoot out the enemy troops with their rifles, bayonets and little else, in another fierce battle of standard infantry tactics. In a landscape that offered no help to friend or foe alike, there was not much time to scoop out a hole to make cover whilst getting your breath back. It was better to jump into that shell hole providing it was empty, must have been often in my Dad's mind as he moved up as part of his section; finding cover, hesitating, firing, killing and advancing again in the classic deliberate moves of foot soldiers in an assault.

The battalion was still attacking at 10pm, long after dusk and darkness, in turn, had spread over the area from the east that stretched in front of them. At 10.30pm the C.O., called a halt, and sent the following message to 83rd Brigade H.Q., recorded here verbatim. "Have advanced on South side of railway until I am further East than the Germans on the N.side of railway, where they are entrenching. It appears to me that the attack on the

N.side of the railway has not got far enough forward to enable me to push on any further. As my position will be impossible by daylight. I shall have to withdraw to the support trench and to railway level crossing in I.11.b as most of support trench is occupied by Shropshires. There are a great number of wounded and assistance of bearer company will be necessary to evacuate my aid post, which is situated near level crossing in I.11.b ". My Father, as part of this battalion of "Diehards", with great vigour and aggression, had spent a long afternoon and evening pushing their enemy back and regaining ground they had been ordered to recover, and as it turned out assisted in no small measure to re-stabilise the army's defensive front protecting Ypres.

In the space of less than six days my Father had experienced, in no uncertain terms and at very close hand, both types of infantry deployment and use in very real and active warfare. A few miles ahead from where he was now, he had marched into a very intense defensive action holding ground against attacking pressures. That afternoon he had added his weight to an attacking force intent on recovering lost territory. Quite a baptism for a quiet family man and modest housepainter to survive and not to mention in his later years at home.

That it was all to be repeated so many times more for him, was one likely reason he chose not to talk about it. Another and more relevant reason was most probably to do with the third activity of the infantry, that of control and occupation after the ultimate victory. This last and easier activity regarding ones enemy was never exercised properly by the politicians, who took over from the Generals, when the war had been won. The other one time house-painter would be allowed to have a lot to do with that and it was to take another generation or two, plus a second world war, to make sure the right prohibitions were put on my Father's enemies to prevent yet another re-occurrence of what he had been forced to endure for more than four years.

Meanwhile, The Battle of Frezenburg was not yet over. Essential ground had been recovered and the men lying out in the fields, amongst the debris and marks of battle, bore witness to that. Young William Jupp was left where he fell, whilst Private, 7428, Harry John Juster was amongst the many wounded needing urgent evacuation from the Battalion's Aid Post. He was another young soldier from Wimbledon on Dad's draft. He too had arrived from England on the same day as my Father, and was now mortally wounded. Tragically, he would die from those wounds on the 17th May 1915, nine days after the battle and before he could be safely transferred back to England. He passed away in the major base hospital that had been established in Boulogne to nurse the seriously injured casualties, many of whom, were unable to travel that extra seaborne leg back to Blighty.

Harry had survived the harrowing removal from the Aid Post under fire, the jolting journey to the C.C.S. at Poperinge, hence by train to the base hospital in Boulogne. He would die amongst his own. The busy but caring Matron of that British Hospital contacted his kin shortly after his death. Her sad account makes poignant reading in his local weekly newspaper, even today, as it did, when it was first published, only a few brief days after the event. Unlike William Jupp, lost forever on the battlefield, Harry had his Christian burial and still lies in his own grave, Plot VIII.D.12.,in Boulogne's Cimetiere de L'Est, with nearly six thousand other comrades brought there from this and many other battle fields of Northern France and Belgium. His name is also amongst eight others who share the same family name and grace Wimbledon's Rolls of Sacrifice and Service which was put on display again in the late Nineteen Nineties, after a long period forgotten and neglected in some storage cupboard belonging to his Local Civic Authority.

The Town's official stone built war memorial could not contain all the names of its war dead, there were too many relative to its proposed design. It was therefore agreed by the local councillors shortly after the war had ended, that they would have commissioned these Rolls, in the form of a hand printed, illuminated book, beautifully bound and which would list alphabetically, the names of the men and women from the Borough of Wimbledon who had served in The Great War. There would be two sections within the one volume, the first a Roll of Sacrifice, listing those who had given their lives, (1200 names), the other a Roll of Service, (8827 names), which would contain details of the men and women who had served in the wartime forces. It was this volume that was lucky to survive the political changes that occurred during the sixties and seventies and reappear late in the closing stages of the twentieth century. Until it disappeared, it was always on public show in an appropriate glass case in the impressive entrance of the Town Hall, as a permanent tribute to the sacrifices and services so freely given by the local people. When the Borough changed its name and its civic venue the custodians of much of the Borough's heritage were sadly lacking, careless or un-aware of their obligations and many important records and documents were lost or carelessly mislaid. Fortunately, this volume was rediscovered by a young researcher who recognised its value and it has been given a place in the local library, in its family history department. Hardly a prestigious resting place for such a volume with all those names of ordinary men and women who served their community so well less than two generations ago. It is better than being totally forgotten or lost. Unlike the card index system, so laboriously assembled between 1919 and 1923, and from which the Rolls were compiled, these valuable and historic cards are now missing, believed to have been thrown out as so much trash. Harry Juster's, William Jupp's, my Dad's, the five local V.C. winner's and more than eight thousand other local peoples' records of service recorded with much detail on those cards did not deserve that fate.

Major G.H.Neale got his request for help to evacuate his wounded shortly after his own communication of 10.30pm. He also received updated instructions regarding the rest of his depleted battalion. He was ordered, as he expected, to withdraw to a line of trenches that ran from the part of the re-established front at the road just west of Verlorenhoek in a N.E./S.W. direction southwards towards the railway. They had to give up part of what they had won as the support was not there north of the railway. Regrettable, but this was being realistic. In this war, where it was all about turning your enemy's flank when you are attacking, but when you are in defensive mode you are not able to use an isolated and narrow bridge head to much advantage, even though it may have cost you dear. 'Ca ne fait rien' or 'San fairy ann' as Dad and his mates would have thought, it was not the first nor would it be the last time that this would happen. War is never perfect.

The front had certainly stiffened up though in the past 12 hours since 3rd Middlesex first attacked, despite this tactical withdrawal. More battalions had been despatched to the area and there was now a solid core of fresh troops occupying the ground that a brief while ago was critically undefended. By 5.50am the C.O., who can only be described as indefatigable, had toured the whole line of trench from the railway to the Verlorenhoek road and found it already full of troops. No room for his men along that line, so accordingly, he informed his masters at Brigade H.Q., by another hand written message, delivered by an equally unflagging runner, that he had positioned his men along the road at the level crossing I.11.b. and in some dug-outs near the railway.

Here, my Father and his Battalion may have got a little rest in the early hours before dawn which brought with it an even heavier bombardment than the consistent crump that went on all through the night.

Fifty five percent of the names called out during the Battalion's roll call, taken at first light on the 9th May had no one to respond to them. So many of the young men who had shouted "sir" yesterday morning had gone. The true extent of the losses were confirmed. Sadly the C.O. must have pondered these lists and again, in only a few days, he had to accept that half his fighting Battalion had succumbed to the enemy's violent fire power of their continuing offensive. Major Neale, a long serving officer of the Regiment had already seen his Colonel lost and now his closer colleagues and staff were becoming victims. Besides some of his best officers, many senior N.C.O.s, Company Sergeant Majors, Platoon Sergeants and Corporals had been killed or wounded and the men on the first rung of promotion, the single stripers, Lance Corporals, were now having to command platoons or sections. Seven officers had been lost amongst the total of three hundred and forty five men who fell dying or wounded or who were now recorded as missing. How would there ever be enough time to write to the kin of these men?

The much reduced 3rd Middlesex, including my Father stayed in the positions close to the front all day, sheltering from the heavy bombardment as best they could, taking more casualties and waiting, if needed, to repel further infantry assaults. The enemy had crept up much nearer to their trenches and now ammunition and many trench stores and tools were needed to replace those that had been lost or used up. Messages were sent to Command H.Q. requesting these supplies and, come dusk, the O.C.'s unit had received most of what they needed to continue the defence of the Battalion's ground.

This defence continued during the evening and night without respite. Near to midnight C and D companies had to move to fill a wide gap of unoccupied trench between their own and the adjacent Brigade. The un-manned trenches were between the 3rd Royal Fusiliers of the 85th Brigade and the 1st Yorks and Lancs belonging to the 83rd. Men remaining, both from the Royal Fusiliers and Yorks and Lancs, had either bunched up closer as individuals had been taken out as casualties or they had got closer to their comrades for extra support during times of specific attack. Whatever the cause, the gap some hundred and fifty yards wide had to be filled. The orders to C and D companies emphasised that there must be no unoccupied gap and if any more men were needed the C.O. was to be informed. Much needed small arms ammunition, rations and water was sent up to these tired men in the line, from the Battalion's command post and all officers and remaining N.C.O.'s were required to assist in their proper distribution.

As the comfortless night merged with the rising dawn of yet another day, my Father and his pals would have, during this time, tried to get some sort of cat nap without really sleeping. Sleeping was forbidden, unless approved by the man in command. Generally a person, if pressed, can stay awake two nights in a row, but eventually the body will rebel over the mind and sleep will take over. For this reason I am certain an hour or so before the usual dawn 'stand to arms' the Officers or N.C.O.'s would have told off small groups of their commands to this sort of rest, maybe a half hour or so, just to relieve the needs of these very weary men. Besides not sleeping, the men had not had any proper food or drink since they left their billets a blurring two days ago and now just blending into the third.

Dad, his Battalion and all those lining the salient, were to stay on this rack. There was to be no relief. In fact, the Germans had no intention to give up their attack and their very heavy shelling continued all the next day. A tired entry in the C.O.'s diary for the 10th May, timed at 11am, describes this situation as normal (can one get used to heavy shelling? apparently these men could and did), and then goes on to record a request to 83th Brigade for more trench stores of all types, Very pistols and Starlights, all of which were again urgently required.

About 2 o'clock in the afternoon more pressure from the attacking German infantry coincided with some British troops from the Rifle Brigade being shelled out of their trenches. About a 100 men started to retire from this ground held by the 27th Division which was on the immediate right or south of 3rd Middlesex's positions. The 3rd Middlesex men were made ready to counter any German break-through by preparing to line the railway embankment on what would be the enemy's right flank if they advanced. This, however, became unnecessary, as 27th Division immediately sent in the Princess Louise's 1st Bn: (Argyll and Sutherland Highlanders) who in a swift and energetic attack recovered the position and restored the status quo.

No other enemy probes occurred that day in this area and with the front fully manned by fresher and stronger units, 3rd Middlesex was ordered back into G.H.Q. lines, the second line defensive positions, that had been established less than a mile back from the most forward British trenches.

At a strength of less than a full company, normally two hundred and fifty men, my Father's Battalion, what was left of it, would have a slightly better night than the previous two had been. There would be no proper beds. They were still part of the reserve troops and as such would have to keep their clothes on together with most of their battle order webbing. They may have been able to change a pair of socks, have a wash and perhaps be given a hot drink and warm meal. They would have enjoyed the pure nectar of that billy can of really hot tea, that special brew, that all British soldiers find so re-invigorating. A sure tonic to relieve the pressure and tension they had all experienced over the last three long days and continuous nights. Things had to be a little better, the enemy was not quite so close, even if the bombardment continued all along this second line perhaps as much as at the front. In the incessant noise, they must have thought 'was there no end to the German supplies of bombs, mortars and shells?'

Unfortunately no, and their battle was by no means over, it still had two more days to run.

The heavy shelling of their positions in the G.H.Q. line had continued all morning, when just after midday they were on the move back to the front again. Out of the frying pan into the fire does not adequately describe it although ones chances of survival may have been minimally better there than they were at the front. The enemy had broken through again at the 27th Division's extreme left adjacent to 83rd's right to the south of that railway that seemed to feature in so much of my Father's first actions on the Western Front.

The same fields positioned either side of the embankment that my family and I visited all those years after my Father had been there, certainly did not look worth fighting and dying for. Plenty of other places to grow cabbages or sugar beet and a bit too low lying to build a house or village. I have frequently studied the photographs I had developed of this place and elsewhere along the Western Front and like the hypothetical line drawn in the sand, only principles can explain why the British were prepare to pay such a heavy price to retain it for the Belgium or French people. There is no other logical explanation, and although the tides of the Great

War may have ebbed backwards or forwards across one field very much like another it was all very much the same as this place. No great rewards, no golden booty, no national prizes or great riches were at stake. Only freedom and decency were being disputed here.

The 3rd Middlesex was immediately required to proceed towards the railway crossing located at 1.11.b. and go into action again with another battalion being sent from the 27th Division to recover and re-establish the line which the British Army was so determined to hold. The 19th Hussars of the 9th Cavalry Brigade, now thrown in as dismounted troops, were ordered to take up the position in the G.H.Q. line vacated by my Father's Battalion immediately and be prepared to move forward in support of them if they needed help.

There was another fierce exchange between the infantry which ended with the line being recovered and consolidated by about 5pm that evening. In an afternoon of heavy fighting the enemy had been driven back and the "Diehards" were digging in again as if they meant to stay. The C.O. informed the Brigade Major, 9th Cavalry Bde: at Potijze Chateau that his officers patrol had been out along the section of front that they had been ordered to recover and with the adjacent units either side of his unit he could confirm that all German troops in the area had been dislodged and that now none were coming through at all along this critical sector. For the present the enemy had spent his force and Major Neale could thankfully report that everything at that time was much quieter than usual. The mixture of 3rd Middlesex men, Argyles, Shropshires and Royal Fusiliers had once more shown what they were worth and the defended trenches were being held with firm resolution and determination.

The Divisional Commander, Major General E.S. Bulfin, wanted this information confirmed urgently by his own man. The 27th Division had informed him via their Brigade on the right of the "Diehards", but the 28th wanted their own people to report direct to them. There is no doubt important strategic and tactical planning was being decided relative to the ability to hold this line. The British Army's political masters did not want to give up Ypres and if this line could be held against violent and sustained attacks, then the army's confidence in its planning, fighting capabilities and morale would be much enhanced.

It is a fact, that the present shape of this salient, as established by these battles in May 1915, remained in place for the next two years or more and I believe speaks well for the tactical choices made by the Generals in overall command. The Germans went back to lick their wounds and did not move on this front again until they were pushed back to that original ridge at Passchendaele in November 1917, exactly where my Father had started his real war just nine days ago on the 2nd May 1915 at this time.

It would take two years before the British Army would be given the power and means to conduct an assault at this place similar to that which the Germans had been mounting since the 23rd April. It confirms how prepared they were and how unready the British nation had been for this war. Meanwhile, my Dad, and his kind, had to hold the line as best they could with the meagre resources that their country could provide.

Hold it they did, until the German offensive became a spent force about the 25th May. During those fourteen days, 12th to 25th May, 3rd Middlesex were kept very busy. They went out of the front line late on the evening of Wednesday 12th May being relieved by 3rd Cavalry Division. Their orders were to work on improving the trenches they were occupying right up to the time before handing over. They then had a six mile night march back to the billets they had vacated five days ago. They did not stay near to Pop: very long, just one day. Early on the 14th May, having had that one day to tidy up, shave off five days beard and attend a company parade, they were relocated at Houtkerke, a small village, an eight mile route march away.

The Battalion grew back its strength here during its five days at this major base area, which was spread over a wide area of farmland west of Poperinghe, out of range of all except long range heavy artillery. Bombing raids by aircraft had not yet become much of a threat. Fresh blood was drafted to the depleted companies whilst the remnants, now almost veterans, like my Father, thanked their lucky stars that they had survived. The church parade was well attended on that Sunday. By then, they had been told they were going east again in two days time.

An overnight stay near Vlamertinghe meant going over very familiar ground on the way to relieve the Cavalry Brigade on the 21st May. That Friday and the day after were fairly quiet at the salient's front positions. On-going, the two days up in front, two days back in G.H.Q.

lines was not too bad for 3rd Middlesex until Monday 24th May. The Germans really spoilt their Whit Monday, their actions being at such variance to the cause of that celebration. What descended on 3rd Middlesex early that Monday morning was not the rushing mighty wind and tongues of fire that blessed the Apostles with the Holy Spirit. 3rd Middlesex were hit by some of the first gas-shells fired by the men with "Gott mit uns" on their belt buckles. Many members of the Battalion were badly gassed by this obnoxious substance, falling on their positions in the G.H.Q. line. The bombardment caused three hundred and sixty men to leave the contaminated trenches and seek alternative positions away from the deadly poisonous chlorine gas. The yellow- green obscene pollution hovered low where it struck until a, perhaps disapproving,   breeze (not quite a rushing wind) dissipated it and moved it on.

This attack coincided with the final part of the 1915 Battles for Ypres. The enemy started his heavy shelling and gas attacks along most of the front but this time concentrated his efforts to the right of where my Father and his unit were located. Dad was on the edge of the Battle of Bellewaarde. A battle that got its name from a small estate consisting of the Chateau of Hooge, its parkland, woods and lake of that name, which was situated three miles down and to the immediate north of the Ypres to Menin Road.

The battalion quickly recovered its composure following its first close exposure to this awesome and terrifying new weapon, and with the very heavy shelling continuing they were ordered back to the front line trenches to reinforce the 2nd East Surreys.

They waited two days and nights under bombardment for an attack that did not come in   their sector. There was plenty of activity going on to their right, small arms fire, machine gun and artillery with the odd field or coppice changing hands as the two armies clashed. No significant gains were made by the Germans and by the end of the second day the attacks ended and to quote the War Diary it was quiet again.

Just to be sure the British Commanders kept their troops at full alert until Friday 28th May, which meant another four days in the trenches for my Father and his battalion. Late on that day the 3rd Royal Fusiliers relieved them from their forward positions. The continuing and never ending changing of the guard had to remain, but the ever present sentinel would be someone else for a while.

My Dad had gone back into billets, many of his mates hadn't and John McCrae found the words again:-

O Guns, fall silent till the dead men hear

Above their heads the legions passing on;

(Those fought their fight in bitter fear,

And died not knowing how the day had gone.)

Extract from "The Anxious Dead".

———————————————

Chapter 7

Bellewarde is no longer remembered as the site of an important battle. Few histories have ever referred to it by its proper name, but the clashes there exceeded in size and probable importance, the Battle of Waterloo, which took place just over sixty miles away. The site at Bellewarde is now a popular and successful Theme Park competing efficiently with Disney World and its kind. The Niagara, Screaming Eagle, River Splash and Flying Carrousel occupy, with many other attractions, the area of several hectares that were much disputed by the British and German armies of 1915 through to1918. Many thousands of visiting adults of all races and ages now enjoy with their children and friends the thrills, fun and fast food, accompanied with screams of delight and laughter, in the place where British soldiers once fought and died for nought but ideals in a war that the politicians said would end wars. Six British volunteer Divisions, consisting of up to one hundred and twenty thousand men, took part in this particular battle around the Bellewarde Lake area towards the end of May 1915. It was the last of four violent and hard fought engagements that make up the Battles of Ypres, 1915 and illustrates, with the later battles of 1917 and 1918 the determination of the British Commonwealth forces not to yield more of Belgium to the Germans. The Duke of Wellington and Napoleon deployed less than seventy thousand men apiece at Waterloo, in 1815, a hundred years earlier, which effectively ended England's long quarrels with France. At Bellewarde, the uninvited German invaders were prevented from taking over and exploiting the last small parcel of what was left of a free Belgium. Thereafter, for three more years an unknown number of British, Commonwealth and Empire soldiers in their rapidly growing army continued to preserve this status to their considerable cost.

The battles that formed the shape of the salient at Ypres for the next three years were an important part of my father's military service which I have researched and investigated together with many of the historical events that coincided with that service. These battles took place at the beginning of his long active army career on the Western Front and I am certain that he would have been very pleased to see the unique use that has been made finally of this part of his old front line. In fact, I can see his bright smiling eyes twinkling at the thought, had he known.

There are no similar fun, amusement or theme sites elsewhere along the Western Front, but there are many memorials and graveyards erected and set out astride its long length as proper and respectful reminders of what took place there. Only a few of these are now much visited, whilst many are all but forgotten. It is possible that this multi-racial theme park and pleasure ground may have the right ring about it, although it was an inordinate time coming, including a five year lapse for a dreadful second world war. The innocent thrills, fun and enjoyment found by so many of its visitors, may conform in certain ways to the expectations of those who fought there for a better world, the theme of which is often projected at these parks. Opened in the nineteen eighties, this park now attracts far more visitors of every age group than "La Belle Alliance" at Waterloo, although whether there are that many who are aware of its previous short lived claim to fame would be difficult to assess. If the name is not in the history books how are they to know?

A British veteran of the Battle of Waterloo, which was fought on the 18th June 1815, became a Waterloo Man. King George III gave him a much prized shiny medal and significant additional time on his pension rights. The Nation showed real gratitude by commissioning this specific medal to be struck and ordering that a soldier's presence in the field that day would count as two whole years of pensionable service. No such gratitude was shown after 2nd Ypres 1915, with its four named battles, or, for that matter, any other named battle of the Great War. It took a long and difficult search for me to establish that my Father was a Bellewarde Man. He had nothing to show for it. He was already a Gravenstafel and Frezenberg Man, both battles of equal importance and ferocity and, as my Father's story unfolded, it became clear he was entitled to, but did not receive, many other distinguished appellations. He received none and certainly no pension rights. All that he and many of his kind were awarded by their grateful nation were varying periods of unemployment and miserly, means tested hand-outs designed to belittle the receivers. Their elected leaders had welshed on their obligations and promises to these men and when my Father's turn came to be shown the proper consideration for his service their gratitude did not exist. Now, of course, the politician's meanness is beyond redemption and it is very similar to the inadequate treatment and recognition meted out after World War II, to those who suffered in the Far East as P.O.W.'s of the Japanese.

The three campaign medals to which he was entitled do not indicate in any way what battles he fought, or in which campaigns he took part. These medals were colloquially referred to by many who received them, as "Pip", "Squeak" and "Wilfred" when three were worn and "Mutt" and "Jeff", if only two were awarded. They were not really even campaign medals although they are referred to as such.

A soldier, who served in a theatre of war for at least a full day between 1914 and 1918 was entitled to three medals. They could be either the "1914 Star", or the "1914-1915 Star", not both, depending on the dates of service, plus, the "British War Medal" and the "Victory Medal". The first and last medals were cast in bronze, the "B.W.M." was cast in silver. A soldier who served after the 31st December 1915 in a theatre of war, be it for a day or three long years received only the last two medals. No bars or clasps were authorised except for the "1914 Star" impressed "5th Aug.-22nd Nov.1914". This bar or clasp, which is a narrow bronze strip, affixed to the medal ribbon, acknowledged that the authorised holders came under enemy fire in France or Belgium between those dates. There was still no mention of a specific battle to distinguish the wearer's service, just those dates. Those who served elsewhere during that time were not authorised and did not receive this bar. Before The Great War, it was customary to have awarded and affixed to the ribbon of a campaign medal a bar or clasp for each battle where the holder had been present. The three Great War Medals that were issued only had the number, rank, name and regiment of its recipient impressed there-on. Even this acknowledgement was omitted from campaign medals that were awarded for service during the Second World War.

My wife's Grandfather, who served as a regular soldier in the South African Campaigns during the late 19th and early 20th Centuries, proudly wore his medals which clearly show where he had served his Queen and later King Edward V11, after the much loved Queen passed away early in 1901. On one of his medals were five clasps or bars, cast in silver and attached to the medal ribbon, which clearly indicated where he had fought. Each bar has the name of a battle or campaign impressed thereon. South Africa 1901 is on one, Transvaal, Orange Free State, Natal and Cape Colony are on the others. The naming on ones personal medals of the actions where the individual has been present, was much appreciated as a proper and adequate recognition of that service.

There are many other instances, prior to the Great War, where campaign medals had much significance and pride for the recipient as well as later providing a wealth of interest and record of the past for researchers and historians alike. The "Die-Hards" Museum have not too long ago managed to acquire and are displaying a wonderful piece of its own history in this form. It is a medal which belonged to a survivor of the battle which gave the Middlesex Regiment its other valiant name. Sergeant Alexander Masters wore on his tunic his General Service Medal 1793-1814 with six silver bars on its ribbon. He, almost certainly, heard his C.O., Colonel Inglis encourage and rally his men with his "Die hard 57th. Die hard." at Albuhera on the 16th May 1811, which coined the apt soubriquet for this tough infantry regiment of the line. Unlike two-thirds of his comrades, who were killed or wounded on that day, he remained standing and unbowed after the battle near the Spanish-Portugese border to the south-east at Badajoz. Somewhat similar to my Father, he was one of the luckier ones in battle as this medal illustrates. It tells a story of other battles he fought through and survived during the long campaigns against Napoleon Bonaparte. These clasps show he and his regiment saw action right across the Iberian Peninsula, over the Pyrenees and well into France. The simple ribbon and attachments fitted in ascending order as they occurred indicated his presence at the engagements between the British and French at "Busaco" situated on the Atlantic or seaboard side of Portugal, "Albuhera" where the Middlesex Regiment became "The Diehards", "Vittoria" well into the north of mainland Spain, "Pyrennes" the mountainous border actions, and into France for the battles of "Nive" and "Toulouse". Only six impressions on a ribbon, but what a story they tell of the holder's service and inform others who seek to know.

Many who have thought seriously about campaign medals are of the opinion that a proper and more appropriate form of recognition was sadly lacking after the Great War ended and was another instance of the penny-pinching meanness shown by Parliament to the returning servicemen. This meanness may explain why such a large proportion of the veterans' British War Medals ended up in the pawnshops of that period. The silver content had some worth but the pawnbrokers would not have put any value on the bronze of the other two castings. The one penny coin of the period would have had as much bronze in it as the two types of Stars and Victory medal and perhaps that is what a lot of the recipients thought they were worth. Bars affixed to ones own War or Victory Medal ribbon, bearing the impressions for example:-"Marne 1914", "Falklands", Bellewarde", "Neuve Chappelle", "Loos", "The Somme", "Jutland", "Flers Courcelette", "Passchendaele" and " Hindenberg Line," or "Zeebrugge", the list is endless, would have made a difference. Such recognition would have increased their relevance and made them much more appreciated by their owners. The men demobbed from this victorious army, throughout its ranks, were indifferent regarding the lottery surrounding a lot of the awards for gallantry being made. They were generally very aware that there were too many anomalies in the impossible system of granting these gongs, that has not been resolved even to this day. The instance regarding the six Victoria Crosses awarded by ballot after the heroic raid at Zeebrugge well illustrates this point. Having their presence acknowledged in the infernos which were their own battlefields, by name, with a bar or clasp system, would have at least distinguished their individual contribution and effort.

It was not to be and my Father still had a lot more soldiering to do before he got his "Pip", "Squeak" and "Wilfred". His "Pip" was the 1914-1915 version without a bar.

The month long battles of 2nd Ypres had left a deficit of sixty thousand killed, missing or wounded in the British army and Dad's battalion had contributed its full share. The actions there became notorious for their particular savagery with much hand to hand killing and violence throughout their full periods. In this way, the British army had held the vital elements of the front which its political masters had commanded it to hold, but it was now in need of a rest. It had to keep its guard up, but it was not looking for trouble until it had revived itself. The German army in that part of Belgium and Northern France was equally prostrate and needed to re-think its strategy.

The nut, the Kaiser and his Generals were so sure they could crack, was harder than they had expected. The failure of the Schleiffen Plan in the late summer of 1914 had been followed with another failure to roll up the enemy's lines at Ypres in the autumn of that year and repeated again in the spring of 1915. The latter attempt failing despite the barbaric use of poisonous chlorine gas on unprotected soldiers whose suffering had been so agonising. Their army was certainly better equipped in virtually every respect than their opponents but they had been unable to deal the coup de grace and thus end of the war.

The heroic French army was still very active, but sadly bouncing off the consolidated and well fortified German positions along all their active fronts to the south of Ypres, losing so many of their young men without making headway or recovering any significant amount of their lost territory. It would be so difficult to replace these fine soldiers, the losses being quite unprecedented. This tactic, the Germans decided at this time, would suit them against the British as well, leaving their enemy to spend its blood and resources battering against their stronger and well built defences until yet another winning plan could be developed. At least it would kill or maim a lot of men and whittle down their opponent's resolution. The initiative was clearly with them and they could choose whether to attack or defend to their own advantage. The ground being fought over was not theirs and all the time large tracts of France and Belgium remained in their possession, damage was far from their beloved Fatherland and besides they had every intention to win eventually.

What was left of 3rd Middlesex went to church on the last Sunday in May 1915. The army chaplain, who had shared in most of the battalion's activities in the past action filled weeks, short of carrying arms, held the Communion service in a church on the eastern outskirts of Popperinghe not far from their billets. By this time, he knew the men in his parish well; and most of these soldiers respected his ministering to their needs both spiritually and physically. They had seen him acting as a stretcher-bearer when the medic had been hit; they were grateful when he gave out the rum ration he had helped to bring round during those bitterly cold morning stand-to's; they were glad to be sharing a packet of smokes with him, when that deep blissful pull on a cigarette felt really good and beat any Number Nine pill the M.O. may have prescribed for what they were feeling. As a substitute for today's stress counselling, Players' Weights and Woodbines were for most a welcome and sustaining prop. There were no Government Health warnings on these packets. The men of the battalion from all ranks had watched their chaplain identifying their dead before giving a common prayer-book form of Christian burial to a much liked friend or mate, often whilst still under shellfire. They had seen him assuring their wounded at the Regimental Aid Post that he would let their folks know they were O.K. They liked him being there. There were pundits even then, although, perhaps, not quite so many as nowadays, who, mockingly, suggested that people cannot live without faith, but most of these men took little heed of this, well knowing, it was much harder to die without it; and they knew, of course, all there was to know about living and dying. That is when Faith really matters. Accordingly, Church parade was not really a chore to these men, although, as was their class, they would often grumble about it. I am sure my Father did. It was also part of company or battalion orders, and, as so it was compulsory, he and they had no option but to attend.

My Father and his friends had a couple of days before this parade getting clean and tidy after eight gruelling days at the front. The parade put a little touch of normality back into their lives. It was so much better than the uncertainties at the front despite the noticeable reduction of the noise from the guns in that direction. After the service, attended by most of the battalion, there was an orderly march back to their billets, where my Father with his mates, enjoyed a hot lunch prepared in the Company's field kitchen and, with not so far to travel, the meal rationed out was much hotter than usual. A luxury in itself, although the fairly basic army fare, served into and eaten from the soldier's personal mess tin, it was not likely to get a best food guide award or recommendation for the regimental cooks. The latter, as a laugh, may have put up a menu designed to tempt their customers, recommending the Boeuf Roti et Pomme De Terre; (after all it was Sunday, the day for a traditional roast) Bully de Fray Bentos en Salade avec Sauce Zeppelin; Fromage Canadian et The Natural but it hardly disguised the same British Army's meat and two veg: on which it fought. The rest of that Sunday was spent "bulling" their kit and themselves for the Divisional G.O.C.'s parade next day.

Appropriately, the 28th Division's Commander wished to personally thank and praise his men from the 3rd

Battalion Middlesex Regiment for their splendid determination and tenacity when fighting those powerful German forces a few days ago. The final engagements at Bellewarde had prevented the enemy from advancing deeper into Belgium and constituting a real threat to the Triple Entente's battle lines across Western Europe. Major General E.S. Bulfin well knew the importance of what had been achieved and shared with the other Senior Commanders the knowledge of how close real defeat had been. He would have also felt the pain of knowing his Division had suffered more casualties than the other Divisions involved. According to some records the 28th Division had lost over fifteen thousand killed, wounded and missing, exceeding the average number of casualties of the other Divisions many times. Such had been the ferocity of their actions in the battles of 2nd Ypres that nearly ninety per cent of the Division's nominal strength excluding reinforcements had been lost. Despite this the line had been held. He would have felt pride at this and privileged to command such men. Men like my Father and the other survivors he met and who were paraded before him. They had certainly earned his respect and now he could express his thanks which, unhesitatingly, he was so pleased to give. The men, including my Father, were also glad that he had taken the time to come out and see them. It meant they had not been forgotten or taken for granted.

Of course, the General would not have been privy to the German plans for the immediate future. Had he been he could have told my Father and his battalion that they were going to be in for a quieter time, much quieter than the last month had been.

He knew, of course, but could not say that another reason for this hoped for marking of time, enemy permitting, was that the British Army was running out of ammunition. He knew it was a fact that all the army's supplies were being used up at an alarming rate and not being replaced nearly quickly enough. It was perhaps only an unexpected stroke of good fortune that it was occurring at the very time when the enemy had decided to rest as well.

Unknown to the British Generals, the Germans were taking stock for a number of very different reasons. The idea of a war of attrition was beginning to creep into their equations as a possible solution to the deadlock on the Western Front. As stated previously, they could sit behind impregnable barriers of trenches, obstructions and barbed wire with plenty of artillery and frequent machine gun emplacements, leaving their enemies to exhaust themselves trying to break through and maybe, in that way, resolve the issue in France and Belgium. They were certainly in a position where they could bide their time, it was not their land that they were occupying. Elsewhere, in the increasing world conflict, the story as seen from their side was different. They were really winning and that gave to them every reason to feel the encouragement born out of success.

The Russians were reeling from the combined German and Austrian victories on the Eastern Front that had recovered all the territory previously lost and then they had followed up by making great inroads into the Tsar's interests in what would be Poland and the Baltic States and on into Mother Russia itself. The Serbs, in the Balkans, were in full retreat and it would not be long before their country would be fully occupied. The Turks were succeeding at Gallipoli and more than holding at bay the British and French Expeditionary Forces who had landed there on the 25thApril 1915. The plan to force a passage through the Dardanelles to gain a safe access for the Allied Navies to lay siege to the Turkish capital of Constantinople (Istanbul) and split the Otterman Empire was not working out. An Allied Schlieffen Plan that was going wrong. On the 7th May, the pride of the British merchant fleet, Cunard's R.M.S. Lusitania, the fastest and largest steamer on the transatlantic service, was sunk by a U.Boat, lying in wait, off the coast of Ireland. The great liner was returning from the United States and virtually in British waters when it was sunk, a fact which did nothing for the prestige of those who reckoned to have mastery of the seven seas. The disaster cost 1,198 civilian lives including a number of Americans who were not combatants in the war at this time, whilst the Germans struck a medal glorifying the deed. Even closer to home, London was bombed for the first time in its long history on the night of 31st May. The Commander of Zeppelin LZ.38. Major Erich Linnarz, acting on orders direct from Kaiser William II, was boasting that he had dropped 119 bombs on the civilian population of the East End Dockyards of London. The dead and injured included women and children in their homes and notched up another first for the Germans regarding conduct in warfare, which many other nations had rejected by manifesto. Importantly for them, they could tell the world they had the capital city of the world's greatest empire at their mercy and could launch a terror campaign without the fear of retaliation. It is a strange oddity how the same man who ordered this barbaric escalation of total warfare, shared a common Grandmother with the King of that

Empire and he had walked next to his first cousin, five years earlier through that same city, paying his respects behind his uncle's funeral cortege.

There was more good news for the Central Powers, this time involving the Italians, who had finally became active on the side of the Triple Entente, by declaring war on Austria. The Italians had found that they could make little or no headway against their enemy, despite having a much larger army to put in the field. The mountainous borders, well defended by the Austrians, immediately started to cost the fourth member of the Entente dear, without achieving any success and the situation there looked ripe for further disasters.

It was not a wholesome picture for those countries, who initially, went to war to defend freedom and for a time my Father was having to take part in a fight using makeshift measures and soldiers' ingenuity to get by. A situation forced upon him and his fellow troops by a scandalous lack of war effort back home in Great Britain. All types of essential armaments were still not properly into production due to the lack of direction from those who could exercise real power if they cared. Even the so-called modest quotas requested by the military staffs were not being met.

Much has been written to lay the fault elsewhere, for those crucial shortages. The trade union's "dog in the manger" attitudes to demarcation and production issues was a cause, the army estimates were too small, the country was not used to fighting on mainland Europe, etc, etc, and ultimately the blame was laid at the door of the British people themselves. It was their fault. It could be any one, provided it was not those ministers and the like in Parliament.

In a democracy governed by the peoples' elected representatives, it is here that the proper vilification should fall. It may have been the will of the British people to go to war at this time, the decision was certainly a popular one, but to hold them in turn responsible for how the war was conducted would be to admit to anarchy. This, patently, was not the case, and the lack of proper procedures and controls, to ensure adequate production and procurement for a war effort for which the country was fully capable, must lay with the men in power. Only the Government had the authority and mandate to swing the country into full production, by issuing lawful directives, allocating adequate labour and material resources, placing appropriate contracts and requisitions and all things necessary to ensure eventual victory. Undoubtedly the men in power were culpable. This war could not be fought on the cheap, but perhaps, at the time, they were still hoping it would be.

Nine months and more had elapsed before they began to realise they had a great deal more very urgent work to do, to adequately conduct this war. It was they, no one else, who had declared war on the Germans and unless they acted quickly to enable it to be fought with all the resources which the country was able to provide, they would soon be negotiating for a dishonourable peace.

The Allies of the British, mainly the French and Russians, had been quick off the mark. They were already fully mobilising even before the Germans and Austrians had declared war on them. It was the British Parliament that had declared war on the Central Powers and by doing so, it behove them, to properly deal with the emergency at once, not wait nearly a year, thus needlessly imperilling their King's subjects more than they were already at risk. An army of over a million men and growing fast could not be supported on the establishment levels of the past and this should have been obvious from the very first day.

The same problems and inadequacies were to occur again, with much greater costs in terms of human suffering and desolation, when the Germans under the banners of the Third Reich attacked in 1939. It begs the question, is a democracy really capable of looking after its people especially in times of danger? I suppose it is, if the right men are there, but in both the instances, when my Father had to go war, once in 1914 and then in 1939, the men in Parliament, at the start, were found to be lacking and not up to it.

The painter, destined to become "Der Fuhrer", in his second war, but at present serving as a corporal on the German side of the trenches in Belgium as summer approached in 1915, held his ground with his fellows from the 16th Bavarian Reserve Infantry Regiment with ample munitions and supplies to fight off their enemies and cause them real pain. The painter from Wimbledon serving in a crack British Infantry Regiment was making his bombs and grenades out of cigarette tins and jam jars. The soldiers in my Father's army had been doing this for some time to defend, attack and deter the Germans troops in the static periods of this new type of warfare and is it any wonder that in times of very active fighting they needed to resort to very vicious and bloody hand to hand methods to hold or recover their ground? They had nothing else and, of course, it was they who paid a heavy price with their lives.   Later, after the euphoria of victory, it was easy to blame the Army tactics for the disparity of the casualty rates. Perhaps a tidy cover up was initiated and the real shortage of shells, guns and other essential supplies for which the politicians were responsible was ignored and hardly mentioned. There was a shell shortage enquiry at the time, and the scandal of which, helped to topple Prime Minister Herbert H.Asquith's Liberal and Coalition Governments eventually in1916 in favour of David Lloyd-George, but these failures have never had the same airing as the lie

It is also small wonder that our immediate allies, the French, became more and more frustrated at the level of support our Generals and troops were capable of giving to their efforts during this period when the joint enemy was also much engaged with the Russians on the Eastern Front. Surely to attack a foe when he is having to fight on both sides of his land borders, puts him at a disadvantage and it must be the better strategy for the maximum effort to be made by both of the opposing nations, not just one, to put every effort into their cause. The British Government patently did not do this and in a number of subsequent histories these demands by the French for help is portrayed as weakness on their behalf. It is, perhaps true however, had the British been quicker off the mark, in putting their full weight into the joint efforts earlier, at the proper time, the final victory would have come long before that far-off November of 1918.

However in 1915, when the shortages were being made known to the public for the first time , disparaging the British Generals was not yet the spin, and, for one in particular, my Father, he would have been very pleased with his Commanders. They were withdrawing his battalion, in fact, his Brigade and the whole 28th Division, from that awful salient for a rest, to heal and become strong again. As May turned into June, with the higher temperatures, and the sun on his back, a man felt better; and even going back into the line was improving, it meant marching in a different direction for 3rd Middlesex. They were not footslogging towards those evil, continually smoking ruins that were Ypres. After five days in billets, on the 3rd June they were moving up for a turn in a quieter sector three or four miles to the south of Bellewarde. The Battalion could march to this front without having to go through Wipers. The trenches they were going to take over from the Royal Irish Rifles lay in front of the village of Vierstraat, which was at the southern end of the new salient. These trenches had not been disputed since they were formed at the end of November 1914 during the race to the sea and opposite to where the future German leader would revisit his old trenches after he had won the Battle of France in 1940. Adolf Hitler, the Fuhrer of all Germany and most of Europe, had returned to the positions he had occupied twenty five years earlier as a Corporal, opposite to where my Father was serving and holding the line against him. My wife and I visited them more than fifty years after the Fuhrer's last visit and little had changed in the countryside during all that time.

The British trenches, along this stretch of the Western Front, were at map reference M2 to N5 located across a small road that ran between the small villages of Viestraat and Wytschaete. This small road was one of several that fanned out from the town of Poperinge, this one abruptly stopping before getting to Wyteschaete with earthworks and shell holes occupied by men in muddy khaki uniforms looking eastwards towards men in equally muddy and soiled field-grey occupying similar uncomfortable excavations. Like most of the old front line there is not very much evidence to be seen of the once continuous systems of trenches and fortifications when I visited this spot. There are numerous graveyards formed after later battles that had been fought after 1915; there are a few isolated concrete emplacements, some still used by farmers to house stock and the like; there is the odd small trench museum, but little else to remind one of those days when my Father and the German Corporal were there. The water filled lakes or ponds caused by the enormous mines set off in 1916 and 1917, by the British, were not features when my Father marched to and from this part of the front nine times in the summer months of 1915. There are now mostly well cultivated flat fields bordered by narrow roads or dykes which drain off the copious surface water from the land. There are also many small villages, hamlets and farmsteads with the same place names as when my Father was there which remain to be located by a map reference from an old diary or perhaps there is a concrete pill-box set isolated in a field for what looks like no particular reason. These latter sad remains can still, however, give an interesting odd clue to a visitor. If the access opening cast in one of the walls, faces the east, one can be certain it formed part of the German positions and fixes their line much more positively, or checks out one's own map reading, just as, if the opening faces the west, it tells it once formed part of the old British front.

The maps used by the British Army even at this early time is another indication of how well organised their army was. My research has shown how quick, precise and accurate the surveyors and engineers of the period produced these vital aids for the men along the whole chain of command. One cannot control and direct great numbers of men and equipment over vast areas of land without adequate and detailed maps, nor can one order a small unit to go to a particular gully or defence post without one. Many of the men from the various units of the CRE (Commander, Royal Engineers), attached to and an essential part of the Divisional Order of Battle, had surveyed and helped map an Empire in the past and providing well founded topographical information came with the general efficiency of the command structure. These facts and many others have been so often forgotten or taken for granted by many a pundit who is only seeking to demur and criticise some fine men's efforts, rather than show the appropriate appreciation for them. A great number of the maps used throughout the war period are now available in the archives and can be used by a researcher, like myself, to retrace very accurately the steps taken by a junior officer and his company of soldiers obeying an order recorded in a diary long ago to go to a five or seven digit map reference on his 1:10,000 or 1:20,000 trench map. The seven digit reference when given as part of an order can still pin-point a feature within a five yard square of territory whereas the more often used five digit one can still direct the searcher to a position or place within a fifty by fifty yard perimeter. Broader areas of the landscape can be and were defined by two and three digit map references when necessary to indentify one thousand and five hundred yard squares respectively. This sort of information gave me great confidence when trying to retrace steps my Father had taken all those distance years ago. The Public Records Office, who keep this National Archive of The Great War Military Maps, record that over thirty million maps of the Western Front were issued to the forces fighting there, most being needed by the Heavy and Medium Artillery men who were not firing over open sights and the infantry who needed to know how to get to that warm billet or that horrendous watery hole in the ground that they were expected to defend with their lives.

My Father, without maps, must have got to know this countryside well. Private R.J.Reed spent three and a half months in and out of the trenches between Vierstraat and Dranoutre, which covered a length of the front not more than five miles long, the latter village being very close to the unmarked French border. Whilst not on trench duty, he spent his time in the hinterland behind the trenches where great tracts of the land and villages, extending many miles back, were being filled where ever possible with all the paraphernalia of war. Extensive dumps of equipment and supplies were being formed; large, mainly tented, cantonments with horse and mule lines were being set out and training and holding areas for all the multitudinous units of the Allied armies were being either established or enlarged. The artillery, that was available at this time, would have been set up at varying distances from the front depending on its calibre. The smaller field guns used for close support of the ubiquitous infantry being nearest to the trench system, the very few heavy pieces being dug in almost permanently, well behind that front. Where the civilian population had been evacuated from the villages and hamlets close to the fighting zones, the army would have taken over this accommodation for its own use as billets or Command Headquarters of various sorts or more often as fortified strong points. In most circumstances, such buildings or features, quickly became wrecked and useless as safe accommodation above ground, gradually being levelled brick by brick to the surrounding contours by frequent and well aimed shellfire that had been zeroed in on them.

I managed only one half day in this area during my various visits to the old front line. It gave me a flavour of the place, but it required research from many other angles to get to grips and imagine what it was really like to spend the sort of time my Father did in this foreign land which was so unlike his peaceful home-town of Wimbledon set in the suburban sprawl of Greater London. From the available sources I have been able to ascertain that there was always some movement or activity happening to the average fully trained infantry soldier and personal rest, relaxation and a degree of permanency was not much on his agenda, even if he had "clicked" in his vernacular a few times, by being billetted with that envied farming family with the attractive daughters. The special billet was to be had amongst the rear areas of the fighting zones, although still within the noise of shell-fire and I hope and think my Father would have been lucky enough to have had his share. Throughout these villages and farmsteads there were many of the indigenous population who had stayed on. They had managed to survive the original ebb and flow of the fighting, probably by securing themselves in the deep basements of their dwellings and now they eked a living by husbanding the odd field not taken over by the military, caring for the few cows, pigs and fowls that they had kept from harm and by taking in paying guests at the expense of the Regimental Quartermaster.

The odd farm-house billet or even barn was the nearest to home comforts the men in British Army in Flanders were likely to get and if there was a wife or even a couple of pretty Mademoiselles as part of the establishment so much the better. These men well knew, as the song goes, although I do not know their contemporary version "there is nothing like a dame" and most of them would have sorely missed the culinary delights and other feminine qualities that would have been provided to each one of them in varying decrees by their ladies back home. It was after all very much the period when each gender's contribution to the other's welfare was clearly defined and generally observed. There were not many men who could knit a cap comforter, do the shopping and cooking properly or carry out a nurse's duties. Likewise there were not many ladies painting and decorating, driving horses or omnibuses or serving at sea. These warmer billets would be alas, but for a few days, before these infantry men would be off elsewhere in the saga that was for nearly four years the Western Front.

The Diaries written up when the battalion was not engaged in a specific battle, become mostly a series of one liners, but they still tell a story of well co-ordinated and positive activity:- 8th June, relieved by 8th K.R.R., relief complete by 3am; 9thJune, marched to Busseboom, rested to 5pm, marched on to Houtkerque; (the distance of 15 miles is not mentioned);10th-19th June, training; 23rd June, won machine gun competition on 30 yard range; 30th June, took over trenches at 03 to P4b--SW of St Eloi from 3rd Royal Fusiers. Whilst out of the line, life for the average infantryman appeared to be one of constant movement, changing billets, a pattern of continual training, parades and route marches with plenty of night working parties carrying essential supplies by hand up to the front. When they were ordered to the front, which was usually for five or six days at a time there was a stark contrast of inactivity with not a lot of detail recorded:-1st-5th July, in trenches fairly quiet; 22ndJuly German mortaring with rifle grenades-cannot retaliate not sufficient a/grenades; 23rd July, rifle grenades explode in D1.D4. asked for 1000 R/Grenades got 30; 25thJuly, more casualties-rifle grenades; 26-28thJuly, working as usual building trenches etc. On the 7th August, the war's first anniversary had passed three days ago, the diarist records an incident in D3 trench which had just received a pounding from about 50 rifle grenades hurled over by the enemy. The British Army replied with jam tin grenades fired from their new trench bomb thrower. It was now several months since the shortage of shells and munitions fiasco became public knowledge and there were still many deficits being suffered by the men fighting a war on behalf of probably the world's No 1 Superpower.

In and out of the trenches became a fixed way of life for the British Tommy, illustrated above from the 3rd Middlesex Diaries but similar along most of the British Sector at this time. There was not much happening on the surface and whilst the British troops were making a lot of their own bangers from what was to hand, the German industrial machine was busy adding fresh horrors to their already long list of superior arms. On July 30th, near Hooge, a few miles north of where my Father was soldiering, and again in the infamous salient, there was a cruel attack by the enemy using their new Flammenwerfer. The flame-thrower designed to pour a jet of liquid fire over the unsuspecting British troops. This local attack by the Prussian Guards was not planned as a sustained action and no significant gains were made. It did however add another brutal instrument of death and maiming, which both sides of the conflict were soon to use as an attack and defence weapon and helped to increase the bitterness, hatred and fury into which the protagonists were plunging ever deeper.

It also added to the reputation of that notorious salient, which had become the principal killing ground of the British sector.

Flame-throwing and other horrors perpetrated there in the summer months of 1915, also included the detonating of one of the first terribly destructive underground mines, this time by British sappers and again it happened close to the village of Hooge. They had tunnelled from their own lines, under no-man's land and they had stacked a large charge of high explosive below their enemy's trenches, which when fired threw up hundreds of tons of earth and the unsuspecting German defenders in an orgy of sudden and unexpected death for the victims unfortunate enough to be taking their turn there at that particular time. This event was, but a prelude, to a much greater bout of mining activity by both sides along many sectors of the battle lines in the coming years. They were spectacular and very deadly in their way but more often than not the resulting deep craters were quickly converted into heavily fortified redoubts or strongholds by fresh troops ordered to fill the gaps or retake the few yards of territory initially lost by the explosion.

3rd Middlesex was out of all this and slowly recovering their losses much the same as all the other British contingents already in Belgium and France guarding the lines to the south of that dreadful salient. These battle tried units were certainly gaining strength at a greater rate than they were taking casualties. At the same time the B.E.F. Command was also being reinforced by more and more trained troops from all parts of the Empire and Commonwealth but with the greatest share coming from the United Kingdom made up by England, Scotland, Wales and the whole of Ireland. Battalions of men were crossing the English Channel to form the new Brigades and Divisions designated by the Chiefs of Staff to strengthen the two armies already in the field.

The tally of killed and wounded in my Father's unit remained quite low both during their duties in the trenches and their sometimes quite dangerous training and support sessions so that come early September the Battalion was at fighting strength again.

In turn, as the whole Expeditionary Force became stronger, so more of the Western Front could be taken over from the French. By mid-summer, the line held by the British extended almost continuously from the Ypres Salient out of Belgium into France, protecting the first large French town of Armentieres, on southwards and nearly through to Arras. It was near here that the French were planning their next big push to take place and they were keen to involve the B.E.F. in their strategy

They were also going to involve my Father who would add yet another unsung laurel to his unrecorded collection. The Battle of Loos would be his and the next British contribution to a war that had nearly been on hold since 2nd Ypres three and a half months ago..

The continual movements around the French and Belgium countryside had kept him and the other soldiers busy in a most positive manner and these men gained confidence as they observed the build up of more and more regiments and the sustenance of war virtually filling the landscape. They were certainly trim and fit. Look at any photograph of this period of the Tommies in Flanders or Picardy and you see men in their prime, just as the Bard observed of their fore-fathers awaiting their test at Harfleur and Agincourt (exactly five centuries previous and in much the same area) "like greyhounds in the slips, straining upon the start". So it was with these men, they were ready to beat the Boche in one more concerted effort.

Their training and minimal guard duty in the trenches had been designed exactly for this end. The General Staff and all other levels of command had been precisely geared to proceed to this ultimate goal of breaking the deadlock and winning a long overdue victory. The men of these New Armies and Divisions trusted their Officers and the Officers had confidence in the Staff. All looked right on paper and as the fresh battalions assembled at their rendezvous locations one unit behind another the question of success did not arise, only how long would it take?

Very soon my Father's unit from the old army and now part of a veteran Division and Brigade would become part of the scheme and they too would be marching towards the angry guns. On the 17th September 3rd Middlesex had been relieved by 3rd Royal Fusliers in the quiet sector in front of the small town of Dranouter close to the French border. They had time for a good clean up, a church parade and a couple of days training before being ordered to leave their tented bivouacs on the 22nd September and march as part of the 85th Brigade to Strazeele in France.

Their Commanding Officer, who led the Battalion on its march into France from Belgium, had been gazetted only recently, promoted to the rank of Lieutenant Colonel, the established rank, for the C.O. of an infantry battalion consisting of about a thousand officers and men. He had barely another week to live. A distinguished Officer, George Henry Neale, age 46, had been the Battalion's C.O. since its previous Colonel, Ernest William Rokeby Stephenson, also aged 46, had been killed in action on St Georges Day, last April, barely five months ago, at the start of 2nd Ypres. As Second in Command of the Battalion as well as C.O., Major Neale had seen much action ever since he had arrived in France the previous January, at the time when my Father was volunteering for his service. The new Colonel had put his life on the line many times as a regular career officer and one like so many of his ilk who did not deserve to be tainted by the armchair historians who have since the conflict ended, willingly endorsed the Kaiser's slander so much as to libel our officer class with distortions of the facts that are now widely believed.

In the Kaiser's phase, this donkey had led his lions in some awful places, even prior to this war. He had shared the dangers with the West African Niger Expedition of 1897 when he was 28 years old; continued during the next seven years, with helping to hold the thin red line during troubles in Tirah, Waziristan and Tibet in what was once Persia and parts of the old Indian Empire. Years of active and loyal service before being called to this major conflict involving the peace and freedom of Europe.

He was about to lead from the front again and have his name join the others of his beloved battalion that have no known resting place. In company with that young nineteen year old mentioned in a previous chapter, who had been at the front just five days, his name would share a space on a memorial tablet to the missing. Only their rank and length of service were different, one was a Private who had joined the army less than six months before he was killed in action the other a Lieutenant Colonel with years of loyal service. In common they fought with the 3rd Battalion, Middlesex Regiment. Both were men of honour and those who say differently are wrong. The silent stone columns tell the truth for these two men and all the others and is the evidence that should be heeded, not some hack's ill-founded misrepresentation about lions and donkeys.

The three lines in Binyon's "For the Fallen" before his famous "They shall grow not old,----" is more appropriate to all these men whatever their rank, be it General or Private, Colonel or Lance-Corporal.

Straight of Limb, true of eye, steady and aglow,

They were staunch to the end against odds uncounted,

They fell with their faces to the foe.

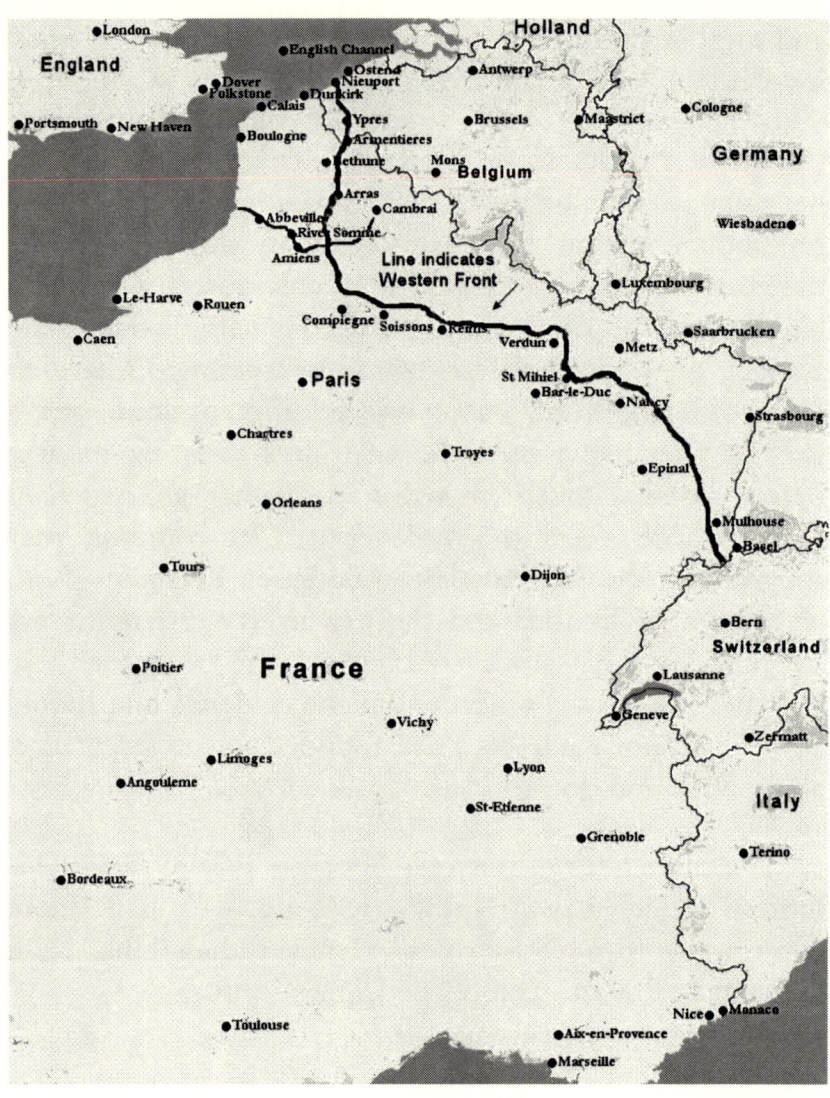

Map indicating the location of the Western Front relative to national borders from December 1914 – August 1918 First World War

Chapter 8

Fourteen Divisions took part in the Battle of Loos, going on to the offensive between the 25th September and 8th October 1915. The British Army's approach to war was being scaled up as never before in its long and active history. More than 220,000 men with their arms and supplies, larger than the Empire's total standing army, but a short year ago, had been assembled on the orders of Sir John French, the Commander in Chief of the British Expeditionary Force, to attack on the left flank of a far greater French initiative. The latters' offensive was planned to occur on two sectors of the Western Front. One sector was to be in the former province of Artois, its left flank near the still thriving coal mining and industrial town of Lens extending southwards on the west side of Vimy Ridge towards Arras, an attacking front of some 15 miles. The other effort was to be in the Champagne area, over 100 miles to the south-east, in the Reims-Argonne region. Both offensives were intended to be the jaws of a very large pincer movement involving nearly one third of the length of the Western Front some one hundred miles plus in length..

Just about this time the British had taken over responsibility from the French forces to hold more miles of the Western Front. The B.E.F. zone now stretched from Ypres in Belgium, across the French border at Armentieres and hence following an zig-zagging direction southwards, to include the towns and villages of Aubers, Neuve Chapelle, Givenchy, Vermelles and Grenay. A substantial distance, more than forty miles in length;

modest when compared with the French Army's front, but still needing to be continuously manned for defensive purposes or from which to launch attacks. The commitment ended at the British Army's command boundary at Grenay where the French poilu, in horizon blue uniform, with his pipe and bristling whiskers, faced eastwards next to Tommy Atkins, dressed in khaki drab and generally drawing on a woodbine cigarette. Neither man had a steel helmet.

The town of Loos was in German occupied France just behind their trench lines opposite Grenay. It was from here that the French wanted the British to be part of their offensive, along a further six miles of the line that stretched northwards.

The attack was to be an ambitious combined attempt to roll back and conclusively defeat the forces of the Kaiser before winter set in. The German forces were well entrenched in front of Loos, which is situated some twenty-five miles from the French border. If most of that captured ground could be retaken, and a large part of the enemy forces trapped and pinched out by the two prongs of the attack, the Allies would be a long way towards winning the war.

Loos was one of a number of small towns in the triangle formed by La Bassee, Bethune and Lens in what was the black country of North Eastern France. The smallest of the mining communities were called "corons", the larger ones "cites". These places had elegant titles like Cite St Pierre, Cite St Elie and Corons de Pekin, to name just three, where much action was to take place. Heavy pit winding gear and slag heaps dotted the area amongst the "corons" and "cites" with their rows of damaged and abandoned miners' houses nearby. Each community had its spired church that stood out from the flat fields between them that were planted out mostly with root crops before the war came to the area.

Many of the French miners, with their families, had fled from captivity by going underground when, as they would say, the hated Boche arrived. Having escaped into the mines, they eventually passed beneath no-man's land through the mining galleries and emerged into the light again in places like Grenay, Mazingarbe and Noeux les Mines, which were in friendly hands and mirrored those places they had left.

Despite the invasion, these people were trying their best to pick up the threads of their lives. Where-ever possible they were achieving this by keeping the mines working and carrying on with the dirty and heavy work that had been their lot throughout several generations in the same manner uniquely characteristic of their society. Of course, the authorities approved. They considered that it was essential that they be encouraged to continue this important contribution to the war effort, as long as they could; despite the odd shell or salvo regularly taking its toll, indiscriminately, on these miners, their wives, their young children and elders alike.

This presence of so many civilians however, living so close to the front and mixing with the troops, was quite unusual along most of the Western Front, which mostly occupied sparsely populated farmland. The Tommies, who had come down from the warzones in Belgium, did not expect to see these people, often, nigh-on sharing their temporary billets in the villages or towns that were well with-in the range and sights of the enemy's guns.

Moving nearer to the actual front, the landscape did appear to be deserted and empty except for the spoil from much digging or artillery bombardment. This was the zone of the communication trenches that had been dug, sometimes well over a half a mile in length, towards various sectors of the ultimate frontline. Each of these communication trenches were linked to its adjacent counterpart by one or more branch links, the whole complicated layout demanding a comprehensive and secret identification system of maps and names, from which the General Staff could instruct their forces to go or assemble thereto.

It certainly stretches ones' imagination to envisage these deliberate earthworks going on for four hundred miles, each and every yard requiring the same back up in depth with its occupants all facing the early morning rising sun every day for nearly four years, whilst the tenants of its equal or probably more elaborate counterpart had the warmth of that early light on their backs.

Although, no sign of life could be observed above the ground in the run up to the start of the Battle of Loos, below the surface, in these deep but open warrens, there was a constant movement going on; that of bringing the necessities of a great battle forward and into the front line ready for the order to attack. Hundreds of troops were involved in these duties that were carried out throughout a period of two weeks before the battle was due to commence and the records indicate that during that time these activities remained unobserved from the enemies lines, a comparative short distance across no man's land.

No man's land, in this area between the two twisting and irregular sets of front line trenches, varied in width. Where the Germans had built outward projecting, heavily defended redoubts, the British trenches were barely 75 yards away. Elsewhere it could be as much as 700 yards wide, a long way to even dash across in a storm of shot and shrapnel without much cover. The enemy's projecting fortresses or redoubts gave them much advantage, enabling them to enfilade or direct their fire both across the width of no-man's land and along its length, when being attacked. The withering crossfire in these circumstances could create awesome difficulties for attacking infantry and needed to be addressed in any battle plan.

The invaders were improving their defences by the day, along most of the long front-line, intending to wear down their adversaries against impregnable positions of deep earthworks, concrete and steel emplacements, protected in front by vicious barbed wire entanglements, many yards wide.

In the otherwise drab and undistinguished landscape of the Loos area they were utilising the existing man-made structures, such as the tall steel pit buildings and cone shaped hills of mining debris, for look-out and additional defence positions. Anything to give extra height and better vision.

One of the most prominent of these steel structures at Loos was quickly nicknamed "Tower Bridge" by the

London Tommies as its twin towers joined by two steel gantries reminded them of their own one across the Thames between Bermondsey and Whitechapel. Thereafter all and sundry used this name particularly when it was acting as a reference or guiding point for the troops fighting in this battle. Like the town of Albert in Picardy had its Golden Virgin and Child, hanging by a thread, from its Basilica Tower, overlooking those who were endlessly passing through towards the battles on the Somme in 1916; and the legendary angels and archers of Mons seen in 1914; so did "Tower Bridge" pass into so many shared memories of those who served and fought at this awesome part of the line in 1915.

In places, second and even third line positions, were beginning to be constructed by the Germans, to double or treble the tasks of the advancing infantry, before the open ground beyond could be safety taken over and passed through. Behind these barriers there were well armed forces with machine guns and artillery which were becoming increasingly more capable of inflicting very heavy casualties and of destroying any attempts by the French and British assailants who tried to dislodge them.

Nevertheless, this was the task facing the Allied Armies in 1915 along the 400 plus miles that made up the Western Front, and many a strategist involved with the two Allies urged for the reasons expressed above, that "time was of the essence", if a breach was to be achieved. Sooner rather than later certainly seemed to be a better option; and it was also important that the two countries began to work together. Large and well equipped forces would be needed.

Strategically, the British choice of battle sites were fairly limited. In the scheme of things, particularly under the informal terms of Entente Cordiale of 1904, they had agreed to support and fight on the left of French forces opposing enemies attacking from the east. This predetermined that Northern France would be the location where the British would fight and led to the place names in Flanders and Picardy becoming such evocative reminders of the sacrifices that were made there, during the four long years that the war lasted. It also happened to be that these places required the shortest supply route for activities outside the United Kingdom and therefore was much to this country's advantage than elsewhere in the world would have been.

When the war was over, many accounts of the events were quick to record that the Battle of Loos was a disaster. They blamed the choice of ground, insufficient reserves, lack of artillery, the inevitable mistakes of Generals and even the wrong type of wind. They laid little emphasis on the fact that the battle, over twelve days and nights, was the heaviest ever engaged by a British army to that date and that this combined clash of arms, determined that every subsequent attack, push or offensive in the future, would need to be larger if there was going to be a hope of it succeeding. How much larger needed to be addressed. What worth, the infallible answer to this question would have been, had it been really sought, found and heeded? It would have been beyond price even towards the start of autumn 1915, long before the Battle of Loos had taken place. In that first year of the Great War, it was well known that the British and Empire's casualty rate stood at 381,982, with an addition of over 12,000 naval men being lost at sea and those figures excluded civilian casualties killed in the bombing and naval shelling of the British homeland.

More than 1,000 men per day, had been lost, killed, wounded, missing or taken prisoner for every day since war had been declared. Three of those Jumbo Jets with British markings, mentioned earlier, were still crashing every day. In terms of numbers our post war standing army had been lost twice over. Britain, and the Government in particular, certainly, had good cause to thank the part-time men of the Terriers and the volunteers like my Father who had filled these fearful gaps. They were more than accruing their merits for, maybe, a National payback when they needed it.

Ninety five percent of the losses had been sustained on the Western Front and I have little doubt, that the Generals already knew what the oracle's advice would have been. Greater armies were needed, stronger and better equipped than the enemy's. They and their French colleagues knew that if the politicians running the country wanted to indulge in a European war, due to commitments that they had made, they should have very large national armies combining total national effort to do it. Conscription and training, stockpiling and producing the means to wage a war in Europe, before the event, was essential. The reality was that one and a half years of war would pass before these essentials would be fully in place. Little wonder this conflict caused the scars the nation incurred then and which it still goes on feeling whenever the war is mentioned.

Even my Father and his mates who had, at least, fought an attacking enemy to a stand-still, back in

Belgium, knew what they had taken on, i.e. to attempt the reverse and get the Hun on the run. They did not need to be a Caesar, Wellington or Kitchener to deduce the enormity of the fight that they had undertaken. As they marched southwards from the Belguim frontier, it was all the same. On their left, wet or fine, was the continuously growling front line, mile on mile of trenches stretching apparently forever that had to be breached and pushed aside to give them access to the countryside beyond. The many Londoners in the Regiments on the march would have said as they passed the unending and similar topography, "same meat different gravy" with a resigned stoicism coupled with a shrewd cockney appraisal of their position.

As I toured this ground and along much of the Western Front, I could see the problem in my mind's eye. There was not and never had been any easy ground over which to attack an entrenched enemy. Check along the whole Western Front and I believe one would find, that there was not one location that could guarantee an easy attack and a complete victory. I am sure that if there had been, it would have been written about long ago.

In spite of this, the red tabbed Staff officers' remit was to try. My Father was one of a generation of young and not so young men who had to try. Many of these men had to try twice, over the same ground, and they would tell you, if they could, that the first time should have been enough. Somebody was to blame for that, but it was not them.

At any rate, the world of 1915 was certainly not yet prepared even to try one slightly more modern solution, albeit, one that was and still is, not totally effective. I have called it the Panmunjom solution. In Korea, the North and South protagonists have been glaring at each other across an almost forgotten truce line of such entrenchments, as were at Loos, since 1953, more than fifty years, and it seems most likely that the unfriendly looks will be extended well into the 21st century. Kashmir may have a very similar line on the sub-continent, much the same as the green line that divides Cyprus. The1915 British and French protagonists did not have the privilege just to glare. The slightest show of weakness demanded blood, much as the politicians demanded action. A combination of French and British Generals, acting under these instructions, eventually agreed and planned a push to end the war that autumn. The French were more keen with the timing and location than the British but once it had been decided, both sides organised the battle with their full resources and much zeal. A look at a large scale map with the whole battle line drawn there-on indicates the scale of French thinking regarding this matter, whilst the smaller sketches of the Western Front in a number of volumes do not convey this aspect all that well.

The early morning attack started by the British Army on the 25th September 1915 along a 6 mile front just east of the French town of Bethune coincided with the French offensive immediately to the right, stretching another15 miles to a position just south of Arras. The French also attacked with large armies in the Champagne sector of the continuous front at the same time. The plans had much merit if all went well. If their forces could batter a wide gap in the enemy's line to allow large numbers of fresh troops to push through into the countryside beyond, the flanks of the German positions would be threatened by encirclement and the Germans would be forced to retreat. If the momentum could be kept going with similar wide pressures keeping the opposing armies in a permanent retreat mode, the Germans would realise that they had lost and they would be forced to sue for peace, or allow the fighting to continue on their own homeland.

So simply a gambit, two simple "ifs", the stark and unchangeable reality of the strategy of The Great War. Winning, losing or drawing a battle did not really count. The Battle of Loos proved that a break-through of the enemy's lines was possible, but the other ingredient was missing and unfortunately remained so even after several other tries made by both sides during the succeeding years. The essential strength of the Allied armies were not yet available, and as a result, so many were to pay the cost that had really been incurred on the day that war had been declared without someone giving due thought of what was needed to win.

The battle actually started on the 21st September. It was on a Tuesday that the great barrage of artillery assembled along the French and British lines opened fire, pounding the German positions for what was an unprecedented four day softening up process. During that time, the British were also assembling gas cylinders every few yards along their front under the cover of this bombardment. It was to be the first time that the British Army intended to use poison gas against an enemy and the officers and men responsible for this new and retaliatory dangerous addition to total war had been well rehearsed as to their important role. It had been simulated many times under great secrecy in the rear areas; and the equipment and over five thousand cylinders of gas had been brought up to the front line trenches without detection or the mishap or being hit by enemy counter-blasts. General Douglas Haig, the then Commander of the 1st Army that were making the assault, attached much importance to this weapon being used, no doubt minding back to the 23rd April, when the Germans first used gas with such damaging effect on the French defenders to the north of the Ypres Salient. They had achieved a break through; but not an on-going retreat, thanks to my Father and his like in khaki.

During this preparatory time the attacking divisions were also assembling. The 28th Division, with its three Brigades made up from fifteen infantry battalions was one of these that had received their marching orders. My Father was one individual in this force of 15,000 men, which was on the move. A total of fourteen Divisions, about a quarter of a million men, with their support units were being co-ordinated for action with detailed and specific orders filtering down from their High Command.

The 3rd Middlesex, with Dad, had come out of a quiet sector of the line known as the "Wulverghem Section-Belgium" on Friday 17th September. They had been kept busy, as always, training in basic trench warfare and expecting to relieve their friends in the 3rd Battalion Royal Fusiliers (City of London Regiment) when they had had their few days out of the line. This routine had been going on, between the two battalions, since the middle of July, about nine weeks in all, most of the summer. Now they were in for something different and even more unpleasant. On Tuesday 21st September they heard the guns start up, just as dawn was breaking. My Father trained with the rest of the battalion that day, as the rumours were finally confirmed that they would be leaving in the morning.

These men had got used to static trench warfare, nine weeks is a long time for doing this in the same place. Despite the stress of the daily casualty count, of unlucky friends being killed or maimed, the cold and awful food, the hard fatigues, the tiredness caused by work or inactivity, the dirt and filth associated with living in holes in the ground open at all times to the elements, these matters became part of an almost tolerable routine when shared by all in the unit. "Trench Standing Orders" had become required reading for all the men in the battalion and set out precisely what was required of them. They were a set of some forty firm, but often benign orders designed to assist and help with their well being in almost impossible circumstances. They were not allowed to take off their equipment either during the day or night whilst in the trenches. At night all bayonets were to be fixed. Every Company was to "stand to" for half an hour before dawn and before dusk, remaining so until dismissed by the Company's Commanding Officer. Each man's rifle had to be kept clean. Time was to be allocated for this task and a very severe penalty would be exacted if a man's rifle was found to be dirty during the regular inspections that were required by these orders. Other orders stressed that going to sleep on sentry duty or leaving ones allocated post without permission were the most serious crimes that a soldier could commit on active service. These orders made it abundantly clear that a man found guilty of these offences was likely to be shot. Every effort was made to limit sentry duty to one hour especially at night when double sentries were to be used if possible. Keeping the trenches clear of waste matter was emphasised for obvious reasons, as was the order to drink, cook and wash only in water brought up in water carts or tanks. Orders governed virtually the whole of these infantrymen's existence whilst they were in these trenches and their rack was about to go up a further notch.

It is hard for me to imagine how my Father coped with his thoughts of going into a major battle knowing that the survival rates were quite low. "Standing Orders" did not tell him what to do. "Devil-may-care", according to the dictionary can describe "happy go lucky", "reckless" or "careless" in the "I could not care less" sense and probably this was part of his attitude. The philosophy that it only takes one bullet or shell to end it all, wherever you are, would have perhaps registered with him. Fear, apprehension, fortitude, discipline born of respect to proper order and authority, self control, duty and "let's get it over", must have all been strong elements in him and most of the men with these British armies. I am fairly sure "esprit de corps" would have kicked in, that pride and sense of shared purpose and comradeship, but I shall never know his personal thoughts that brought him through. I did not ask him.

I do know, however, that he marched with the rest of his Battalion and their whole Brigade, in long columns of four, the first nine miles towards his next rendezvous with those four horsemen, many swore they saw riding, the dark, smoke and shot filled skies, over the battlefields of Northern France, where such terrible events were taking place.

Geographically, he was marching away from the front at first, going in a westerly direction, towards the

French town of Hazebrouck well away from possible enemy shellfire which could decimate long columns of marching men. The strains of "Tipperary" and "Pack up your Troubles" would have blotted out some of the noise of the guns as he skirted the nice old town of Bailleul before using the N42 main road which ended for him just before reaching Hazebrouck at the village of Strazelle set at the cross road with the D947. It is recorded that upon being billetted in the village, he and his unit were engaged in a sharp bout of attacking infantry training for much of the next three days.

Good rehearsals over similar ground conditions as would be faced in the actual assaults were becoming a strong feature of the training methods prior to battle. The battalions were told their likely slot in the massive and carefully planned scheme involving large numbers of men and units that were about to make history. They were expected to perform their allotted tasks at certain cues in the course of the battle, which was anticipated to last many days but really of unknown duration. Obviously, it would be expected to be more on going, if things went well and defeats and failures were not features that were practised in this training. It was explained to these fighting battalions that they would not have to continuously assault the enemy during the offensive. They would be given an objective to take and secure within a reasonable short time and then await relief from other oncoming units. These units would either provide extra back-up to maintain possession of the captured ground or pass through to assault the next objective in a pre-planned order. All this seemed to work well as they trained; and invariably my Dad and his mates captured the make belief trenches represented by the tapes stretched out across the fields in the training areas. They felt some relief when they were told that they would not be in the initial assault battalions, little knowing that they and the whole of their 28th Division were about to be instructed to hold itself in readiness to meet quote "unexpected eventualities".

That meant being at the disposal of General Sir Douglas Haig and Dad's cue for the real thing that came in on the very next day after the first units attacked, to start the Battle of Loos proper. It was Sunday the 26th September when his battalion was ordered to get kitted out for the fight and march southwards, fifteen miles, to Bethune, towards the guns and the noise of the fighting. They arrived at 9pm finding the town teeming with troops and groups of walking wounded endlessly moving to or from the front that glowed and banged away along the whole eastward horizon from the town.

The 3rd Middlesex needed some rest after their long march, loaded down with their equipment and they were very glad to be billetted quickly by the staff elements working with their own quartermasters, in the town that had been mostly taken over by the military and had become the capital of the British Army operating in the area of the north-east French coalfields. No Michelin stars would have been given for their accommodation or the victuals they received at the end of their long day. They felt lucky to get a meal but the orders as they were dismissed were laced with an element of foreboding. They put reveille at 5.30 am., first parade after breakfast at 6.30 am, dress, battle order, fully armed and ready to move. Most knew they would be in the fighting the next day, the battle lines were now less than 4 miles away.

Sharing their billets, or being housed close to the many French families staying in Bethune, no doubt brought memories of civvy street flooding back to my Father and these other young and active men deprived of the benefits of their normal existence. All ranks missed their previous way of life and they could catch glimpses of the same whilst in these still populated towns or villages that were so different from the militarised zones they generally had to occupy. Young girls and women, as through all wars, well saw, understood and sympathised with, to varying degrees, the universal hunger and desire they saw in the eyes of these men who so missed their own loves. These men in khaki deserved the support they received in the smiles and other tokens given without regret. They had all become part of this colossal bubbling cauldron, a "pot au feu", that was boiling away to rid the land and homes of these civilians from their common enemy and they all knew the distressing reality that so many of these young soldiers did not have a future.

Many of yesterday's young men, in the sector that my Father's Battalion was about to attack, had already lost their future. They had lost it making progress, only to have much of it taken back by a heavily reinforced enemy determined not to yield up their spoils of war. The British objective here, on that first day of the battle, had included one of those fortified redoubts,   mentioned earlier. This particular one was known as the Hohenzollern Redoubt and many who fought there knew it as a place of evil repute. It was captured on the first day of the battle, partly lost two days later when the enemy held one side and then after many more rounds of hand to hand fighting and bombing it was regained completely by the enemy on the 3rd October.

Ownership of this strategic sore remained to be disputed many days after the rest of the Loos offensive came to an end. It was the 46th Division, not one of the original Divisions detailed for the battle, who recovered the western part of it on the 13th October and the final sparks of the fighting at this place spluttered out a few days later with each side laying claim to a part of it by sheer, constant and bad tempered force of arms.

Before this however, on the 28th September, it was my Father's lot to try to help to hold this captured hell-hole, before the actual out-come of the battle had been decided. He and 3rd Middlesex were about to pay heavily for that privilege and their efforts went un-rewarded despite the verve they put into their attack.

The day before, 27th September, they had been ordered to march towards the British lines and assemble near the small town of Vermelles. They arrived there at 1p.m. after the short trek on busy roads and through busier communication trenches after their one night stay in Bethune. They knew as they waited there in the open, with the rest of the Brigade around them, that the offensive was now at a critical stage. For nearly thirteen hours they remained there, exposed, watching the action from an uncomfortable short distance, awaiting their orders to join it. They witnessed the gun-fire, the explosions, the smoke and noise and perhaps the most awful, the sights of stricken men, wounded spectres emerging through the gloom. This really brought home to them what they were about to face and the drag from many a shared Woodbine probably helped to allay their fears just a little. As the afternoon slowly drifted into night, 2 o'clock came and the long wait was over. It was time to move. It was their turn to try.

Their appointment with the enemy, arranged a long five days ago, was close by the ugly Hohenzollern redoubt that smoked and snarled like an active volcano about to erupt. Instead of lava boiling and bubbling, bombs and bullets seemed to whizz in all directions from its inner cone, the sides of which, in places thirty feet deep, steeped with sand bags and infested with bolt holes was populated with men in khaki killing those in field grey that were trying to get into it. All along this part of the battle-front it was much the same. The Diehards in battalion strength, all four companies, were ordered to join the fighting by approaching via a deep communication trench, still named Central Boyau from days when the French army manned this part of the line. Central Boyau terminated at the British front line trench that was opposite the redoubt. As the Battalion spread along this trench getting ready for their first "over the top" attack, stretched either side of them were the remainder of the their Brigade preparing to do likewise or help support those holding existing captured ground along a battle front of some one thousand yards.

The Germans were trying the exact opposite, using all means to recapture their redoubt. It was the key to this part of the line, and all the surrounding areas from which they had been prised twenty four hours ago. In face of this the British Generals from Division up to the Army Commander felt that there was still a chance of gaining that most sort-after break-through. If only their forces, now being reinforced, could hold and push through to that open ground beyond this moonscape of tortured chalk and barren earth, much littered with their dead and dying, it would indeed justify the efforts that had been made already.

Accordingly, it was my Father's turn with his Diehard friends to back up the modest gains, by more shooting and bombing, just as soon as the British artillery bombardment, designed to help them on their way, had ceased its work. It did so at 9.30am on the morning of the 28th September and the 3rd Middlesex advanced in the open on the south or right side of the redoubt towards a feature known to them as "The Dump". In front of this spoil heap of mining debris there was a trench built as part of the German line, which was now back in hostile hands and needed to be retaken. Big Willie, Little Willie, the Chord, South Face trench and several others on various sides of the Hohenzollern redoubt were still in British hands and 3rd Middlesex used South Face trench to approach their target. The action started in earnest at point 35 on the C.O.'s map in front of the German held Dump trench which was quickly taken by the attacking "Diehards". Good progress was made until the battalion ran out of bombs and there were no more to be had. Without bombs it was very difficult to hold the ground they had recovered when being attacked by an enemy better equipped and armed. Heavy casualties from the fierce counterattacks started to amount and Colonel George Neale their commanding officer ordered the battalion to slowly withdraw fighting as they went with whatever they had left.

All four companies gradually withdrew down the same South Face trench as they had used to approach Dump trench. It was a matter of trying to remain unexposed to the wicked cross fire and bombing coming from several directions from the higher ground held by the enemy.

The German pressure was building up and as the Diehards withdrew they were ordered by their Brigade Commander, to hold, at all costs, the first trench, Big Willie, captured by the assault yesterday after a costly dash across no-man's land. The Brigade Commander, one of the many senior officers in the thick of the battle, had set up his command post H.Q. central to his Brigade's zone of attack.

It was costly to 3rd Middlesex going in the opposite direction to get to the comparative safety offered by Big Willie. Their Colonel was killed outright and amongst many others my Father received his first packet, as he would have called it. I have wondered if the same shell that injured my Father, did for Colonel Neale. The gallant Colonel became one of the twenty thousand missing from the Battle of Loos and he, with the others, is commemorated on the Loos Memorial which forms the side and back walls of Dud Corner Cemetery, a short distance from the village of Loos-en-Gohelle.

Dad kept his shell fragment for the rest of his life, embedded in his skull. It is one of a few hazy recollections of mine, buried deep in my adolescence and early adult memories that my Mother would remark on certain occasions that dear Father carried the relic of this wound with him, even to his grave. I have no documentary proof of this particular fact, it certainly did not seem to affect him in any way, all the time I knew him, but on 28th

September 1915, late evening, I do know, it meant Blighty to him, even if he was far from sure.

The poet Philip Edward Thomas, who was killed in action during a battle that took place much later in the war, had had similar thoughts as my father was thinking at this time, and he committed them to verse........

'No one cares less than I,

Nobody knows but God.

Whether I am destined to lie

Under a foreign clod,'

Were the words I made to the bugle call in the morning.

—————————————————

Chapter 9

The blast of the exploding shell knocked my Dad over, sending him tumbling into Big Willie, with blood pouring down the side of his face. Perhaps, he and the Colonel would have been spared their injuries, as with so many others, had they been issued before the battle with that most recognisable symbol of the British Forces of the two world wars, the steel, or to give its correct name "shrapnel" helmet. Unfortunately, like many other items, these helmets did not become standard issue until well into the next year and one consequence of this for my Father was that his "gorblimey" field service cap was ruined, being scorched, holed, ripped and very bloodstained and he became in urgent need of stretcher bearers to take him to the Regimental Aid Post, for the doctor or medic there, to determine whether 'he' now had a future.

Whatever was to be decided, if he ever got there, the Battle of Loos was over for him. He had become one more casualty amongst many who needed that urgent attention, but he was unlikely to get it, while his fit companions had to battle against those enemy troops who were counter attacking with such deadly intentions.

Fortunately he had fallen into the trench. If he had remained above ground, he would not have made it. A comrade would have probably straightened him up against the steep side of Big Willie and tied a rough dressing around his head to check the bleeding until there was some-one who could attend to him properly. There was nothing else the fighting troops could do for him, and it was too hot at and above ground level for any of the appointed First-Aiders to try, whilst so much pressure from the attack was happening. There were too many mortars, bombs, bullets and shells being aimed at Big Willie to make a move yet. The only hope for my Father was that his blood would stop flowing. Unattended open wounds like his could quickly drain a man's life blood and become fatal.

He did not have much of a priority. He was only one amongst the bulk of 327 Diehards who were now either dead, dying, maimed or wounded, lying where they fell or, like him had fallen or dragged themselves below ground level to escape another more likely mortal blow. Three more of Dad's mates listed on the medal rolls either side of his regimental number had been killed in this action. They would never answer the daily roll call again. G7448, 7449,7465, Privates, Wickens, Standerwick and Kearley paid the supreme price for our freedom that day when my Father was wounded and they too would be remembered, like their Colonel, in Dud Corner Cemetery, their mortal remains having no known resting place.

The remainder of the 3rd Middlesex continued to hold on to the captured German trench and as dusk settled the German assault eased and eventually stopped. There was always tomorrow to try again and all troops, friend or foe alike, needed respite after the efforts that they had made continually for nearly twenty four hours. That decision of the Germans to stop for a rest also went a long way, I believe, in saving my Dad's life. If they had continued and eventually forced a retirement from Big Willie, Dad would not have been in any state to get up and go in a fighting retirement and the enemy were not taking prisoners at this stage of the battle where the British were not acknowledging defeat.

Despite this lull, there was not much time for rest however, and getting as many of the wounded out of the line would be one of the many activities ordered by the few remaining officers and N.C.O.s in charge of 3rd Middlesex. In this time, my Father would have come round from his concussion and shock and he was able to put his thoughts together again clearly enough to tell his platoon N.C.O that he could walk with a little help. Although his face was drained from shock and loss of blood, I think he would have been quite pleased to be told that he and another chap, slightly less injured than himself should try to make it back to the rear and the dressing stations that could help them properly.

Whatever they thought, they had little other option, they were 'hors de combat' for a time, and they would be too much of a burden to their mates next day when everyone knew the action would be renewed. Accordingly my Father with his wounded friend dragged themselves towards the Regimental Aid Post (R.A.P.), that they had been told had been set up in a dug-out which was part of Central Boyau close to its junction with the British old front line trenches. It was not an easy journey though not too far, about 600-700 meters in all, with plenty of others that were going their way. Squeezing pass cases far worse than their own took it out of them perhaps more than all the other obstacles. Men wounded so badly, that they could not survive. They were just about holding on to the last vestiges of their existence, having been made as comfortable as possible. Most were now moaning with pain and asking for their mothers as, variously, a padre, priest or friend tried to give them that last comfort drawn from them being there. More of my Dad's mates had become this casualty type but there was small chance for a proper farewell from him, someone was always behind wanting to press on. Others in front of him, mostly the stretcher cases, held him up until there was sufficient room to pass; and there was always the tortured terrain, above and below ground level to try to negotiate in one's anxious and fragile state. Regardless of these horrendous and disheartening difficulties my Father got there. Waiting his turn at every phase in the evacuation system he would have gradually become more confident that he was going to survive.

The Regimental Medical Officer at the R.A.P. in Central Boyau trench, under the dull, shadowy yellow light from a dimmed hurricane lamp, probably looked at Dad's dressing, ascertained that the bleeding had stopped and decided to leave well alone, instructing him in the same breath to follow the others towards the A.D.S (Advanced Dressing Station) not more than a mile behind the front.

This A.D.S. was situated along the Vermelles to Hulluch road and it was approached by a further series of communication trenches and traverses that led there and provided better protection than travelling above ground. Today it is the site of the St Mary's Advanced Dressing Station Cemetery where nearly two thousand men have their graves or memorials. Many of these were the seriously wounded who had been taken there by the Herculean efforts of their friends, or by anonymous and courageous stretcher bearers, detailed before the battle started to do this epic work. Sadly, the long struggle that my Father had managed, was too much for them, especially, when coupled with the fact that the ultimate medical assistance was still two or maybe three difficult and uncomfortable legs away in the relay race to survival. If, instead of the hard and wearisome evacuations by stretcher bearers, horse powered carts or ambulances and then a slow train journey, there had been a squadron of those helicopters working with the efficient field hospitals depicted so well in the television series "MASH" this graveyard might not have been so crowded with fine young men. Less than a third of the British and Commonwealth soldiers laid to rest here are named, the remainder are unknown warriors, sharing in theory, I suppose, that Victoria Cross, awarded to that other unknown soldier lying in Westminster Abbey. Who's to tell whether they deserved it, the same as he did? Anyhow, the dates on the head-stones of the Die-hards from the 3rd Battalion buried in this smaller plot in France has much importance to me. They bear further and poignant witness to the presence of my Father in this battle, his contribution to it and his brief visit to this same spot. It makes my hairs stiffen to think I have seen and visited this special place as he had done.

When I came here in the late 20th Century, my wife and I stayed at a nearby chateau which is run now as a good hotel. The hotel boasted a gourmet restaurant where we indulged, once or twice in its excellent French cuisine. I have since calculated that the cost of that visit would have easily paid for my Dad's total four year service on the Western Front with a couple of his Die-hards friends included for good measure. It followed in my reckoning, that only my father and his like had paid the true price to make my visit possible and in his time there, his nation could get so much, for less than a shilling (5p) a day.

Many of the wounded, brought to the A.D.S., of course, did survive and went on to complete the additional medical hurdles. My Father was one amongst them. The Medics at this A.D.S. would have, minimally given him a hot mug of tea, sweetened with plenty of tinned condensed milk, the only sustenance he had had since he went into action twenty six hours earlier. I do not know if he was much rested here, or that he had his wound inspected, but by most accounts and research, it was usually an in and out procedure for the walking wounded.

The Main Dressing Station (M.D.S.), or Casualty Clearing Station (C.C.S.), one or both in that order, would now give him their attention when he arrived. This is where he would become an official casualty of war, an important aspect for his service record. A serving soldier of whatever rank was allocated a place somewhere in the service, by order. That person was not a free agent, some document would give him authority to be where he was and what he was doing. Whether on active service with a unit, on seven days leave at home or occupying the attention of the Medical Services etc, his time there where-ever it was, had to be properly authorised and his name and number included on an official list. There was no such thing as freelance activity as a civilian may exercise and if a soldier's papers did not match his whereabouts, that soldier would be in serious trouble, all the more so in any theatre of war.

The medical officer (M.O.) and his staff at either of these units would document him, inspect and treat his wound, rest, feed and water him, before sending him on. If he was lucky there would be some nice young female nurses helping the doctors here, and one of their jobs would be to give him a dose of anti-tetanus serum as well as clean bandages and that little bit of sympathy he needed. I believe, as the major town of Bethune was less than six miles from the A.D.S. he attended, and the route was along fairly decent although very busy roads, he was told to go direct to the C.C.S. that had been established in that town. It was not necessary for him to go to the M.D.S. as an interim stop; he did not have any broken bones to be reset from possible very rudimentary splinting or major redressing of larger or gaping wounds that needed more aid at every one of these deliberate stages.

At the C.C.S. in Bethune he was told that he would be sent back to England to recover. Was he glad? I believe his smile nearly reappeared. He had been relieved of most of his fighting kit and equipment back in the trenches where they were still needed and he literary owned just what he stood up in. He had been washed and cleaned up after his treatment but the Medics were not giving the walking wounded new uniforms unless absolutely necessary. Seemingly the lice inhabiting his clothing would make the return journey with him. The brown official label tied to his filthy tunic listing his details and bona-fides and the bandage around his head made him feel somewhat fragile, but at least there were many more men like himself, sitting and waiting for that hospital train to take them back home, away from the horrors that they had witnessed so recently on that six mile fighting front that formed the Loos battlefield. He was not given a bed, there were none to spare for his type of wound. Doctors, nurses and orderlies tended to go for the label, tied to one of his tunic's buttonholes, which gave his details: Number G7458, Private, Robert James Reed, 3rd Middlesex, Shrapnel head wound, loss of blood, evacuate to England; rather than speak to him directly when they approached him. It saved repetition, one may suppose, for very tired men and the attention given at these military casualty stations was reckoned to be very good and adequate by any standards of those days. Certainly enough to start the healing process of all but the very seriously wounded.

Along the front at suitable intervals the Clearing Stations had been set up as part of the overall battle plans. The C.C.S. diaries, now archived at the Public Records Office at Kew, indicate how efficient they were, especially when dealing with the enormous numbers of wounded men resulting from major pushes by either of the protagonists. One such place, set up at the College of St Joseph in Bailleul and designated Casualty Clearing Station Number 8 was dealing with battlefield wounded within two days of the buildings being taken over. Its C.O., Major H.Rogers, R.A.M.C. (Royal Army Medical Corps) records in his diary for May 1915 that the hospital admitted a total of 9639 cases in that month, during the peak of the battles of 2nd Ypres. No doubt his returns would show similar figures for the end of September taken during the actions at Loos. The Diarist praises his staff of all ranks, in a note dated 19th May1915 for the good work done and states that even the largest convoys of sick men were accommodated without a hitch. A failing National Health Service, in the early part of the twenty-first century, would do well to study their methods even to get a third of their efficacy. For research purposes

I have scanned these diaries for names of individuals without success. They are not recorded in any I have examined, only the number of patients are noted, how many admitted, how many sent on, and, sadly, how many who did not make it any further. Quite often they also mention the types of casualties dealt with, giving the numbers of stretcher cases and those still capable of proceeding on their own without too much help.

Both Bailleul and Bethune C.C.S.s were on a direct railway link to the channel ports of Calais and Boulogne as well as a major Base Hospital near the latter port. This almost permanent establishment was mainly set-up for the seriously injured who could not travel further and convalescent cases that were not being sent back to their home country. Many Colonials and men from the Dominions came into the latter category, Canada, New Zealand, Australia and India were much too far away for them to be sent home unless they were heading in one direction for a medical discharge and they were out of the fight.

The sooner my dear Father could get on that hospital train heading towards those ports the sooner he would be back in France and in the action once again. That was the policy worked out by the army staff officers and it worked on over eighty percent of the soldiers wounded on the battlefields and sent back to England. These valuable veterans were returned to active duty generally within one to four months of being wounded. Private Robert James Reed, although temporary damaged, should not take too long to send back.

In the meantime, until Dad got well again, the Middlesex Regiment would have to manage without him. In fact his battalion had to remain at their post, in those costly German trenches for another forty-eight hours. Just before dawn at 5am on the 29th September the south face of the Hohenzollern Redoubt was heavily attacked again by German forces in great strength which was later backed up with further pressure on Big Willie and the West Face. Whilst Dad was waiting for that train, 3rd Middlesex was fighting desperate actions to hold on to the small gains like Big Willie and Dump Trench. It was not possible and they eventually regrouped company by company into the German first line trenches on the 30th where they remained until they were relieved at mid-night of the 30thSept/1st Oct.

The remains of the battalion left the battle-ground by much the same route as my Father had done on the night of the 28th/29th, forty-eight hours earlier, using the same communication trenches, until reaching the A.D.S. on the Vermelles to Hulluch Road. Here they assembled and marched the two and a half miles to Annequin where billets were available for those battle weary men. My Father did not know, when he left his friends in Big Willie two nights earlier, that he would not be rejoining them when he was well again. 3rd Middlesex had just three weeks on the Western Front to do, they would be shortly embarking to another completely different theatre of war.

The Battle of Loos which started with our infantry attacking with great spirit was coming to a close without much gain. The on-going fighting for the next few days was mostly to hold on to the gains made earlier on the 25th-27th September. It was hard going to defend all that was gained on the six mile line from which the attack sprung. In fact, for two of those miles at the northern end from Cambrin, on to the Brickstacks then to the Hohenzellern Redoubt, only the bare narrow width of No Mans Land had been taken and held. Southwards the German front line had been breached for over four miles to depths exceeding two miles in places, but the breakthrough into open country was not achieved. There was to be no easy victory yet. Even a quarter of a million men in arms were not sufficient a force to smash through and hold the enemy's second line and reach the countryside beyond. At the critical time, the German ability to move and provide fresh reinforcements directed at the fast diminishing British reserves in the lines so far reached, was destined to ensure, that the same stagnant, bloodstained, foul and mud ridden sector, would remain as it was for the next three years.

The French armies to the immediate right of the British for twelve long miles down to Arras had fared no better. Neither had their lone and gallant attempt in the Champagne region achieve the hoped for advance to the Ardennes. General Joffre's small gains on both these fronts, did not justify the losses, according to most writers propounding with hindsight, when the war was over. No one came up with a lasting alternative then or during the war. It was not suggested, but could the Panmunjom solution have been the best way to resolve the problems of the warring nations of Europe? It begs the question was there anyone in authority who had the nerve to suggest it, and try diplomatic persuasion? It would need both sides to agree politically, but a continent divided by a permanent inactive Western Front in this way did not suit anyone in 1915. The Central Powers still intended to win and keep their gains and perhaps a lot more, and the Allies were intent on stopping them and they too perhaps would not go away empty handed afterwards. That the loser would have to pick up the tab, was the only perceived prospect, whoever it was. The hollow slogan "the war to end all wars" had not been coined quite yet. It would be another thirty-five years before a sinister and threatening barrier would arbitrarily divide this continent without an ensuing bloodbath. The alternative to this, then, was just too horrific to contemplate. In 1950 an iron curtain would become acceptable and tolerated across the heart and cradle of Christendom. Two accrued arsenals of H-Bombs, the outcome of another world war, made it acceptable. So-called war had become cold without lots of fighting, as had occurred twice within the living memory of most, despite the above much quoted political exposition first made public whilst the Great War's killing and maiming was reaching its crescendo. It was the certainty of total mutual destruction that focused the minds of the politicians of the great powers of the First and Second worlds to stop their warring in Europe. They came up with the cold war, defined in the Oxford Dictionary as "a state of political hostility and military tension between two countries or power blocs involving propaganda, subversion, threats etc". Consequently there was no publishing of endless casualty lists in the newspapers for the forty years that the cold war lasted and the rusty curtains had been taken down. The slightly different version, which makes up the United Nations on-going truce in Korea is still in place, another cold war, with similar intentions. It is speculative, but if mushroom clouds had pierced the skies of test sites of the warring nations in 1915, I am fairly certain the cold war syndrome would have been become a factor much earlier in national politics. There is not another explanation. Deterrents seem to work, where solemn promises, treaties and agreements can be broken or ignored before the ink is dry.

A detente of any sort did not happen in 1915 and dear old 3rd Middlesex was still not quite off the hook as far as the Western Front was concerned. They were still doing their bit despite the reduction in their numbers. They slept late in their quarters in Annequin, paraded just before tea-time at 4pm to march to the town of Beuvry just south of Bethune a distance of not more than four miles. They were here two nights then back they went to Annequin to be nearer to the front. They cleaned up there but on the second day, they received sudden orders to move to the reserve trenches as part of the 83th Brigade. The high toll from all battalions of the 28th Division's three Brigades made it necessary to condense them into one. The survivors from the 85th and 84th were transferred to the strength of the 83th Brigade, forming one that could reasonably hold a sector of the front line without spreading the defence too thin. The offensive was dying out but the Generals wanted to hold the small gains that had been won. The village of Loos, what was left of it, was in British hands, and consequently as part of this holding action, 3rd Middlesex relieved the men of the 2nd Battalion Cheshire Regiment whose usual order of battle was with the 84th Brigade. Holding the same front line trenches briefly near the Hohenzollern Redoubt, they were subsequently ordered out of the line and left this battlefield for good on the 6th October1915.

The Battalion spent fifteen more days in France doing a lot more marching and training around the towns of Gonnehem, Lillers and Essars, as well as having to defend six hundred yards of the Givenchy sector holding the Givenchy Redoubt, Marie Keep and Gunner's Siding. Although they sustained two men wounded at Marie Keep, 3rd Middlesex's strength was built up again in this time, with fresh drafts from England, before they embarked for sunnier climes. On the 22nd October they entrained at Fouquereuil near to Bethune for Marseilles, in Southern France and a major port for activities in the Mediterranean area. It was a two day train journey away. The 28th Division had received orders to move to Salonika and the restored 3rd Middlesex (in Brigade as a part of that Division), consisting of twenty five Officers and eight hundred and six Other Ranks sailed eastwards on the H.T.Transylvania at 11am on the 25th October out of Marseilles harbour. They were not yet privy to the ultimate destination and they little knew they would end their war as conquerors in Constantinople, capital of the Ottoman (Turkish) Empire for well over the past six hundred years.

By the time his friends were setting off for their undisclosed destination, my Father had been back in Blighty for nearly three weeks. He had waited just one day in Bethune after seeing the M.O. and getting patched up ready to board the train heading for the port of Boulogne and the hospital ship that would take him across the Channel. He had managed to send a field postcard to his wife letting her know in the briefest of terms that he had been wounded, admitted into hospital and was going on well. Such cards made it fairly easy for him to get in touch with his family. They were much quicker than trying to write a letter that would need to be approved by an officer. They were an early type of pro-forma, designed with set sentences, to keep relatives informed regarding the soldier's health, if he had received any mail or parcels from them, and if he was expecting to write to them. This army postal service was particularly efficient and of course it was very good for morale at home and easy for a soldier to keep in touch with his family.

It was part of the B.E.F.'s movement system to get its wounded men back to England as quickly as possible. The procedure did not generally select individuals from the batches of wounded in any way connected with where they lived or where their Regimental Head Quarters or barracks were located. Groups of men as they left the Casualty Clearing Stations were sent on to complete their journey to a hospital in Blighty via train, ship and train again. On the French side of the Channel the carriages often could still take those 40 men or 8 horses but some improvements had been made for the walking wounded by providing carriages with proper seating and specialised hospital trains to take the stretcher cases. There were no drive-on, drive-off facilities at the ports yet for trains or other forms of transport. The wounded men had to be embarked and dis-embarked as quickly as possible in the continuous process of evacuation. It was reasonable for cases like my Father but very labour intensive and traumatic for both the badly wounded and their helpers. Back in England the trains, always full, would depart to a destination unfamiliar to most of its passengers. Most did not care a jot, they were out of it for a time and they had the prospect of seeing their loved ones again, a reality they hardly dared hope for, during their great endurances on the Western Front.

My Father's train took him to Matlock in Derbyshire to its then General Hospital set a little outside the main town. The records were long gone but my Mother told me he had been there during the war to recover from his wounds. When I visited this spa town so many years later, to pursue the lead, I ascertained that, in fact, this hospital had been much used to help the likes of my Father and I am now certain that Private R.J.Reed did recover in this place close to the heart of the England, for which he had so recently spilt his blood.

Much blood had been shed in this greatest clash of arms between the British and German forces to that date. A contemporary report by the Prime Minister, Mr Asquith, in October 1915 put the losses sustained at Loos at over sixty thousand. By this disclosure it was deduced that the five day offensive and subsequent counter attacks had been seen then as the most terrible battle ever fought by British troops. It is also still perceived as an example of the most vicious form of hand to hand fighting by infantry clashing at close quarters; with that other grim reaper adding much to that daily tally, the well sited machine gun, designed by an American, Hiram Maxim and manufactured at Germany's armament factory in Spandau as the Maschinen-gewehr 08.

As a vignette which illustrates how all strata of our society bore the frightful burden of this particular battle and generally throughout the war I add this to my story. Each year over the past thirty years to my knowledge at least, one casualty from this battle has been remembered by name in the B.B.C.'s TV broadcast of the Service at the Cenotaph in Whitehall on Remembrance Sunday. He is Captain the Hon.F. Bowes-Lyon, 8th Battalion, The Black

Watch Regiment, whose sister, Elizabeth, later became Queen of England and then the much loved and respected Queen Mother for fifty years. Another, not mentioned quite so often, is the son of England's favourite and most read poet. This battle cost Rudyard Kipling the life of his only son, Lieutenant John Kipling, age18, who was serving with Irish Guards. Both were killed in action on the same day my father was on the battlefield; the late Queen Elizabeth's brother being struck down on the 27th September and I believe, still lying in the same area around the Hohenzollern Redoubt where my Father was wounded a day later. The two young men had no known graves for many years. If they had been interred as individuals the inscription on their stone markers would have read "A Soldier of the Great War Known unto God" the phase coined by the Father of one of them. Their actual names are recorded on that long list of the missing at "Dud Corner". Much later John Kipling was interred in grave VII.D.2, St Mary's A.D.S. Cemetery., after much searching and forensic identification.

So many aching hearts had murmured the plea put concisely by another fine poet and then found it answered with such ambiguous random such as to be beyond comprehension:

....

To-night I smell the battle; miles away

Gun-thunder leaps and thuds along the ridge;

The spouting shells dig pits in fields of death,

And wounded men, are moaning in the woods.

If any friend be there whom I have loved,

God speed him safe to England with a gash.

....

Siegfried Sassoon[*]

---

* Copyright Siegfried Sassoon by kind permission of the Estate of George Sassoon.

Chapter 10

The 16th Bavarian Reserve Infantry Regiment of the German Army, including a certain Gefreiter or Lance Corporal Adolf Hitler, had dogged or shadowed my father's Brigade, as it marched south from Belgium into France for the Battle of Loos, which took place amongst the coalfields of the French black country. This Gefreiter, despite his dangerous duties as a regimental runner, had managed to escape death or injury by the same unexplainable selection where-by Private Reed had survived his gash. The future Fuhrer of Germany, and, for a time, of most of Europe, unlike my father, continued to serve for many more months in the same area. It was near the small French town of Fromelles, a short distance north of the now shared Hohenzollern Redoubt which had been at the centre of the Loos' battle. The Redoubt, named after the last kings of Prussia and emperors of Germany, remained a much disputed part of the Western Front until late in 1918 when the British ultimately broke the line and made their lesser recorded advance to victory.

My father and Adolf could have swopped many a yarn about this area and period of the war, had they met and had a mind to, similar to the hundreds even thousands of men, from both sides, who had also been on active service along this front. However, the autumn Battle of Loos in 1915 was the one and only time a serious try to alter the course of the war was made from this place.

Taking a more defensive stance, and intending to keep the ground that they had captured, the German Command did not switch their units about so much as was the wont of the British Commanders. The latter, minimally charged with recovering occupied France or Belgium, tried to make sure that their sections of the line did not stagnate into some cosy type arrangement, but there are instances where this did occur. Not quite a truce but a "I won't shoot, if you don't" situation. Generally that type of tolerance of the status quo, was not accepted, and the British units in the frontline were expected to frequently probe and test their enemy on the other side of no-man's-land. This was the deliberate policy of both the French and British armies and it was additional to the planned offensive or big push, as such actions were commonly called, in those days.

The war diaries of the infantry battalions on the Western Front, mostly tell a story of much activity and movement and my father, although he had been wounded, was not given much time before he was part of that again.

Although deadlock existed between what now seems the equally matched opposing forces, the reality was that, in the time between 1915 and 1918 this was tested continually by daily skirmishes and no less than thirty-five major British led operations before their war winning advance. It is clear that the Allied Commanders had the confidence to win, they made most of the running, as they were gradually given more and more men and equipment to bring them up to the European standards needed to fight this war.

The German effort, during this same period, amounted to only seven strong initiatives against the British armies and one against the French at Verdun. They were on the attack during the four major battles of 2nd Ypres, April and May 1915, in which my Father was first involved and their three other major offensives, all in the spring of 1918, one in Picardy and the others in Flanders and Champagne. The first series managed only to reduce the size of the salient in front of Ypres. Three years later, despite having won the war on their Eastern Front against the newly formed Soviet Union under Premier Vladimir Ilyich Lenin, they could not sustain their attacks and achieve the "coup de grace". The German army failed at the last hurdle, although the Kaiser and his generals well knew how close they had come to taking all Europe by conquest.

At that critical time, after four hard years, it was backs to the wall stuff for the Entente and particularly the British. They were rallied by the famous "Special order of the day" dated 11th April 1918 given by Field Marshal Sir Douglas Haig, who had been Commander in Chief of the British Armies in France and Belgium since December 1915.

This man certainly did not deserve having his reputation so badly damaged, albeit posthumously and well after the war, by many historians and writers, that, was in turn, to influence, unfairly, much public opinion against him.

Although it is somewhat early in my story, it may be helpful to pause and consider the quality of his all important message to the full; it may remind one of other famous calls made by other fine British leaders at times of similar grave national dangers:-

Special Order of the Day, By Field Marshal Sir Douglas Haig, K.T.. G.C.B., G.C.V.O., K.C.I.E. Commander in Chief, British Armies in France. "To all ranks of the British Forces in France:-

Three weeks ago today the enemy began his terrific attacks against us on a fifty mile front. His objects are to separate us from the French, to take the Channel ports, and destroy the British Army.

In spite of throwing already 106 divisions into the battle and enduring the most reckless sacrifice of human life, he has as yet made little progress towards his goals.

We owe this to the determined fighting and self sacrifice of our troops. Words fail me to express the admiration which I feel for the splendid resistance offered by all ranks of our Army under the most trying circumstances.

Many amongst us now are tired. To those I would say that victory will belong to the side which holds out the longest. The French Army is moving rapidly and in great force to our support ------

There is no other course open to us but to fight it out. Every position must be held to the last man: there must be no retirement. With our backs to the wall, and believing in the justice of our cause, each one of us must fight on until the end. The safety of our homes and the

Freedom of mankind alike depend upon the conduct of each one of us at this critical moment."

General Headquarters.   signed:

Thursday 11th April 1918.   D.Haig. F.M.

These surely are not the words of some General floundering in a battle he did not understand, he knew full well that all would be lost if his men continued to fall back. He is telling his tired soldiers the truth as he sees it and he feels confident that they will respond to his call.

In fact in less than three weeks the real crisis was over and the enemy's advances in both Flanders and Picardy were stopped. By the 29th April 1918, the German Armies, that had been massively reinforced with many Divisions from Russia, had been fought to a standstill in front of the key towns of Ypres, Poperinghe, Hazebrouck and Bethune, thus leaving the Channel Ports safe.

Further south, all those hard won gains on the Somme of 1916 and 1917 had been lost to similarly reinforced German forces, together with the important town of Albert with its leaning Golden Madonna and infant Christ, hanging from the tower of its shattered Basilica. However, the next German objective, the important railway town of Amiens was not given up and by the end of April, this town too, was no longer in danger of falling to the enemy. The vital junction between the French and British armies had been seriously targeted so as to split and isolate the two allies, with the clever plan of finishing them off separately. As in Flanders, the German ploy in Picardy did not succeed, both due in no small measure to the British Commander's leadership.

There is now no comparison between the strategies that have evolved since my father's war with Germany ended properly in May1945.

Since then almost permanent truce lines have become the norm for settling international disputes and territorial claims. Generally after an initial flare-up, peace-keeping of a sort is put in place and thereafter, terrorism taking many forms, often aided and abetted by the factions from both sides, keeps the killing and maiming to what seems acceptable levels. My so called "Panmunjom solution" that I believe has fitted most of these situations, stays in place ad- infinitum. It includes the long period of the cold war and the shortest of fights in the African state of Sierra Leone. The former had the North Atlantic Treaty Organisation (NATO) and the Warsaw Pact to keep the peace and the Iron Curtain in place, whilst the latter has not much more than a dozen Royal Marines keeping the status-quo. Both fairly blood-less.

That was certainly not the case for my Father throughout the Great War, no peace-keeping efforts for him. War was fought to win or lose regardless of the cost.

After receiving the first notification of him becoming a casualty, Dad's young wife with his children aged four and two years soon learnt that his wound was not life threatening. They were quickly informed that he was back in England and on the mend. My research has shown that when the news of an individual was not good their relatives did not have to wait long before they had the details. Even when men were posted as missing, their where-abouts unknown, their kin were notified quickly after the event, and any subsequent details relayed as soon as they were known and/ or confirmed. The post office system worked with great efficiency, and its efficacy was not diminished by not having first and second class post. There were often two or three deliveries every day, as well as a telegram service, which transmitted its messages often with-in one or two hours of them being initiated.

I have a cousin, whose mother's first husband was mortally wounded in France less than nine months after their marriage. She was informed very promptly. My Aunt's husband was a Private in the 2nd Battalion of the Hampshires, a County Infantry Regiment, very much like my Father's own Regiment. He became a casualty towards the end of the great Somme battles of 1916 where every yard was much disputed in terms of blood and effort. I have seen the original documents that indicate that in less than two days of this personal tragedy, my aunt had received a telegram telling her that her dear husband had been dangerously wounded. The same telegram informed her that he was receiving treatment at a Casualty Clearing Station not far behind the battle-lines and that the authorities regretted that permission for her to visit him could not be given. Two days later she was officially informed that he had died of his wounds, a communication the poor lady probably received with a letter of sympathy from the nursing sister who had attended her husband, as he finally succumbed to his wounds. She told how he had died in the early hours of the morning, 4.35 a.m. 25th November 1916.

It is remarkable that this same personal letter, dated the 25th, told my aunt where her husband would be laid to rest, and that a cross would mark his grave. For one so close to the horrific consequences of the fighting, the caring nurse wrote with much compassion that he was going to be buried in Grove Town Military Cemetery. This was a well tended burial plot close by the 2/2nd London Clearing Station from where she was writing.

The Tommies fighting in this part of the Somme area had named it Grove Town in 1916 and it has kept its name to this day. In fact, two Casualty Clearing Stations made up Grove Town, the 2/2nd London and the 34th. Both had been established in September of that year as the British and Commonwealth forces painfully advanced at the most southern end of their 20 mile front. The location is a few kilometres from the village of Bray-sur-Somme and it is now well off the beaten track amongst the acres of featureless fields of this farming countryside .

That same grave and cemetery set amidst the chalk uplands just north of the River Somme survived at least two later battles being fought across them. The first was as the Germans advanced in the Kaiser's Battles of March-April 1918, only to be driven back fighting during the final British offensives, starting on 8th August and known as the last hundred days, which ended with the armistice of November 11th.

The Uncle, I never knew, received my respects in nineteen ninety eight, during a visit to this lonely place eighty-two years after he died. I stood at the exact same spot as his wife had done when she made her pilgrimage in the nineteen twenties. The cemetery was new then. Her visit was not long after Sir Edwin Lutyens had redesigned and supervised its permanent re-construction from a plot with wooden crosses into one of stone markers and flintstone walls. This English Architect noted for his designs and plans for New Delhi in India as well as much of the memorial work associated with The Great War incorporated in his layout of Grove Town, the Stone of Remembrance shaped like an altar with its inscription "Their Name Liveth for Everymore" together with a stone cross signifying sacrifice.

These two monuments had been commissioned by the then Imperial War Graves Commission to be included in virtually all British and Commonwealth military graveyards through-out the world. Sir Edwin Lutyens designed the first whilst his colleague Sir Reginald Blomfield designed the inspirational Cross of Sacrifice with a bronze sword affixed on its front face depicting the predominant religious and military allegiances of the 1392 dead of Grove Town and the countless others interred elsewhere that it honours so graciously.

The tasteful dignity of Grove Town Cemetery, its typical Britishness, is perhaps fitting as a permanent and lasting memorial, but it should not be forgotten that the surrounding fields were terrible killing zones where these resting warriors gave their all for our dignity today.

Its raison d'etre is the same as this noted architect's cenotaph, or empty tomb, in London's Whitehall, that also does for my uncle and all our fallen heroes in their own capital city; only Grove Town is not nearly as well frequented.

The visit of my wife and I to this grave all those years later, owes much to my mother, who had kept three small pictures that were taken on her sister's visit and then given to her as a keepsake. My mother, no doubt, had also known the young volunteer soldier, although she had only been the young adolescent sister of his wife, at the time of his death. These box brownie images confirmed the precise location of the grave and showed the image of my aunt during her visit; and although they were not precisely dated, it is not difficult to judge the time or period by my aunt's Sunday best and stylish clothes.

My wife Ellen, remarked whilst there, that these men should perhaps have been brought home to rest amongst their own. She knew and felt concerned that we were the first of his kin to visit his burial-place since his own wife had been there more than seventy years earlier. She also questioned, perhaps knowing the answer already, were we also the last to go this particular grave? This perhaps, also, begs another question. Will this always be "some corner of a foreign field" as land becomes ever more precious especially to the local people of Northern France, where so many graveyards are sited?

My aunt started to receive her widow's pension six months after her husband's death, her separation allowance being stopped as her pension began. She received all of thirteen shillings and nine pence a week (68.75p) paid at the post office every Wednesday in advance. It was thus, how the bulk of the widows of the fallen were provided for by the world's most wealthy Empire that were using its men-folk to fight for its very existence as well as its most high and honourable principles. Who thought that 68.75p or just over one

Euro was enough, I do not know. The Chancellor of the Exchequer's budgets of the period would be a good place to look for the culprits and that sum compares somewhat to the meanness of the 75p increase bestowed to the millennium's senior citizens as a good start to a new century.

An even more unforgiveable indictment of these guilty men, the authors of these paltry reimbursements; can be assessed when comparing the amount of this widow's mite with the not over generous basic state pension paid out for the year 2000. This was set at £67.50 per week and is nearly ninety eight times more than my aunt received for losing her husband. Allowing that her pension would increase at the yearly rates of inflation that occurred from the times my aunt received her pension in nineteen seventeen; her pension in the year 2000, would have reached the dizzy heights of £10.35 per week!

The British people were certainly not fighting this war for personal gain, or even reparations. Set at these rates, on a million war dead, the cost would not have dented the Fuhrer's coffers as he prepared for round two; and regardless of that, the country's political leaders had already decided not to collect them.

The Empire did not have to bear this particular weekly expense of 68.75p for long however. My Aunt remarried. She fell in love with her first husband's friend in arms, the pair having joined up and fought together until that day on the Somme when they were separated. About a year after peace had been declared my Aunt married the Uncle I did know, and my cousin more recently related to me a tender postscript to the story. She told me that before she was born the young couple saved to be able to travel to France together and visit the young man's grave at Grove Town Cemetery. This visit was the farthest they would ever travel away from England in a long and happy marriage lasting many years and represents the deep feelings they both could share without envy or jealousy, long after they had managed to move on and rebuild their lives. My cousin told me they both wanted and needed to go on that pilgrimage before they finally laid that part of their past fully to rest. They never forgot or be-littled that sacrifice that still symbolises the standards of their age.

My Dad's wife did not have the type of heart-ache that my aunt suffered, she got her soldier husband back home for a few days and she knew he would get better. The wounded that were convalescent could get leave and I am sure he did not have to wait very long before he was travelling on a warrant back to his home in Wimbledon from Derbyshire. His filthy and blood stained uniform would have been discarded and burnt to be replaced in the general clean-up he had been given by the medical services in Matlock. He would have travelled to his home smart in his re-issued kit. A khaki great coat, new army cap with his regimental badge and most likely he was dressed in a uniform known as hospital blues. This was a pair of trousers and jacket, made of rough woollen serge, similar to his khaki ones but of a Dutch boy's trouser patch blue colour, worn with a soft collared white shirt and red tie. This blue uniform identified to all and sundry a soldier who had been hospitalized and who was not yet ready to be returned to active service.

Wimbledon, approaching its second Christmas at war was not much changed from how my Father had left it six months earlier, except probably in the attitudes of its people. The German Zeppelin raiders were not dropping their bombs near the town, although the danger existed generally on a nightly basis for the whole of London. Fortunately for most of the south west suburbs, the enemy was concentrating more on the East-End docks and Central London if their navigation was up to the mark. The war news mostly from France and Gallipoli left little to be happy about and personal grief or worry was affecting many. There was still a degree of confidence and there were not many shortages in the shops, with much more money being earned by increased work opportunities to buy more. The biggest change was that the whole population was becoming more involved in the war. The first volunteers could not do it on their own. All people of working age, male or female, were beginning to be required to register that fact.

For the first time in the country's history conscription and direction of the country's labour potential was being set in place. Despite the great fervour of 1914, not enough men were now volunteering to make up the losses or generate the enormous efforts needed to achieve victory. Nobody could foresee when the war would end and its popularity had waned as the spirit of adventure and glamour of fighting noble battles, had significantly changed. Differing stories were filtering back to the homeland from men returning wounded or when they had been given a spot of leave. This leave was the same for Officers and Other Ranks alike. A precious six days, which included the time taken to travel from their unit at the front and back. Perhaps it was a little unfair to those with the farthest to travel but it did allow a faster turn round and back to duty for all concerned with the ever seething Western Front.

All attempts by the Allies, since the gas attacks by the Germans at Ypres in April1915, had been less than successful. The newspapers reported excellent gains but these were always measured in yards rather than miles. My Father's six months of active service could not be glossed over as a resounding triumph, as it had been in certain reports. He knew better and there were not many conquering heroes disembarking from the endless troop and Red Cross trains.

Although he would not want to worry his family, he and his fellows in arms knew that they were living on borrowed time and a bit of luck. Probably most significant, the population as a whole, now knew that they were fighting a dangerous and tough enemy. All the signs added up to make an enemy that they knew would take some beating and the good old British Navy gunboat of old, fronting the Pax Britannia, would not be anywhere near sufficient in this war.

Little wonder, that those at the sharp end, made much of being gay, in the old sense of the word. Enjoying the fullness of family life, drinking and eating well, being merry and loving, resting properly and leaving the tears until it was time to say farewell and return to active service those few short miles across the water.

Accordingly my Father would have made the most of his precious short leaves from the hospital. The first was when the Medical Officer (M.O.) felt he could travel without help. Three or four glorious days at home without any lien on his time only an ability to lie-in. In all, it took the M.O. eight short weeks to decide that Private R.J.Reed was fit to return to service, and in that time he probably enjoyed two or three further passes for home leave away from the hospital and the staff that were under pressure to get him back on the army's fighting strength as soon as possible.

It came all too soon. He was not allowed to have even Christmas in Blighty. Certified fit for active service again by the M.O. at Matlock General Hospital on 23rd November, he was ordered to report to the Middlesex Regimental Depot at Millhill Barracks in North East London for forward posting back to the war.

In the time since he had been wounded, he had come to realise the quality of the work done by the nursing profession. He had experienced their help and humanity at first hand. He had also been in receipt of this largesse at a time when one of the needless atrocities of this war had been committed on a much loved member of that calling, an act that had needlessly upset and saddened these caring ladies, including the ones helping my Dad. Nurse Edith Cavell, a lady past her fiftieth year, had been shot by a German firing squad at 2 a.m. on the morning of 12th October 1915 in occupied Brussels. She had been found guilty of helping allied soldiers to escape into neutral Holland. It was a harsh and brutal summary execution which took place less than twelve hours after the sentence of death had been given by General von Sauberzweig, the German Military Governor of Brussels. The courts martial found all twenty seven of the group on trial, guilty, but only five including Miss Cavell were sentenced to death. She and her friend Philip Baucq, a

Belgium architect, had their sentences announced to them in their prison cells in St Gilles Prison late afternoon on the 11th October informing them that they would be shot in a few hours time. They were told that no pleas for clemency or mercy would be considered. Unknown to them however, there was a desperate late night appeal by Mr Brand Whitlock the senior American political representative in Belgium. He tried in vain to have the sentence stayed. Shortly before 2 a.m. Edith Cavell and her friend were taken to the Tir National, the site of their execution, and the details of this brutal act were posted outside on the streets of Brussels for the public to read.

It is difficult to understand the German action of killing an ageing English Matron who had been employed at the Belgian School of Certified Nurses since 1906. It was common knowledge that she and most of her profession nursed wounded men whatever uniform they happened to be wearing. These nurses certainly did not believe they were betraying their own or any nation when offering assistance to soldiers needing their help.

It has been said that Miss Cavell's last thoughts were embodied in the words "Patriotism is not enough", implying the need to do more. Although my father did not know it, her thought, closely mirrored what his own had been when he first enlisted and now as he returned to Millhill Barracks, accepting that he was going back to France; and that he would not be filling his children's stockings on Christmas Eve.

I can appreciate and that he must have been also very saddened to learn that his old battalion had been ordered to the Middle East and that he would not be rejoining them. He still had friends in his company that he would miss. Neither would the fact that he was being posted to the 2nd Battalion instil him with much confidence as to his future. He knew of the scrapes this unit had been in since arriving in France the previous January, not the least, their efforts at the Battle of Neuve Chapelle in March. As another first line infantry unit of the old regular army, 2nd Middlesex had certainly taken many a knock and needed more men to make up its fighting losses. In fact, all eight battalions from the Middlesex Regiment that were on the Western Front at the time my Father was wounded, had taken part in the Battle of Loos or its subsidiary operations, so really, there were no long straws he could have drawn, they were all short ones regarding a choice of battalions. His masters in Millhill Barracks could have chosen to post him to any one of the following battalions if he was going back to France or Belgium. They were in numerical order the 1st,2nd,(the 3rd now left), 4th, 1/7th, 1/8th,11th and 13th. The Battle of Loos was still much in the minds of virtually every man of these seven battalions. Most of the surviving members had well and truly cut their teeth in this large scale operation which has become of very special interest to all later Die-Hards and others who study the Regiment's history. As parts of the 2nd, 28th and 24th Divisions respectively the 1st, 3rd and 13th Battalions fought in the main battle area between Grenay and Givenchy, whilst the 4th Battalion attacked just to the east of Ypres in a Divisional action to pin down enemy forces likely to be directed to the main battle front as reinforcements. The 11th Battalion as part of the 12th Division were engaged in the subsequent actions on the Hohenzollern Redoubt as I related earlier. Finally, the 2nd,1/7th and 1/8th all part of the 8th Division saw action at Bois Grenier south of Armentieres with similar intentions as the 4th Middlesex nearer to Ypres.

The 2nd Battalion diaries are, if anything, sparse on many occasions and for their contribution to the subsidiary action launched in Brigade strength on the 25th September through to the 26th they are no exception. It literally takes a couple of lines to record that as part of the 23th Brigade, the battalion marched and assembled at Rouge de Bout, subsequently taking position for the attack on Rue Biache. Two days later the diary reports that the battalion is occupying front line trenches just east of La Boutillerie having one company in support at La Croix Marechal, a small hamlet situated at the crossroads of the D176 and Rue des Davids less than a mile to the rear.

The Serie Bleue Maps of France are most helpful tracing these places, and with their help I have seen the country around Bois Grenier and the battalion's records do little justice to their efforts in this period of hard fighting. If anything the land south of Armentieres is even flatter than it is around Ypres and even the approaches to a small road bridge either side a stream gives elevational advantage to the occupier. The fields can only be worked when the massive drainage systems are in order and these ubiquitous water-filled ditches that occur in every field must have become difficult and deadly obstructions for attacking infantry. Of course the artillery fire from both sides added much to the problems of occupation as well as attack when the damage done to the drainage turns the land into deadly quagmires. Another very difficult place to force an issue. Our Generals can, I think, be thanked that they did not try too much here, holding the wallowing line was hard enough as the frequent spate of "Cim. Britanniques" bear sad and rather neglected witness. No stirring fights grace the names of the frequent hamlets and villages hereabouts. Only the Kaiser tried it very late on with his offensive between 9th-29th April 1918 when it took twenty three British and one Australian Divisions to hold and stabilise the line, after losing a number of well known towns. Ypres did not fall but as the famous Iron Duke would have put it "it was a close run thing" after Armentieres, Bailleul and Merville were taken. Field Marshal Douglas Haig's famous appeal made a strong contribution and the acknowledged finest army on the continent he had helped to create, pulled it together again as mentioned earlier in this chapter.

The Rue David's cemetery half way between la Boutillerie and la Croix Marechal still clings to its links with the past, although this is an example where new housing has been built right up to its boundary walls. It was here I walked more ground that my Father had helped to defend on his return to the trenches after recovering from his nasty head wound.

A few days at Millhill sufficed to get him re- kitted into his standard khaki uniform again, his hospital blues being returned to the Quarter-Master. He signed for a complete new clothing and boots issue, a rifle and the necessary accoutrements he had lost when he had been sent back to Blighty by the Medics. He would have also been allocated a place in a holding company and the barrack room bed that went with it. As a trained infantry man he was not wanted at Millhill for any longer than was necessary. He was scheduled for onward posting a.s.a.p. from the 5th Training Battalion at Millhill Barracks as part

211

of a fresh draft being formed from men like himself, returned to active duty, and new recruits, who had passed their six to twelve week basic training programme. Generally in the army, if you are not fighting, you are drilling, training or retraining or preparing for guard duty, so until his full draft was assembled he was not sitting around thinking what to do next. It was likely he managed to get another short leave home during his three weeks at Millhill Barracks but the records indicate he was back in France on the 15th December 1915.

As part of a draft of forty-three men he became a member of 2nd Middlesex less than two weeks before Christmas in the small French town of Morbecque, where the battalion was in billets. This time it was not new to him, and the fact that the battalion was in proper accommodation, perhaps a brick-built barn with a watertight roof, was certainly better than camping in tented bivouacs or going straight into the line as he had done on his initial introduction to this awful war. The cold winters to which Northern France is prone, however, was not all that inviting to him; he would much rather be home with his family.

On arrival the men on his draft were allocated to the various companies A,B,C and D, the way all infantry battalions are divided. The company officers would then select each new man for a specific platoon and section which dealt with a particular aspect of fighting skill. The men in these groups depended much upon each other, whether they were bombers, riflemen, in a machine gun team, etc and bonds of friendships were usually quickly struck up in these circumstances. It was hard to be lonely or aloof with each man sharing the common hardships of a soldier in these conditions. Unfortunately companies, platoons and sections in later years remain only in the memories of their individual members, very much like a man's Regimental number. The man does not forget those aspects of his service but unless another has asked the right questions of him personally, it is almost impossible to obtain that knowledge by research.

An individual's service number has been made comparatively much easier to find by the Public Records Office's systems of documentation but an individual's actual company, section etc was very seldom recorded in the documents now available.

I have been unable to find this type of detail regarding my Father but it is fortunate for me, researching his service, that the Battalions in which he served generally acted their war out as a body and I am therefore confident that in following 2nd Middlesex's activities I am following in my Dad's footsteps.

Ten days before Christmas 1915, there he is, sharing a billet again with six other men of his section in the small French village of Morbecque, straddling the main road a mile or so south of the important town of Hazebrouck. Like a million other soldiers just like him, he must have felt, particularly at this time, the longing for his own warm hearth which was less than one hundred and thirty miles away and wishing for a few more of those halcyon days with his wife and children that he had left just two, may-be three, days ago. The escorted and darkened out night ferry in which he had travelled, took no longer than the well appointed and brightly lit modern ones do now, the only stark difference was what lay in the purpose of his visit to this un-assuming area of Northern France. Somehow he and his kind were able to shrug off, smile and joke so as to not give way to this very natural and common yearning for home. The men of the British Army kept this attitude throughout its many trials and disasters and this inbuilt quality enabled it to maintain its first class morale especially when the going was at its toughest.

The battalion part of the 23th Brigade and 8th Division had been out of the line for a number of weeks as General Head Quarters Reserve when my Father arrived. This period in reserve, gave the battalion time to take in more men as reinforcements, send its soldiers on various courses, such as learning the latest trench mortar techniques, machine gun and bombing strategy, or the use of gas as a weapon. There were also good news for some, they were in for a spot of home leave. Its Commanding Officer Lt. Col. R.H.Hayes, C.M.G. (Companion of St Michael and St George) had come back from his six days at home a week before my Father arrived. One "lucky" other rank not mentioned by name was granted a month's leave, according to a diary entry on the 8th December, on condition that he agreed to continue his service that was about to expire. I believe he must have been an old soldier of some repute to get that sort of special treatment. The diary makes no mention of his return on the 8th January 1916; I only hope he survived that year, quite a bad one for 2nd Middlesex., and, for that matter, the rest of the war. Whatever happened, it was certainly another "beau geste" by an unknown and unrecorded patriot, who, one must assume by the diary entry, really did have the option to leave it to the others, and take, in their own words, a very cushy option.

Some twelve miles to the rear of the front the noise of the guns did not have quite the same affect on my Father as they had done when he approached Ypres for the first time, although I expect his knowledge and experience now recalled vividly in his mind's eye the horrors wrought by those sounds.

He had five days to get into his new routine, let his family know he had arrived safely in France and that he was missing them, before he was on the move again. The Battalion left for a four day exercise with the whole 8th Division on the 20th December. It was very much a marching tour of the area to the west of Morbecque, towards the G.H.Q. town of St Omer. Officially, the exercise was designed to test the fitness of the force and its ability to re-deploy en masse. This mid-winter exercise included spending a night in the open, marching some twenty five miles in the two days they were on the move, assembling in an area defined by map reference only and setting up a defensive stance using the topography at hand. For my Father, he had only to do as ordered and keep up with the others. I can only hope and trust that he and his new found pals got enough bully to make up for all the energy they were using. At that time of the year it would not have been a picnic but I think they probably thought that it was very necessary. Unlike peacetime exercises, it was no game they were playing, and they certainly knew that they had to be fit for whatever they were expected to do.

The 2nd Middlesex returned to Morbecque late on the 23th December as the exercise came to an end and Dad's first Christmas in the army was spent in the same billets he had vacated a few days earlier. He remained there for the beginning of the new year of 1916 and getting towards the anniversary of his first full year in the army. At that time the English did not make much of Hogmanay; those celebrations were generally the reserve of the Scots and possibly some border regiments. Christmas day, however, was made much of by the British army where ever possible, with quite an emphasis on the religious aspects of the feast, and a true spirit of goodwill to all ranks. Traditionally, the sergeants did the rounds of the men with some welcome hot toddy to start the day right and they were later joined by the officers to serve the main meal at lunch time, or at least see that there was that bit extra to mark what everyone considered to be a very special time. There would have been a great effort to ensure the post from home was delivered and distributed and most likely a church parade and a Christmas service with carols held in the local church. If such a place was not available, a drum-head service in a convenient open space would have been held. The army was certainly adaptable but unchanging in its attitude to Christmas day whether it was at war or not.

Probably that day in 1915 was one of the better days experienced by my Father during his long service on the Western Front. I believe it was also like that for most of the Die-Hards of the 2nd Battalion.

The New Year was not very old before it changed. Strengthened by several intakes of new men, the last arriving on the 9th January, the Battalion's period out of the line came to an end on the 11th.

The 23rd Brigade with 2nd Middlesex, all four companies, leading, marched eastwards the dozen or so miles to the front line area, a zone just in front of the towns of Estaires and Sailly-sur-la-Lys. The rivers Lys and Law together with the numerous canals were the main collecting points for the myriad of field drains and ditches along where this part of the front line was formed. These waterways, of course, were the reason why, the whole area extending from Ypres south to Armentieres and Bethune, became such a difficult place to fight a long and tedious campaign which would have finished lesser men and their leaders.

The access roads remain as in my Father's time, formed on an embankment a metre or so above the normal lie of the land. The numerous villages and hamlets are also still there giving accurate identification to match the Battalion's diary entries and sundry map references provided in certain notes of the period.

My Father celebrated his first full year of service,15th January1916, in the wintery and water-logged trenches in front of Sailly-sur-la-Lys. He could have boasted, but never did, that for over two months he never left the area. Until the 27th March the 23rd Brigade defended the line being in and out of the front line trenches mostly on a four days in four days out basis.

After the 25th February, he and his pals of the 2nd Middx shared and relieved that part of the sector in front of the village of Laventie, with the 1st Battalion of the Grenadier Guards, the most senior Regiment of Foot of the King's army. L/Corporal A.Hitler of the 16th Bavarian Reserve Regiment was serving opposite Laventie near or in Fromelles, a small French town stubbornly held by the invaders with a trench system manned in depth by strong forces heavily armed and determined to stay there.

The Germans had no intention of attacking in strength the British troops opposite them, their remit was to hold their ground and fend off any intrusions. The line was drawn and it was not for moving. The opponents did carry out actions on a relatively small scale, trench raids to bomb or take a prisoner, shelling and shooting designed to keep all human life on tender-hooks, well below ground level and generally wet, threatened and uncomfortable. Men of all ranks from both sides were killed or maimed regularly, but as many an old soldier would have put it, "if your name ain't on it you'll survive" or conversely, "if your number's on it-----".

Of all the endless bullets and shells fired off in either direction that did the killing, not one had the names R.J.Reed or A.Hitler inscribed on it. Had it been so, one would have had to wonder, who would have led Germany between 1933 and 1945 and who would have been writing this true tale today. The two men in question could not have known this positively at the time, although their contemporary thinking was yet another version, amongst many others, expressed by a Persian Astronomer-Poet of old in his Rubaiyat, the stanzas particularly featuring his potters and pots.

The later wide-spread fatalism fitted the awesome conditions of the Great War; even when my Father was about to leave the perpetual, foul smelling, churned up mud and slush of the wet Flanders plain.

In the spring of 1916, he and his friends of 2nd Middlesex, were about to move south. They received orders to embark to a less active area of the Western Front. Another thirty mile extension to the British front-line had been taken over from the French Army to ease the pressures on that Armyand its man-power, now required urgently in the developing Battle of Verdun.

My Dad was to pay a visit to the chalk downs, dotted with farming communities, of an out of the way area in Picardy that was drained by the gentle, sluggish and meandering Rivers Somme and Ancre. A schoolmaster poet, the same age as my Dad, saw much of this same area that was cruelly to become his final resting place. We are very fortunate that one of his works sets out precisely the mood of innocence and confidence during this early time in a place that was about to be changed irrevocably:-

The Magpies in Picardy

Are more than I can tell.

They flicker down the dusty roads

And cast a magic spell

On the men who march through Picardy,

Through Picardy to Hell.

T.P. Cameron Wilson. (1889-1918).

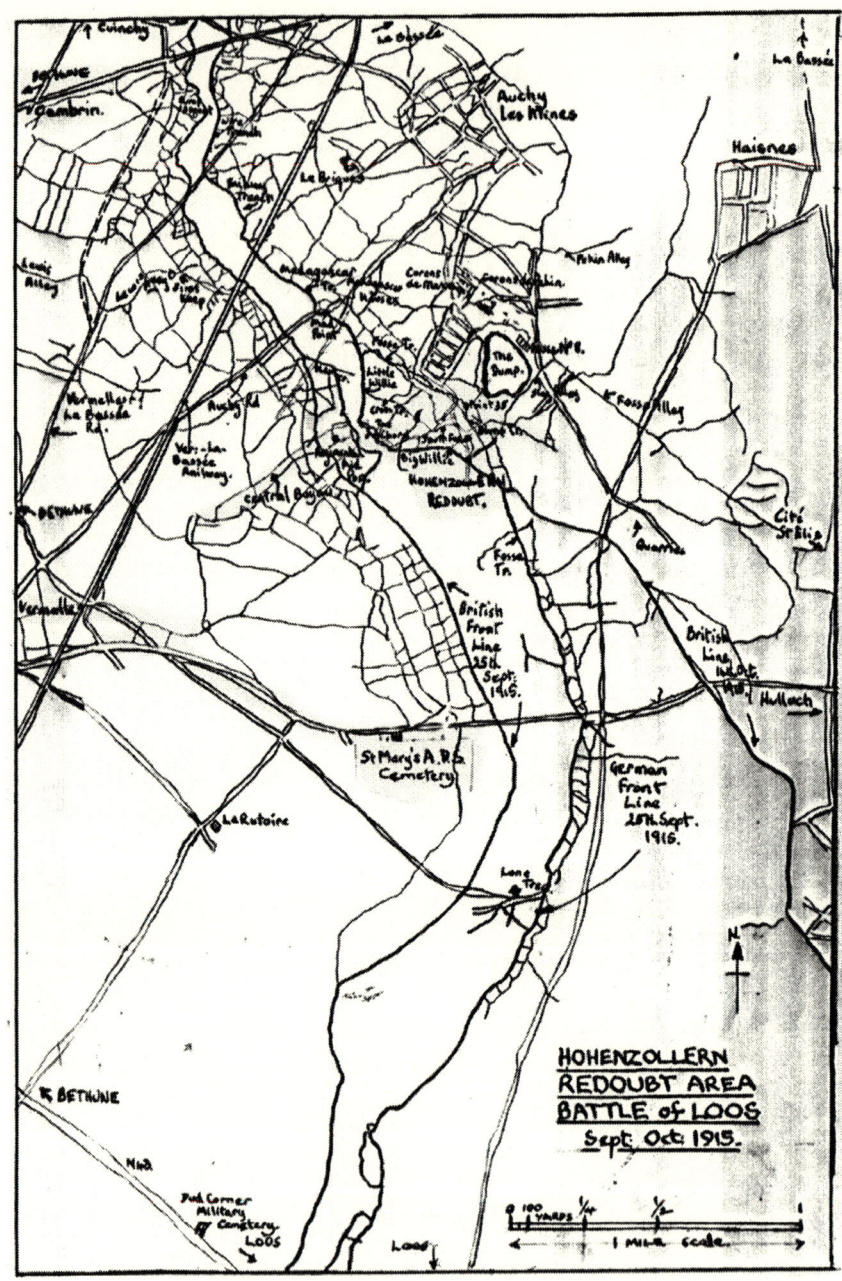

Battle of Loos Map – Sept – Oct 1915

Chapter 11

If "The Somme" is talked about today, the conversation will generally recall bitterly, the selfless sacrifices made by a generation of young men whose images remained very much as those sepia photographs retained in old family albums or in the classic flickering movie clips used in Television Documentaries. Prior to July 1916 it was quite different. As the new British Third and Fourth Armies, Kitchener's Men, gradually assembled behind their irregular and zigzagging line of the front stretching for approximately fourteen miles there was a whiff of victory and much confidence in the air.

The line of the proposed frontal attack facing the enemy started, on the British left, with the German held village of Serre, situated at the most northerly part of the line to be assaulted. This village was followed by familiar and revered place-names now forever to be associated with a battle noted in the Guinness Book of Records as the bloodiest in modern history, leaving over a million men dead or wounded in its initial four and a half month course. Beaumont Hamel and Beaucourt followed to the right of Serre, down across the slow moving River Ancre to St Pierre Divion. The line of the attack would continue opposite Thiepval, Ovilliers and La Boiselle, the latter village situated on the south side of an important major road left by the Romans, that ran for nine miles in a north-easterly direction, between the towns of Albert and Baupame. The front line trenches cut across this road a mile or so from the outskirts of Albert and were the central axis of the well planned "big push" that sought to achieve the early capture of Baupame and the area about it thus causing a major division of the enemy's forces. If the plan was to be successful an advance was required to occur, simultaneously for all of seven miles each side of this road and the flanks at each end of the advance would have to be maintained and well defended. A little more than a mile south-east of La Boiselle is the village of Fricourt where the front began to run due west with the enemy held villages of Mametz and Montauban a further five miles from Fricourt. All these small towns and villages were the very initial objectives of the British and just east of Montauban was the point where the British Command gave way to French Forces. At this juncture our French allies held the line continuously to the Swiss Border more than three hundred miles away.

As the plans were originally laid the French forces hoped to extend the attack along a further twenty miles employing the likes of another forty divisions additional to the hoped for twenty-five to thirty-five British ones. Field Marshal Douglas Haig in this, his first major offensive as the supreme British Army Commander on the Western Front, also intended to attack opposite the village of Gommecourt to the north of Serre as a diversionary tactic and remove a troublesome small salient.

There were quite a number of these projections along the length of the Western Front, all were weeping sores, whether occupied by friend or foe alike. Sheer cussedness and a great reluctance to give up land were quite often the reasons for maintaining them, when an evacuation would have shortened the line to be defended to the probable benefit of both sides; not that that would have been a motive for such action. The origins of other salients were often very different and two, set good examples, of this point. At Ypres, it was a political decision between the British, Belgium and French to retain at any cost, a few square miles of muddy polder, rather than lose all of precious Belgium to the enemy: whilst the Germans kept their salient at St Mihiel for strong strategic reasons. It was a thorn, thirty kilometres deep, piercing the French lines south of Verdun and try as they might the barb could not be removed. Both these salients were doggedly held for nearly four years at unbelievable expense in blood and sorrow. They remained firmly in place until the very last phases of the war. It was then that the British broke out of their Ypres Salient in September-October 1918 and advanced towards the German border and at the same time French and American Forces, working together, nipped out part of their thorn with a classic pincer movement that straightened their line ready for further attacks which later secured other modest gains.

The opposing lines, established in the area of the Somme in Picardy, were the farthest the Germans had managed to penetrate into mainland France since the earlier advance to Paris, in 1914, had been repulsed. It was at a distance of between sixty to seventy miles due west of the Franco-Belgium border just south of the Belgium town of Mons. The front lines here had remained static, although they had been heavily consolidated on the enemy's side since the Schlieffen Plan had gone wrong. It was considered to be a quiet sector where there were no large scale activities, only sporadic trench warfare.

It was no wonder that there was much optimism in the British ranks, with over a full Division (18,000 men) spaced behind every mile of front to be attacked, ignoring the reserves and artillery to match such massive forces. The pendulum seemed at last, to both General and Private alike, to be swinging in the Allies' favour; they no longer had less than Jerry and my Dad was getting a first class view of the much planned preparations. He was probably also at this time "in the know" that his 8th Division had been selected to be at the centre of the attack and that his 23rd Brigade would provide the initial assault troops. More short straws perhaps, but he, like the whole British Army, wanted to get this dreadful war over. He wanted to end the anguish, disappointments and suffering endured in all classes and sections of his society since August 1914. Every-one in the forces now knew the calibre of the German Army and did not think it would be easy but at least it was time to try again on what they thought were more equal or even better terms than those that had been tried previously.

Whatever the case, my Dad was not sorry to have left those damp, very muddy and water-logged areas he had been guarding and helping to hold for the previous three months since he returned to active service. The men of 2nd Middx had learnt to keep their heads down during their sojourn in front of Bac-St Maur, Fleurbaix and Laventie in the Pas-de-Calais area of Northern France a little south of the town of Armentieres. They had had no deaths since the end of January when four men had been killed by a shell hitting its mark in their trenches. After this incident, up to the 26th March, when they left this sector, a number of men had been wounded, all by shell fire, and I believe the absence of a lot more casualties was due to the good state in which their trenches were kept, and the soldierly prowess that had been quickly learnt by this quality battalion regarding how to deal with this unique type of static warfare.

During this time they had been sharing alternate trench duty with the 1st Battalion of the Grenadier Guards, and as with all Guards Regiments trench discipline, tidiness, turn-out and good soldierliness was a matter of course. I have noted from my research that, similarly, the Die-hards took with them, as good a reputation as to the way they too conducted themselves. It was the same whether they were guarding the front or carrying out endless supply fatigues when "relieved" and so called out of the line.

The village of Merville was just over six miles from the front at Laventie, from where the Battalion marched with their full kit in the late Monday evening of the 27th March 1916. My Father and his Battalion had been ordered to entrain at its small railway station just past midnight, this hour being chosen to avoid enemy shell fire. The area was still within the range of the larger calibre guns and shot could be zeroed in, in daylight hours, even at this early stage of the war, by observers using light aircraft or observation balloons. Using the cover of darkness did not exclude all the dangers. Quite often a shell fired at a pre-registered location would find its target that was situated well behind the main front.

Obeying their orders nothing much went awry and the complete Battalion left the First Army in Pas-de-Calais to become part of the Fourth in Picardy. The Fourth Army was one of Lord Kitchener's famous New Armies assembling in the south in a part of the line recently taken over from the French. My Father and his friends remained men of the 8th Division and 23th Brigade and that meant that there were a lot more men and their back-up equipment also on the move, a whole Division's worth at the very least.

It was for 2nd Middx, in all, a rather interminably slow journey, getting on for twelve hours, to go from one Province or County to its neighbour. There was little difference to travelling from Surrey to Hampshire, or Lincolnshire to Nottinghamshire; Pas-de-Calais and Picardy were next to each other. I do not know, but it was most likely the same for all the various units on the move, the reason being that the Western Front did not take into account the directions in which the railway systems were built. Most of the existing lines travelled eastward from the English Channel in Northern France and tended to end in No-Mans Land. They were adequate for transporting men and material from the French Channel ports to the war zones of Flanders and Loos, but to transfer by train southwards was more difficult. There were not many routes going in that direction, and accordingly the routes chosen were not direct. It was however, much kinder to the feet and the bumpy wooden second class seats were better than the hard pave or cobbles of the early twentieth century French roads.

Dad passed into Picardy quite near to the English Channel across the River Authie having had to follow a lengthy detour westwards via Hazebrouck, St Omer almost into Boulogne before heading southwards, through Abbeville, and only then in the right direction, east, to their ultimate destination of Longueaux on the south side of the River Somme close to the city of Amiens.

General Kitchener, as he was when fighting his desert war in Sudan in 1898-1899, had built his own railway line from scratch across the empty Nubian Desert to move his army then. He built it to avoid most of the tortuous twists, bends and cataracts of the River Nile between Wadi-Halfa and Abu Hamed. The British Empire was fighting the Madhi and his followers who had taken over most of the country after killing General Gordon in Khartoum fourteen years earlier. Before this railway, a boat on the Nile or a few caravan trails fit for camels were the only means of travel across this vast country. This railway is still in use today, marked on modern maps of the area, that bear very few other lines of communications. In the Sudan of Kitchener's time planning permission was not required or sought but in 1916 the homeland French authorities certainly would not allow him to do likewise, to suit his present war plans and preparations. The British had to make do with existing services, limited as they were, for any fresh initiative, although, more often than not, these initiatives were the result of French representations and requests.

Using the railway system to hand, the British troop movements were certainly not as efficient as their enemy's. The Germans had designed their transport routes, both rail and road, primarily to suit such a war as this. The Central Powers, by their very name, realised that they were facing the possibility of conflict along at least two of their borders. Consequently, their systems allowed for this by providing suitable junctions for movements should they be needed towards any point of the compass.

227

Accordingly, most of their operations included detailed and precise railway schedules and timetables that actually worked properly, and these were an essential and important part of their battle plans and most helpful for moving reserves or reinforcements to defend their lines.

Despite the slowness of my Father's journeys, I believe, he never thought about them in terms of time and even if he had wanted to, he had left his one and only Sunday best pocket watch at home. His sergeant and the company bugler generally looked after his time now, the wrist watch was not very common yet and so wake up calls and deadlines appropriate to him were expressed verbally through his N.C.O.s or a blast from a trumpet or a whistle.

He certainly never carried a Michelin to be able to check where he was going and the changing directions of travel must have been quite dis-orientating, notwithstanding that he and his mates were largely ignorant of the more detailed geography of Northern France. In fact, I am fairly sure that in these rural areas the place names, even if they were marked by some sort of notice, would have meant little and these soldiers' situation is summed up precisely in one of their popular songs either of this war or the later one ".... we don't know where we're going until we're there! la la...". It was still to them, where ever it was, the same meat, different gravy, shared hardships and many dangers.

The 2nd Middlesex's diarist, brief as ever, records, "arrived at 12:40pm 28th March 1916, detrained and marched to Bourdon" which was seventeen miles away and where a new C.O. was awaiting them. He was Major

E.T.F.Sandys appointed to train and lead the Battalion in the coming battle. This was a task all Commanders viewed with much pride tempered with a feeling of onerous responsibility. This man would have known that it was now only three months or less to the off, and the men of his Battalion needed all the assault training they could get to stand the best chances of success and survival.

Major Sandys received his promotion to Lieutenant Colonel, the established rank for a battalion's Commanding Officer, not long after he took over the battalion. Several veterans I met expressed their liking and respect for this man and he did his best to ensure that they were as familiar as possible about what they were expected to do. All around them the evidence was collecting for a clash of arms the like of which had not been witnessed previously by them or any of their forebears. Dad, who had seen at first hand the substance and paraphernalia needed to keep the Ypres salient in position and the attempted break through at Loos six months earlier, was very impressed. He and his fellow soldiers-in-arms could literally see the efforts being made to put an end to this terrible war. They thought with confidence, that no one would be able to stand up to all of this power and force.

His part, as was the whole of 2nd Middlesex's, in the impending events, centred initially on a "disputed barricade" a mile or so east of the town of Albert. The Battalion was on the way there on the 4th April to get its first view of the actual enemy positions that they were expected to storm in the coming fight. It was a week since they had arrived in Picardy and they had already been told by their new C.O. that they were part of the plan being carefully hatched, in great detail, at Fourth Army Headquarters in a somewhat modest chateaux at Querrieu, a small village, situated astride the main Amiens to Albert road, which was not far from their own very temporary billets at St Gratien, from whence they were now marching.

The Commander of the Fourth Army was the recently appointed Lieutenant-General Sir Henry Rawlinson. He was fifty two years old, a former infantry officer who would have remained on half pay had it not been for war being declared in 1914. Like most or perhaps all of Britain's senior staff officers he had much experience in maintaining the peace and preserving the Empire up to the end of the Second Boer War in 1902. He had had no first-hand experience of command in a war between an equal or similar industrial power which would involve the deployment of massive armies. The British Government had not provided the means for the establishment of such a force before this war had started. His country, had for many years, tended to keep Continental Europe at arm's length, as much as her own interests would allow; and the rest of the world, except for a comparative few independent countries, were mostly colonies, protectorates or dependencies of the British and European Powers. These colonies etc had mainly an agricultural or semi-industrial economy involved in the production or extraction of raw materials for shipping to and processing by their various masters in Europe. The British contribution to the policy of a balance of power in Europe was her navy, not a large and conscripted army.

Of the rest of the world, Canada, Australia and New Zealand were parts of the evolving British

Commonwealth of Nations and much involved in the present fight. The United States of America, whilst developing internally at a rapid pace, generally and politically did not want to take sides. Their constitution was set on strong democratic lines and a majority of her politicians favoured the Entente Cordiale, but it was the very mixture of first generation Americans from all the European States that clouded a clear preference and kept them sitting on the fence until more outrageous acts were committed against them. Japan had joined the Alliance and declared war on the Central Powers in the early days of the war, but did not send troops to fight in Europe. China, as a nation, protected their own interests, as much as they dared, but did not officially participate in the conflict. They did, however, provide a very useful contribution to the British war-effort on the Western Front by supplying labour to provide a non-fighting work corps. More than fifty thousand Chinese were eventually employed on the heavy construction and groundworks needed. Many came from the United States and Canada where they had helped to build long stretches of the trans-continental and branch railways that had opened up the vast development of these countries. They were non-belligerents but they shared many of the dangers and hardships causing them also to have their own rolls of honour and graves which are dotted along the old front line to this day.

The Republics emerging in Central and South America had too much trouble internally to be concerned with matters outside their own boundaries. Africa had few states not affiliated with a European power and conflicts there most often followed the European allegiance or fealty of a particular area.

231

Lastly, the Ottoman or Turkish Empire, could and did threaten the Allies' interests and, most importantly, the way the war was conducted. They joined the Kaiser early, hoping to recover possessions that had been lost to various European nations throughout the nineteenth century, and of course make further gains after their victory. Before the Great War broke out the Empire was known as the sick man of Europe. It had not really kept up with the industrial and hi-tech developments to any extent, and needed a stout partner to significantly frustrate their chosen enemies' interests. For many years both before and after the Crimean War of the mid-eighteen fifties, skirmishes and crises between Britain, France, Russia and Turkey, frequently broke out across the vast areas of the mainly Moslem Middle East, Balkans and Southern Russia, which had been euphemistically called "the great game" along the various corridors of power. The Turks had backed the British and French against the Russians in the Crimea; they fully appreciated the potential of the oil reserves across Arabia and the Persian Gulf and they would have liked to challenge the Raj's control of a great part of its Indian Empire, especially the large areas with a predominant Moslem population.

The Kaiser joining "the great game" for the first time in 1914, to the British and French chagrin, quickly got the Turkish Empire on his side. As a result, this Empire, in 1915, twisted the British Empire's tail until it hurt too much in mainland Turkey and ensured once and for all that the war could only be won on the Western Front with all that that meant in horror and suffering. The alternative plan to attack the so-called soft under-belly of the Central Powers from the South, and thus get round, the un-assailable and blood soaked deadlock in Europe, was an utter and sad failure.

This was due mainly to the unexpected tenacity of the Turkish soldiers defending the spot chosen to attack, the Gallipoli peninsula, the hostile nature of the terrain that favoured the defenders and the shocking toll on the fitness of the attacking forces, who were plagued by bouts of illness and disease, caused by the excessive heat and unhealthy conditions in their cramped and limited toe-holds on Turkish soil.

The Allied plan had been originally designed as a naval attack, that would use a strong flotilla of battleships that would force its way through the waterway of the Dardanelles, proceed to the Turkish capital of Constantinople and intimidate the Turks into submission. This plan did not succeed. Well sown sea mines and the narrow, easily defended, waterway could not be breached by naval power alone and unacceptable loses of Allied warships called for a change of plan.

The failure led to the landing of military forces from Britain, Australia, New Zealand and France on the 25th April 1915 on the narrow peninsula of Gallipoli with the intention of securing the safe and easy passage through the Dardanelles and Sea of Marmara for the Royal Navy and, of course, the eventual capture of the Turkish capital of Constantinople. These forces tried for nearly eight months to dent the Turks resolve but failed, and had to be withdrawn as 1915 ended.

Winston Churchill took the blame for the flawed plan and resigned as the First Lord of the Admiralty and left politics for a time. Now at the age of forty one he joined his old regiment, the Oxfordshire Hussars, to serve rather humbly as a major in France before returning to England in 1917 to restart his career in the House of Commons.

As well as their success at Gallipoli, the Turkish winning streak continued elsewhere in 1916, when they caused another dangerous defeat to British and Empire forces in what is now Iraq. At the desert town of Kut built on the Banks of the River Tigris south of Baghdad, a British expeditionary force intending to secure the oil resources of the area were forced to surrender to superior Turkish forces after a siege that had prevented any relief reaching them. This last Ottoman victory excelled anything even Saddam Hussein's substantial and well equipped forces could muster against the U.N.Coalition eighty years later.

However, the Turkish power did fade, and eventually British and Empire Forces soundly won their desert war under General Sir Edmund Allenby, and occupied cities and land that had not been under Christian control since the crusades of Richard the Lionheart.

The Ottoman or Turkish Empire, by October 1918, ceased to exist. The last of the long line of Ottoman Sultans, who had controlled much of the Balkans and great cities such as Constantinople, Baghdad, Tehran, Jerusalem and Damascus, (reputedly the world's oldest and continually lived-in city), for more than seven hundred years, was banished into exile.

The vast areas and great cities of the Middle East came under the control of the British or French victors for a brief time. The whole area then came to be reconstituted under mandate, treaty or agreement and now some eight or nine decades later, after seeing at least six more dangerous wars, numerous treaties, full scale United Nations involvement and even road maps for peace, there is still little of that commodity in this important and very wealthy area. What the Ottoman rulers exercised for seven hundred years that maintained and secured their Empire for so long, has escaped a modern solution. My recent tally of two hundred and twenty one independent United Nations member states, each one separately or together have failed to find a lasting answer and this failure cannot realistically be blamed on the cult of Empire. They have all gone and is this what is missing?

General Rawlinson probably knew what to do, my Father did as well, but politics were not their forte, they were going about their own business as ordered by the politicians. Dad as a volunteer soldier in the army for the duration of the war, Henry Rawlinson as a busy Commander of the Fourth Army.

In the decade before the Great War the latter had gained good and merited promotion from Brigadier-General to Major-General. He was an able and thinking soldier who had realised quickly that the type of war that he was now fighting was very unlike the skirmishes and peace keeping roles that had been required within a global empire populated by relatively friendly or lightly armed native populations. He knew the industrial nations on each side of this conflict had weapons of mass destruction and that it was vital to keep ahead of this technology to stand a chance of winning. He knew that wars could be only won by those with the most up to date artillery and well equipped infantry and support units. He had studied the recurring strife in the Balkans that would fare up and settle nervously, usually under armed guard. He also knew, as we know today, that solutions could not be trusted or be of very long term. He had studied the Russo-Japanese clashes between 1904-1905; the advances in military aviation and communications etc; and they all demonstrated to him how the influence of new weapons and the methods of parrying them affected a modern conflict between industrial nations. The blood-bath, what was the American Civil War was still much featured in staff studies with many lessons to be learnt. Like the rest of his fellow senior ranks, he appreciated the needs to be ready and militarily superior if one was to successfully engage an industrial enemy on proper terms, which was unlike most of his political masters, who had taken his nation into this war completely unprepared and perhaps, it is reasonable to say are still doing much the same all these years on.

In 1916, the task had been passed to him. He was charged to devise the best way to carry out this fresh initiative on the Somme and win. He was starting with that proverbial blank sheet of paper and ultimately having to incorporate every need of a war which was being fought on a hither-to unprecedented scale. Care, morale and fortitude there was in plenty but only overwhelming power to smash the enemy would give the slimmest of chances of coming good in the end.

Five miles out from Amiens my Father's column joined the main road at Querrieu, where all these great problems were receiving much attention from the staff of Brass-hats under General Rawlinson. Dad and his Battalion were just one small but vital statistic in these endless needs but at least they knew where they were going that day. They turned left to proceed towards Albert that was another ten miles along the very straight poplar lined road ahead of them. Passing through the Fourth Army's Head-Quarters town they marched to attention to provide the necessary respect and compliments required by the bustling senior staff officers and their transports swarming the area. To the soldiers these men were their winning team. Even if all wars and battles are uncertain and not very predictable, except in hindsight, at least the swagger of the troops of 2nd Middlesex indeed, manifested the will to win to the busy senior officers, like all the many other khaki-clad thousands who marched that way along Picardy's own Voie Sacree in the spring, summer and autumn of 1916. They were well named, the very flower of British manhood and well trusted by their Generals to do the task their country had imposed on them both.

As they marched towards their front, my Father and men of his of Battalion would have given thought to another terrible battle raging between the French and German Armies for the Fortress town of Verdun. They knew that this battle had been making the headlines for more than five weeks and the tales of the heroic French defence and counter-attacks were filling many column inches in the newspapers. The Verdun battle and their own expected one, would unknown to them, change history and man's relationships with his neighbours. These battles would simmer down through their own survivors' and future generations' perspectives that the fundamental error and stark horror of solving national disputes by war must cease..

The Verdun battle had started as a major assault by German artillery in the last week of February 1916. It would have a profound effect on all that the British Army was expected to do on the Somme. The massive French contribution on their right would, eventually, have to be significantly reduced and the B.E.F.'s efforts would become prolonged and attritional towards the main enemy's army.

Knowingly, the German High Command under its Chief, General Erich von Falkenhayn intended to suck into the Verdun battle as many soldiers from the French Armies as was possible and kill or maim most of them in the process. He would use the bulk of his weapons of mass destruction firing every calibre of shrapnel, high explosive and deadly poison gas missiles into the soldiers defending their beloved homeland. Falkenhayn had deliberately picked a target dear to French hearts and a symbol of their protection against their rival in the East. Verdun and its fortresses had to be held or France would go under the German yoke and the victors would become the conquering super power of Europe dominated by a lust for expansion and gain at the expense of their victims.

As my Father marched that straight road the outcome of that battle was far from certain and still had many months to run. His own had yet to start and he and his pals could still enjoy a break by the side of that road to rest and let the inhalation of a Player's Navy Cut or Will's Woodbine do its work, before the sights of the town of Albert began to come into view for the first time. The crackle of gunfire had been heard throughout their march, it only got louder. This town had been under enemy fire for more than eighteen months and it was showing the scars of much destruction. My dear Father had seen this before, like the town of Wipers, he knew Albert was dying, as its proud structures were reduced to dusty rubble by modern high explosives.

The beautiful golden Madonna with the Christ child held aloft in her upstretched hands, that my wife and I could see standing on top of the dome of the tall red brick tower of the Basilica of Albert, as we travelled that same road as my Father, was not the one he and the men of his battalion saw. The Virgin he saw was laying seemingly without suspension and against all the rules of gravity at a precarious angle below the horizontal, threatening to crash down into the ruins seventy meters below. The stone image that he saw was an object of a Great War legend. The one I saw was a replacement standing vertical and proud.

Albert, before the Great War, had been a quite prosperous town, with a population of several thousand whose incomes came from local industry, farming and what we would now call tourism and a legend of its own. The Basilica of the Golden Madonna or Notre-Dome de Brebieres at the centre of the town attracted many thousands of pilgrims who visited a relic of the middle ages which was reputed to have healing and miraculous properties and which was consecrated in the church. So many devotees were making this pilgrimage that by the last quarter of the nineteenth century Albert was being likened to Lourdes in the Pyrenees of S.W.France where a great number of Christians believe a vision of the Virgin Mary had been seen.

The new Basilica had not been finished twenty years, when the war stopped this traffic and the lovely town could no longer play host to the pilgrims who wanted to go there. It was too near the front to survive as a proper town and suffered much from bombardment. As early as January 1915, one such shell from the German Artillery exploded at the Virgin's feet but failed to send her and her infant crashing into the debris below. Some would say the dowel work was especially good, designed to with-stand the wrath, of what insurance companies call, Acts of God, in the form of Tempests and Storms, let alone a shell from a five-nine. Most soldiers, however, thought it was a sign. Legions of troops from both sides had their own versions, that had perpetuated over many months running into years during which these legions of soldiers could ponder the awesome spectacle not only in the town but from considerable distances in the surrounding shelled and trench scarred chalk downs and woods of Picardy.

The French poilu and the British Tommy, both, reckoned the war would end on the day the statue hit the ground, whilst their opposition the German Schutze thought whichever side toppled it , that side would lose the war. Schutzes' seniors obviously did not aim that high again, whilst the French and British, it was said, stealthfully re-secured the vision, as it was, to keep the war going.

For nearly three and a half long years of unspeakable agony and adversity for the men fighting and dying in Picardy, the Virgin and her Infant remained displaced, much as the ending of the war and its losers remained uncertain and unpredictable. It was not until the British were pushed out of Albert by the Kaiser's spring offensives of 1918 that the matter was resolved. Shortly after the town was captured, the British, in April of that year, with a fine piece of artillery marksmanship brought down the tower with its third shot. With the tower, the statue went, never to be seen again. The war ended within six months not quite as predicted but were the Tommies, les Poilus, der Schulzes very far out?

Back to 1916, the population of Albert had been all but evacuated and replaced by troops, who had turned most of the buildings into bunkers. There were a few facilities in the more sheltered places, the odd canteen, a Battalion or Brigade H.Q., and the communication systems spreading there-from.

It was here in Albert on their first visit, 3th April 1916, that unambiguously the Battalion's diary records "Bath had by all". Obviously it was a major event for the diarist not known for the exuberance of his verbosity. Certainly it is difficult for me to imagine four companies of officers and men, numbering nearly one thousand, participating in this luxury in one day. No doubt, as it was written, all did take their bath, and it can be further said, whether they needed it or not; and no doubt they all felt the better for it.

Bath times were well organised affairs, much mentioned in accounts but how many changes of the cleansing hot or warm waters there were, is not recorded. The bath generally followed an issue of new or clean underwear for everyone, the discarded garments often sloping away under the power of its own pediculosis!

All the same a very clean Battalion then spent the next six long days in the trenches beyond the town, becoming familiar with areas they were likely to assault in the near future. The targets were viewed from a few inches above ground level for a second or two at a time. To view longer would invite very unfriendly reactions and very soon if the viewer did not fall back dead there would be spurts of chalk or dirt that would zip their stark onomatopoeic warnings to get down.

Three months would pass whilst the men of 2nd Middlesex were learning what would be expected of them; and during this time all the men became very aware that this part of France was becoming packed to overflowing with the men and materials needed for the approaching battle. A complete khaki conurbation sprawled out behind Albert towards Amiens becoming the equivalent of city of over a million souls. Temporary accommodation for men and beasts, temporary transport parks, temporary dumps and shelters for every type of store, equipment, ammunition and explosives. The feeding and watering requisites for such a host of men and animals had to be provided and stored. These victuals then had to rationed out, distributed then prepared and cooked for battalions of hungry and thirsty men. Railways, tramways and roads had to be designed, surveyed and constructed with great speed and urgency. These routes often led into freshly dug trenches or embankments for protection and unobserved movement from a very interested enemy. Medical services needed many new Aid Posts, Casualty Clearing Stations and Hospitals to be established, staffed with doctors, nurses and orderlies and stocked with medicine and dressings etc for the expected victims of the coming fight; whilst someone had to ponder the requirements for suitable last resting places for those who would be beyond help after their battle.

All this and much more had to have an efficient system of law and order imposed over it to ensure its smooth working. This was provided by the Corps of Military Police (C.M.P.) and to a more limited degree, Regimental Policemen (R.P's). The system did work well mainly due to the spirit, morale and loyalty of the British Army but, like most of our civilian police forces, the "Red Caps" kept themselves apart and they did not enjoy a surfeit of popularity from their charges. Ask, any ex-soldier, about the C.M.P. and he will probably tell you that the sight of a pair of "Red Caps" on patrol would have immediately prompted him to straighten up, make sure his cap was on straight and his buttons were all fastened properly. Such was and most likely still is the affect this force had universally throughout the army; but in turn, lack of discipline and selfish behaviour was always very minimal and exceptional in the armed forces and even more so when the men were doing their service in a war zone.

Driving through now-a-days from Amiens to Albert and on to Baupame one can easily see in ones mind's eye the enormity of this under-taking. The countryside has reverted back to how it was before 1914 and it is clear that in military terms there is nothing there to fight a war. The land is empty; agricultural and farming land stretching for miles, virtually uninhabited. If you want a drink or any other sustenance whilst there you have to take it with you. I believe, starting from scratch the Fourth Army did well just to bring enough water for the thousands of men and animals occupying the area yet alone start a major offensive within six months of arriving and taking over from the French army who had been defending this quieter sector along a rather relatively narrow strip of land.

Halfway through all this activity taking place on the Western Front in France, to add to the problems of the people of Great Britain, at the end of the Easter break on the 24th April 1916, a small faction of Sinn Fein took to the streets in Dublin, seized a number of public buildings and declared an Independent Irish Republic. They were not well supported by the majority of Irishmen, although the seven men who signed the Declaration on behalf of the Provisional Government did expect that more subjects would join them in their fight, adding to the aid that they had been promised from Germany and their kin in America,

Certainly, most of their guns and ammunition did come from Germany, but little else was forthcoming. Consequently this lack of support caused, the only revolt that occurred throughout the vast British Commonwealth and Empire during the period of The Great War, to collapse with the leaders' surrender to the British Army six days later.

History has shown that the sharing of power democratically in the whole of Ireland was still many years off and much more bloodshed would occur before that would be achieved. However, I think, it well worth remembering that there were far more many men in battalions from Dublin and what is now call The Republic of Ireland fighting for the common cause on The Western Front between 1914 and 1918, than the numbers of Irishmen that took to the streets at Easter-time 1916 in Dublin. t

It was not long after this event that on the night of the 10th-11th May 1916, my Father and seventy four men of 2nd Middlesex carried out a raid into the German trenches from their own front line. It was just something more to send their pulses racing when the men first heard the news, as if thinking about the coming big push was not enough.

The records show that the group left their own front line trenches from between two communication trenches known as Dorset and Longridge Streets and I have been able to study and walk the ground over which the raid took place helped much by these pointers. The ground was difficult and dangerous and can be visualised, as it was then, when using a detailed 1:10,000 trench map titled Ovillers, Sheet No 57d S.E.4. Edition 2.B. "with trenches corrected up to 11th June 1916", produced by Ordnance Survey 1916. A copy of this original map and many others are kept at the Imperial War Museum's archives in South East London. They are good and usually very accurate indicators of the positions of the trenches and strong-points of both sides at the times when they were dated.

The helpful stains of white chalk from the diggings have mostly gone, eradicated by nearly ninety years of ploughing and reaping except where the deepest and most violent mines were set off. Now only these records can assist to locate a particular spot, other than where the land has been preserved, as it was, in the form of relatively small enclosed memorial parks, generally kept with infinite care by the Commonwealth War Graves Commission.

Fine examples of these parks can be seen at Beaumont Hamel, Vimy Ridge and Deville Wood, whilst the Lochnager Crater site at La Boiselle is the only remnant left of the Western Front near to Mash Valley where my Father fought the first parts of his Somme battles. It was and still is but a short walk from Lochnager, the site of the greatest explosion and mine crater of the Great War fired a few minutes before zero hour on July 1st 1916.

The many other craters, blown that day, have been filled in over the years mostly to reclaim a scrap of farming land, although I believe someone has built his house over one of the sites. Even Lochnager, this volcanic-like pit, all of ninety metres in diameter and thirty metres deep was not secure for the coming generations to see until the site was purchased by an Englishman in 1979 over sixty years after its big bang. Now it is one of the most visited sites along the popular "circuit des souvenirs" or "remembrance trail of the Battles of the Somme 1916", as well as the location of a moving service of remembrance every 1st July at 7.30 a.m. commemorating the selfless tragedies of that day.

The route the raiding party, which included my Father, were expected to take was across the length of the infamous Mash Valley which formed a wide stretch of no-man's land before reaching the enemy's positions barring the way to the village of Ovillers-la-Boisselle and to the right the Albert to Baupame road. The seven to eight hundred metres along the valley was virtually the same approach that they would have to take when the main offensive was called and it was pitted with shell holes and overgrown with at least two seasons of rotting and un-harvested corn and weeds. Walking, running or crawling would not have been easy on this terrain, and at night loaded down with arms and equipment, very hard.

Colonel Sandys had been told that the 4th Army Staff at Querrieu wanted to test the German resistance along this pivotal part of the line of the attack and if possible to capture a prisoner or two for their Intelligence Staff to interrogate. Something stronger than a furtive patrol was required. A selected group at platoon strength, heavily armed, well trained and briefed would be the right force.

As well as the four officers, forty six N.C.O.'s and men would be armed with revolvers with three refills of six cartridges. They would also carry a vicious knob-kerry each and at least four bombs. These were the men who would do the initial in-fighting and take the prisoners and bring them back to their own lines. The remaining twenty five men, who would stay out in no-man's land to secure the retreat route, would carry rifles with fixed bayonets, plenty of small arms ammunition and their share of four bombs a piece. There were also a number of other necessary items to take and use on this nocturnal raid; five sets of wire-cutters and heavy hedging gloves; most men would carry one of the fifty-seven torches that were issued and they would drag two ladders, two ammonal tubes with five detonators along with them. All these and more would go with the raiding party, including an optimistic twenty pairs of handcuffs, in case they got lucky with the prisoners. The ladders to get in and out of trenches are not items often associated with such a mission but since falling back on this part of my research, I have remembered that on the clip most frequently shown on TV of another much more epic event, that the second and third soldiers to leave the British landing craft making towards the Normandy shore on D-Day 1944; they too, are carrying a ladder between them.

Just who indented for and who supplied the fifty knob-kerries obtained from the Quartermasters' stores I have not researched. I am not aware that there were any special drills or training hints on the uses of these blunt instruments or how large was the total British arsenal of these items. It proves, I suppose, that it was not all shell-fire, machine-guns and bullets in this infantry-man's war.

My Father and the others were given a couple of limited rehearsals whilst out of the line, designed to assimilate the real thing and get to know what they were likely to be doing, but it was not long before they were marching from their billets in Hennecourt Wood the five miles into the front lines again. The 8th May saw my Dad in Dorset Street trench pondering the future and for a long two days gearing up and observing the target area with the others. What happened at night over there? Was it usually quiet? Was there much regular activity initiated by the German troops living out the same unnatural and wretched existence as themselves?

I shall never know, I can only surmise from the incomplete evidence. However, I do know that after those couple of long days and nights of rather stressful anticipation, on the night of the 10th-11th May, Dad in the party of seventy-five men, faces and helmets blacked out, wearing leg protectors, heavily armed like brigands, with no I.D.'s or gas helmets used their ladders to quietly climb over their parapets and crawl out into the semi darkness of no-man's land.

In three groups, the actual trench raiding party, those armed with the revolvers, went first, spreading out as they advanced to approach their enemy targets along a line of about sixty metres wherein they were instructed to take their prisoners and cause much killing and mayhem before being rumbled. The remaining men followed fifty or so metres behind.. They would act in support from chosen positions in front of the enemy's barb-wire and parapets as the others made their retreat.

The raid went quite well by Western Front standards, the first men of 2nd Middlesex across Mash Valley got through the enemy's wire in sufficient numbers to sneak over the parapets and into the trenches killing silently as they went until they had established enough of their own men to intimidate and take prisoners. This did not last long. Only two terrified German soldiers had been dragged out of their trench handcuffed to their captors, on a two to one basis, with one escort and these two groups of four men each were quickly crawling or scrambling on their way back before the enemy became more aware of what was happening. The silence did not last long and very soon unfamiliar guttural oaths, shouts and gun-fire broke the silence and caused the Die-Hards also to change their tactics. They began shooting or bombing any enemy unfortunate enough to show themselves above the parapet or come round a transverse occupied by a man or group of men in khaki.

There was too much opposition to stay for long. With the element of surprise gone they knew it was time to leave. Once out of the enemy's trench they joined their friends behind the parapets and in turns controlled by their own officers or N.C.O.'s moved away in small groups, as fast as a crouching zig-zag run would allow. They retreated through the back-up men in no-man's land, who in turn, were successfully trying to keep the nearest enemies' heads down with their own rifle fire and bomb throwing.

Until it was fairly certain that the enemy was not going to pursue the raiders across Mash Valley towards the British lines the senior officer organising the retirement kept a line of men facing the German front to give cover to those of his men with their backs turned. Soon, however, much more enemy fire was playing across the valley from the adjacent fortifications, German shell-fire was also raking the area and it was obvious nobody with a choice was going to stay put. Like old Bill, they all knew a better 'ole in their own lines, and their seniors ordered the remainder to go to it, toot-sweet!

In all they were out on the wrong side of their own wire for not much more than an hour, but they certainly were a brave lot. Two men were killed in the action and had to be left where they fell, twenty one others, including two of the four officers, were wounded by enemy fire and needed assistance getting back. Only one of the prisoners taken survived his nightmare journey and was interrogated by a grateful staff at G.H.Q., who had initiated the raid.

Col: Sandys' reports taken from the officers and N.C.O.'s who had participated in the raid, also went to swell the gathering intelligence at 4th Army H.Q. but did nothing to defer the intended offensive. The attack date, privy to but a few, was still seven weeks off its scheduled start and although it needed all this time to get everything into place, the determined response to a raid of platoon strength was not considered significant.

2nd Middlesex's C.O. did not like it. He knew his men faced a resolute and dangerous foe, well dug in and well armed. He felt, maybe, that the artillery would provide a better balance of the odds that he instinctively knew would be needed. Stoically, he was also resigned to the fact that he could little affect the die that had been irrevocably cast long before he even got there.

Ten men out of the seventy five of the raiding party were awarded medals for their actions that night. Two Military Crosses (M.C.'s) went to the officers, four Distinguished Conduct Medals (D.C.M.'s) and four Military Medals (M.M.'s) were awarded to the N.C.O.'s and men. My Father was not on the list that was gazetted on the 23rd May 1916 two weeks after the successful raid, but I believe that the inscription on the reverse of a D.C.M., "For Distinguished Conduct In The Field" is probably appropriate to all those brave men who left their trenches that night to go across Mash Valley.

Walking that same field gave me goose-pimples, how did so many men like my Dad do this not once but many times in similar or slightly different ways? They never said and of course, there could never be enough medals to go round.

May dragged into June for the mostly New Armies stretched along this eighteen mile Front. Hundreds maybe thousands of orders were being issued to put into precise place the infantry and their assault equipment, the gunners and their artillery, the sappers and pioneers with their explosive charges and construction and trenching equipment, the follow up reserves, the airmen buzzing and observing the area, the medics with their field ambulances, dressing stations, field dressings and splints. Each and every person and item had an order and place to go; Brigade Order No 37 dated 17th June 1916 told my Father as part of 2nd Middlesex where to assemble for the attack and how he and his fellow soldiers would be armed. An intensive barrage was ordered to open fire at 3am on the morning of the 24th June, a noise that would rumble across Northern France and the English Channel to be distinctly heard as a shudder of the glazing in many a window in London including my Father's home and the cabinet room in 10,Downing Street early on that Saturday morning. It continued all week. Surely after the days of this type of build up and much other activity the troops and their officers really did begin to think it would be a walk-over.

Of course, the common enemy was not exactly idle either in France or elsewhere during this time. The German Army was earnestly waging its own savage war at the gates of Verdun, battering the Russians in the East as well as striving to strengthen their defences along the rest of the Western Front.

The German Navy was active too. On the last day of May their High Seas Fleet's brief presence in the North Sea led to the greatest encounter of heavy warships of all time when it clashed with the British Grand Fleet. This most significant naval battle of the war, known as the Battle of Jutland, was swiftly followed on the 5th June, when the enemy's underwater service killed a man considered by the British Nation to be its best and most respected soldier.

Both of these happenings brought much sorrow collectively and individually because the death and injury rolls were so high. In the case of the earlier event, fortunately the tragic losses were tempered with a perceived and well hailed important victory. The same was not mitigated when Lord Horatio Herbert Kitchener of Khartoum, the Secretary of State for War, became the highest ranking casualty of the conflict. All Britain had lost its much loved senior Field Marshal, its number one on the army list and favourite son, as well as most of the crew of eight hundred men manning the fast armoured cruiser H.M.S. Hampshire. This warship had been taking Lord Kitchener and many of his staff on a mission to Russia when it struck a German mine, sown by one of their submarines near to Scapa Flow off the western coast of the Orkney Islands. The atrocious seas that were raging at the time, firmly sealed the fate of all but twelve men from the stricken ship.

The British soldiers on the Somme were mostly his men, they liked specifically to be called a part of

"Kitchner's Armies", they had responded to his famous appeal and to hear that he and his Staff perished, at a stroke, was a bitter pill indeed. The event was so unexpected. So much again, for the risk free lives Field Marshals and Generals were supposed to lead, add then the other tally of Senior Naval Commanders present and going down with their ships at the Battle of Jutland five or six days earlier and this abject claim is seen again for the travesty it really is.

Over time the Battle of Jutland has also had its many critics, not quite as many as the Generals have received, but except for contemporary accounts, this greatest of sea battles has suffered much in the telling. My concerns here are limited to the place they lie with my Father's activities on the Western Front but I think it is interesting to note, that the German High Seas Fleet never ventured out again from their mine-protected and secure moorings in the Heligoland and Wilhelmshaven bases sited in Northern Germany until the war was over. They came out then to surrender themselves in accordance with the Armistice terms. Obeying those terms, their officers and crews delivered this once powerful force of warships to the Royal Navy's Grand Fleet moorings in Scapa-Flow. There was certainly no fight left, most of the Imperial German Navy sailors had mutinied long before the ships left Germany and were not on board. Those men that were, promptly scuttled their vessels and their rotting hulks remain there until this day.

The painful and tragic loss of Kitchener did not delay the start of the Somme battles of 1916 by one day. The weather did. It gave more than twenty thousand men an extra twenty four hours of life. The unseasonable wet and murky weather postponed the start scheduled for 7.30 am on Friday 30th June, six days after the unprecedented artillery bombardment had begun. The offensive was ordered to start at the same time on the next day. A massive infantry assault involving well over one hundred thousand men, (some estimates put the figures at one hundred and forty thousand) from eighteen divisions would be ordered to leave their own lines at the appointed time, to advance across no-man's land, kill, maim or capture all enemy forces they met until they had reached their specified objectives. They would then consolidate until a second wave or force took over from them to make further advances until the full day's targets had been secured.

My Father's Battalion accordingly moved up to their taking off positions on that Friday, the last day of June. Like most of the infantry they were dressed in battle order, leaving their large packs and kit bags with the Quarter-Master whilst carrying their small haversack at shoulder height. They carried a loaded rifle with bayonet, two hundred and twenty rounds of "small arms ammunition" and two Mills Bombs. Dad and his companions also carried two empty sand bags a-piece with a trenching tool, either a pick or shovel and their water bottles filled with cold tea. Unlike at the Battle of Loos nine months earlier, all the soldiers were wearing Shrapnel helmets for the first time in battle. They were also equipped with the vital anti-gas 'PH' or Phenate Hexamine helmet which was to be replaced later in the year with the more familiar box respirator commonly worn with its square webbing container on the chest.

Many or most of the men making their way to their appointed assembly points had never been over the top before, for my Father he had last done it nine months ago and he well knew its life or death perspective or prospect. Facing the unknown in such circumstances is hardly something one can get used to, no matter how frequently it is that you are called to do it. Each battle has a beginning the lead up to which had to be endured, those last few waiting hours and then minutes are different from all other experience in life before the full horror and action changes the reflective mood and stark reality snaps into place. Going "over the top" has come to personify "The Great War", the unbending courage and fortitude of this age of mostly young men, so unsung and particularly un-rewarded in the years that followed, it is now so hard to comprehend. At the start of the Battle of the Somme there were some fourteen miles of trenches or more filled with such men or boys each one with his own premonition.

Rupert Brooke's soldier had doubt for his future: "If I should die, think only this of me; that there's some corner of a foreign field that is for ever England". William Butler Yeat's Irish airman knew and was positive "I know that I shall meet my fate, Somewhere among the clouds above". Britain's Sovereign and Naval King, the late George VI, in his Christmas Broadcast to the Empire of 1939, when he and his people once more stood on a similar threshold, suggested a line or two, which proved to touch as the best advice to the vast majority of his people's inner thoughts and Christian beliefs then, as well, as I believe, it did when my Father and those many thousands of fine men were finding it hard to doze before daybreak on the 1st July 1916.

Paraphrased very slightly to suit the middle of the year rather than the beginning, the King's words, taken from a 1908 poem of Minnie Louise Haskins went:-

I said to the man who stood at the Gate of --'tomorrow',

"Give me a light that I may tread safely into the unknown".

And he replied, "Go out into the darkness,

and put your hand into the Hand of God.

That shall be to you better than light,

and safer than a known way."

Chapter 11

Chapter 12

As an adolescent in 1944, I vividly remember watching a doodle-bug, or V1 flying bomb, heading roughly in my direction across the sky whilst I was cycling home one afternoon from a visit to a friend. The reason I was not attending school that day, was not that the second London blitz (the attack by Adolf Hitler's unmanned vengeance weapons) was at its height, but because, rather inconveniently, the Nazis had chosen to start it during that year's summer school vacation. Going to school would have been a bit of a farce, if not near impossible, due mainly to two reasons. One was that most youngsters, who had returned to London after the first blitz of 1940-1941, had been re-evacuated; and the second was the frequency of the attacks. In reality and with hindsight, regarding this incident, I suspect that I should have taken shelter instead of continuing my journey. At the time, I wanted to get back to my house and family and air raid warnings were very common and not of too much consequence to a young teenager. During the period of that summer, starting just after "D" day, June 6th, the siren's noisy high and low pitched wails were sounded very frequently to tell Londoners that more pilot-less bombs were approaching, only to have the constant pitch of the all clear going shortly afterwards, when the danger had passed over. This time it was different, I heard the bomb's engine cut out when it was at about eleven o'clock from where I was watching, at an elevation at about 70-80 degrees from my horizontal sight line. It was approaching from the south and I said to myself that I was going to see the thing hit the ground and explode, and so I did.

I knew only too well, having heard but not seen many in the continuous day and night attacks, that the flying bomb's engine was set to stop to allow the weapon to fall on its random target somewhere in the capital's metropolitan area. All the time the engine could be heard, it was likely to miss you, if it was loud when it stopped, it was time to say your prayers.

I had a perfect view of this bomb as it pitched from the sky and exploded harmlessly about two hundred yards away to my left onto some waste land alongside the Southern Railway's main and suburban lines between Earlsfield and Wimbledon Stations, not far from a small local electricity power station. Had its German controller in Northern France timed the flight just an extra second more it would have destroyed six sets of railway tracks, consisting of the up and down mainlines from Central London to Portsmouth, Southampton and the South West, two important suburban lines and two lines for freight. A strategic target if ever there was one. Instead, on hitting the ground, the bomb, sent a huge plume of black smoke and dust into the air but its blast was well dissipated before it reached me as I was peering, crouched behind the comforting brick parapet of the road bridge over the railway tracks, where I had stopped to watch.

I remember feeling that I had been somewhat wayward getting into that position and mentally debating and deciding that it was not the sort of thing best told to ones parents or siblings. It was best not to mention it.

Whether on the 1st July 1916, my Father had similar thoughts, or other reasons, why he never told me or his family that he had seen, heard and felt the mighty explosions of the Lochnagar and Y Sap mines minutes before the whistles blasted the message for him to advance and attack the enemy. There can be little comparison of my flying bomb with the Lochnagar and Y Sap mines, which although he never knew them by those names, were enormous detonations causing huge eruptions that violated the very ground and trenches with the force of an earthquake right where he and his Battalion were standing less than a mile away. In fact, the mine at La-Boisselle (Lochnagar) was the loudest and largest explosion ever detonated by man until the Second World War and nuclear fission.

The noises and sights he heard and saw on that fair Saturday morning must have stayed with him, if my comparative trifling experience on the 27th July 1944 had etched such a deep memory within me. The fact that it took more than sixty years before an interested private individual volunteered to preserve the largest of these forgotten sites (Lochnagar),as with much else connected with the Great War, did influence the sharing of his memories and he like most veterans decided to leave their experiences generally un-said.

It was only much later when these Great War soldiers had aged and were fast dying out that a few of the younger generations started to realise that these men would soon be gone forever and there was a need to get at least some records whilst the first hand authentic witnesses were still able to tell their own stories.

There were many other underground mines blown under the German trenches along the front that day before the infantry assault began. They were expected to be the coup-de-grace to an enemy already reeling, it was thought, under the most sustained artillery bombardment ever used. Unfortunately, that was a fatal misperception or assumption and the Big Push to end the war, became instead, a four and half month long horror of death, mutilation and attrition that would dig deep into the attacker's and defender's resolve alike; no matter what the rank or status of any particular individual happened to be.

It is frequently stated that the Divisions used on the 1st July were from Kitchener's New Armies, inexperienced and green. This is not true. There were quite a few battle tried Divisions and Battalions in the mix containing men who had fought on the Marne, Ypres 1and 2, Neuve Chapelle, Loos etc:. It was not the fault of the men who attacked that day that the tragedy happened, war had become a vast battle of wills viewed from both sides of the trenches.

Just how long would it take to break the enemy's expansionistic designs, after the 1st July 1916, would become the new and vital prediction and target of the British Generals. They knew for certain now, what they had suspected for some time, there was no quick fix. No single action, offensive and advance would be enough.

In the Commander in Chief's own words, after that first day on the Somme there had been a subtle change of objectives. A great break through to roll up the German line and advance to victory through Baupame, Cambrai and Mons was no longer included in the motivations for these actions. Haig described the plan as "the wearing out battle", with three main justifications:-(a) To relieve the pressure on the French Armies in the desperate fighting at

Verdun, (b) To assist the Allies in the other theatres of war by preventing any further transfer of German soldiers from the Western Front and (c) To wear down the strength of the enemy.

It can be said with good reason that these aims were certainly achieved. It did help to win universal recognition of the horror that this war deserved, and that this battle, if any, should have been a part of the war that was to end all wars. That it did not, is no fault of the Armed Forces, their Generals, nor my Father and his like.

The initial consequences caused by what happened on 1st July 1916 were the trials and sufferings of thirteen individually named battles, the last of which ended on the 18th November 1916, although there were on-going actions after that to exploit certain advantages that had been gained. Combined, the battles up to this point, secured a territorial gain of a few square miles of contaminated and dangerous landscape often with better tactical aspect, about thirty villages and a few farmsteads all demolished to just rubble and brick dust. It also tipped the war in the Allies' favour, although it cost each side an equal share of over one million men killed or wounded and it brought about a universal change in the common public's attitude to war forever.

The official battle nomenclature for the 1916 Somme Battles gave bare references to small woods and modest towns and hamlets, but they would soon become the places of lasting and sincere, although often unspoken memory, for those who had fought there and survived. For the rest of us, particularly those who enjoy a democratic freedom today, these scarce remembered names should be perhaps likened to that once obscure Pennsylvanian town of Gettysburg. The soldiers who battled on the Somme with such selfless concern for themselves are entitled to and deserving of an Address equivalent to Abraham Lincoln's words spelt out on that battlefield and so graciously enshrined in the Lincoln monument in Washington.

The battles of High, Delville and Mametz Woods, together with Thiepval, Guillemont and Morval are but some of the many places in the Somme Department of Picardy that justify and deserve a similar and proper Prime Ministerial Address of equal weight and political will to sustain. Sadly, had they been spoken, they would have been but hollow words which took much less than twenty years to become meaningless. Repeating just a few of Lincoln's words at Gettysberg shows just how hollow and insincere it would have been. ".......... The world will little note, nor long remember what we say here, but it can never forget what they did here. It is for us the living, rather, to be dedicated here to the unfinished work which they who fought here have thus far so nobly advanced. It is rather for us to be here dedicated to the great task remaining before us--that from these honoured dead we take increased devotion to that cause for which they gave the last full measure of devotion-- that we here highly resolve that these dead shall not have died in vain---------.

My Father, at the start of all this, with the noise of the two great mines close to Ovillers-la- Boisselle still ringing in his ears was alert when the shrill whistles blasted out. He was in the second of four waves of men to leave their front line trench in the Die-Hards' plan of attack. He had watched some of the first wave of about two hundred men slip over the top of their parapets to creep forward just before zero hour and then he had heard the dreadful rattle of the enemy's heavy machine guns and rifle fire that had started immediately, even as the British artillery barrage subsided. Although my Father and his wave could not see the killing from below the parapets, their own officers and N.C.O.'s, with the best foresight, ordered them to make their advances across no-man's-land quickly at the double.

There was only an approximate fifty yard gap planned between each wave, about thirty seconds in time to provide such a space, which meant that in less than two minutes the bulk of 2nd Middlesex was out amongst the noise, smoke and fire of lethal shell and shot that was sweeping across Mash Valley. They were heading for the German's first line which was, unexpectedly, very active and pouring incessant cones or arcs of machine gun bursts into their midst and the other on-coming British infantry of the 8th and 34th Divisions. Inky Bill, Major General E.C. Ingouville Williams, destined to be killed before the month was out, commanded the 34th, whilst the 8th Division, my Dad's, was led by Major General H. Hudson.

The men of 2nd Middlesex were situated on the 8th Division's extreme right with the 102nd Tyneside Scottish Brigade of the 34th Division on their right. Men of the 2nd Battalion of the Devonshire Regiment, part of the 8th Division, were placed on the left of the Die-Hards and it was these three Battalions of the dozens that were attacking on the 1st July (2nd Middlesex centre, 2nd Devons on their left and 20th Northumberland Fusiliers right) that had the furthest to go to reach the enemy's trenches that day, virtually at the centre of the whole, miles long, line of attack.

I believe that the mix of battalions from regiments from three very separate corners of the United Kingdom was not a fluke just for my Father's central section that morning. The diverse make up of the Divisional and Brigade quotas of Infantry Battalions was deliberate. Army Staff Officers ensured that the dangers and risks of battle was spread throughout the army and generally the battalions included men from many towns and counties of the British Isles.

Unfortunately the Pals Battalions formed and recruited by enthusiastic employers and the like early in the war proved to be a disaster. When confronted by heavy fighting and losses such as occurred on this first day of the Somme battles, the grief experienced by close communities in so many working class areas when the slain and injured figures were announced was too great to be allowed to be repeated or even risked again.

Quoting from the War Diary of the 2nd Middlesex Battalion, it records in such a matter of fact, short and cryptic style:-

---

1st July.   "Assaulted Front line in 4 waves, 50 yards gap.

1st Wave		2 Platoons from	"B" Company.	
		2	"	"A"	"
2nd	"	2	"	"A"	"
		2	"	"B"	"
3rd	"	2	"	"D"	"
		2	"	"C"	"
4th	"	2	"	"C"	"
		2	"	"D"	"

Bombers amongst the 4 Waves, 8 Lewis gun teams amongst 2,3,4 waves.

on Rt Tyneside Scottish 34th Div:

on Lt 2nd Devons.

Heavy machine guns caught 1st straight away on leaving trenches 2nd wave doubled forward, before anyone reached German front line the original wave formation ceased to exist.

About 200 all ranks succeeded reaching German line passing over they entered 2nd line of trenches. After short fight half casualties forced to retire to German 1st Front trench. Survivors under Major H.B.W.Saville consolidated.

By 9.15 handful of unwounded men perhaps 12 forced to retire to shell holes outside enemy front line. They stay there until darkness enabled them to return.

Of 23 officers 1 remains unwounded. 650 O.R.s took part in the assault 50 answered their names early hours of 2nd July

Lt:Col: Sandys and Major Saville wounded.

6 Officers Killed.

9   "   Wounded.

7   "   Wounded and Missing.

It is not much for a day for which probably more words have been written than any other day of the Great War. It does however clearly indicate that the superior and confident forces that left their trenches sharp at 7.30am were quickly whittled down by a comparatively much weaker opponent who had managed to remain out of harm's way, well below ground, before the attack started.

The rain of the previous day, which had delayed the assault, had stopped, the sun was out but a mist still hung over the ground as my Father moved as fast as he could as soon as he was clear of his own barbed wire. The slopes from the British trench and into the long churned up field of Mash Valley was not a place to stay long. Even so, near the start, it was littered with many khaki clad bodies as well as the normal debris and shell holes of a no-man's land of nearly two years standing. The Die-hards' dead or wounded had to be avoided as well as the obstructions, by running and turning, dodging, ducking and jumping as fast as his fitness and kit would allow. He knew, as every man knew in the mass of British Infantry that morning, as they left their trenches at zero hour, that there was only one way to go. Forward and into the enemy's trenches and barricades.

The loaded rifle, at the port, across his chest and his battle order equipment did not impede his movements or progress, but five or six hundred yards offers a good chance to be mown down by a determined well armed defence. The German machine gun bullet that struck my Father's right leg, in a convoluted way, almost certainly saved his life. The air was thick with them coming from three directions. On his left, they came from the German defences in front of Ovilliers-la-Boisselle; his right was covered by the machine guns his worried C.O. had observed still much in evidence at la-Boisselle, despite the British week long barrage. Finally, only some of the German guns facing him had been silenced as he raced towards them. They still fired from positions that went back in depth, stretched across Mash Valley half way up a slope topped by the Albert to Baupame Road. He had achieved most of this initial advance before he was brought down. That same bullet could well have done for him as so many others had killed that day. Every rank was well represented, but, for Dad, it caused no fatal damage, although he never reached his goal, or met his enemy face to face, as he was expecting. In fact, very few did, and those who did were certainly not enough to remain and hold the ground until sufficient numbers could get through the killing zone that was no-man's land..

Unexpectedly, the same awful scenario occurred along most of the greatest frontal attack ever planned and launched by a British Army, which had been well trained and equipped to do so, if only the enemy had been softened up as much as most of these men believed.

The line, which had been my Father's primary target, was the first of three that defended and barred the way to the important highway, and each one was just an early objective for him that most significant morning. The small village of Pozieres another two and a half kilometres on in the same direction was where he was expecting to answer his name at the normal company muster that evening. That roll was never taken, nor was Pozieres, or even Ovillers-la-Boisselle, or that first enemy trench until much more blood and effort had been expended.

The latter village was not cleared finally of Germans until the 16th July; and it was more than two months, 3rd September, before a tough and tenacious enemy relinquished its final hold on my Father's first day objective. The dreaded but inevitable bite and hold strategy would replace the quick fix massive offensives that had failed along two thirds of the British front. The German defences were too strong for a full scale frontal attack by infantry supported by artillery. Some other way was needed.

Remarkably, my Dad was only hit once before he stumbled and hit the ground. A bullet from the guns of a battalion from the 180th German Regiment, whom he was expected to engage after his charge, had put him out of the fight. Although a rather nasty flesh wound the bullet had not struck a bone nor done any permanent damage to his leg. The enemy battalion, with the help of artillery and their thinly spread friends to their right and left, had wiped out most of the attacking Diehards before they had even reached the first line of enemy trenches. More than four hundred men of 2nd Middlesex lay hugging the earth or, past caring, were out-stretched where they had fallen in no-man's land twitching or jerking if their broken young bodies took further punishment from the constant enemy fire of bullet and shell that was sweeping the whole of the attacking British front with fury and without respite.

Whilst my Father, spurting blood, from his wounded leg, was carefully choosing his time to crawl into a deeper shell hole in order to stay alive, nearly 200 men still able to respond to their Officer's or N.C.O.'s orders fought their way through to the first German held trench and were bombing or bayoneting their way into the next. Despite this display of sheer gutsy determination and courage by this typical British infantry regiment, in less than two hours, it was over.

The Divisional or Brigade Commanders could see that the ground across Mash Valley was crowded with British dead or wounded. It was constantly under a sustained enemy bombardment and by that time it had become obvious to them that to send even more men into Mash Valley could not be justified. The same would happen to them.

Consequently, without reinforcements, those men of 2nd Middlesex in the German trenches, so dearly won, were unable to hold them on their own. Bravely they hung on until their own casualties and an enemy calling up fresh troops, made it impossible to remain. Taking more casualties in the counter-attacks, they were forced to give up the second line and to retreat back into the German front line. They held on here until the few men that were left unscathed decided to avoid capture or death and take their chances in no-man's land, being fairly certain they would not be pursued. Prudently, like my Father, they spent the rest of the day below ground level awaiting the cover of darkness to eventually make it back to their own lines.

During this wait my Dad was able to patch up his wounded leg, check the bleeding and no doubt wonder if he would survive in a place where so many in his group had been killed or maimed. He had not been alone for long, alert to every awful sound of the raging battle, before he was joined by first one fellow wounded Diehard, then another and another until it was very crowded with men in various forms of shock and hurt. Shelter was at a premium and every projecting hump or depression quickly became occupied. Some soldiers were much worse than my Father but many could probably thank Providence that they too had been knocked down. Did they comment on their plight in the debacle? I certainly do not know. By anyone's standards it was as bad as it could get. I do believe, however, that, if they said anything, it was more likely to have been about the sharing of a fag or drink, patching a wound and "let's get back to the right side as soon as possible". Strategy and tactics were someone else's problem to plan and order, it could not matter to them, they certainly knew that their battalion was napoo (gone) but they weren't, even if they had seen too much to be good for them.

It was not only over for 2nd Middlesex that day. It was also over for a large part of Rawlinson's 4th Army as well as the 3th Army's diversionary attempt between Gommecourt and Hebuterne under General Sir Edmund Allenby, who is usually remembered for his later successes in Egypt and Palestine.

The salient at Gommecourt would remain as it had started at zero hour on the 1st July 1916 until August time1918, two years on. There were many more British dead in no-man's land and on the German wire there, than before. These beheld for many months the price that was paid to keep reinforcements reaching the main thrust of the offensive. With sad irony and hindsight they were never needed. Comparatively few German troops were needed that day to hold back the heroic efforts of so many gallant British battalions.

It was only after the 1st July that the German High Command would have to deploy masses of their best troops into the on-going, slow grinding, attritional battle. Their Commander, General Erich von Falkenhayn insisted that every lost yard would have to be retaken, regardless of its cost in German lives or strategic or tactical value.

Douglas Haig would have preferred to have made his main efforts in Flanders with his 2nd Army under General Sir Herbert Plumer, believing that the route to winning the war was more likely to be achievable there.

However, shortly after he was appointed Commander in Chief of the B.E.F. just before Christmas 1915 (19th December) replacing Field Marshal Sir John French, he was directed by his political masters to fight in Picardy alongside his French allies. Six months later he had tried and put a great plan to the test. The first day had not gone well along two thirds of the British front but there were successes adjacent to the French Army's somewhat scaled down efforts.

The 1st July 1916 is often quoted as being the worse day ever for the British Army. I am not so sure, only the post war spin has called it that with the inclination to condemn in turn most of the British efforts sometime after the war had been won. I could mention the loss of the American Colonies in 1777, Dunkirk 1940, and the surrender of Singapore in 1942 as being far worst. It is true that nearly sixty thousand casualties have been quoted as the toll for that day but that is very difficult to verify. The figures cited are often not accurate and whilst any number is a tragedy, it was not possible to avoid huge losses in the type of fighting that this battle in particular and the Great War overall had generated.

During the planning of any attack or type of action an assessment of probable gains and losses are made, be it the Battle of the Somme or Verdun, El-Alamein, Stalingrad or D-Day etc etc. The estimates are never right. The Japanese got it wrong at Pearl Harbour when they failed to take out the American aircraft carriers in their surprise attack, but they did lose far fewer aircraft than they had expected to lose. The Somme, Verdun and Stalingrad costs were much greater than the estimates made, the gains harder to assess and easy to criticise. The battle in the desert was nearly right and on D-Day, even with Omaha, far fewer casualties were sustained than were expected but land taken targets fell short. Like all crystal balls they are seldom as clear as they are after the event.

On the first day on the Somme, it had gone very badly from the extreme left at Serre, through to the Albert to Baupame Road. Six Divisions the 31st, 4th, 29th, 36th, 32nd, 8th were back in their starting trenches, no-man's land and the German front line wire was littered with their dead, dying and wounded. My Father's 8th Division was so badly mauled that it was relieved immediately and taken out of the line. British Army policy was not to keep units that had suffered much, too long in the immediate battle zone. It is a sharp pointer to the Staff's concern and knowledge that ordered this course of action as regards to the 8th Division that had perhaps sustained the longest casualty roles for that particular day. By very competent staff work, the 12th Division from the Army Reserve, replaced the shattered 8th before daybreak on the 2nd July.

The cadres of selected officers and men L.O.B. in the military parlance (Left Out of Battle), who would become the embryo around which battalions or other units could be rebuilt in the event of heavy losses were aghast and much saddened by the shattered remnants that were returning to their various assembly areas. It is recorded in the case of 2nd Middlesex, that only twenty eight men and one officer went back to their people L.O.B'd. Young Second Lieutenant H.C.Hunt had used up more than his nine lives that morning but he was safe again for a time. Unfortunately I have not been able to find the names of the meagre twenty-eight other ranks but

I do know the 2nd Battalion's grief must have been very hard to bear. A pitiful few more got back to their pals by morning. That early morning tally on the 2nd July records that there was a tick behind fifty names of the six hundred or so that had originally made up the list.

I know that my dear Father was not amongst them; he had crawled back after dark with his wounded pal to the nearest friendly trench. He was one of the more than forty thousand of one estimate, who, in his vernacular, had "copt'd a packet". A veritable army of wounded men, each one in urgent need of some sort of care and assistance.

The dead remained where they had fallen or expired and for most of them, they would become names added to the legion of missing, without any known last resting place. Only a   fraction of the killed in action would be recovered from that battlefield and given a proper burial. The priority given to stretcher- bearers and medics was to help and try to bring back those still breathing and this operation was not even nearly over after at least three or four days of sustained and determined effort along the length of the front.

The state of the wounded men varied through a whole spectrum of pain and hurt. There were those with just a spark of life remaining in their broken bodies, there were those without limbs, without faces, and without minds, and every other sort of wound, down to the ones that would live to fight another day. They all needed help. First those able to crawl or stagger with or without help came through their own lines, through gaps made for them by the survivors or replacements guarding their part of the battlefield. Of course, the serious side of the war had not gone away, even although I have read that, by the end of that first day, a number of the enemy really did think that they had killed and maimed enough Tommies for one day.

The soldiers being brought in by the endless stretcher parties as well as under their own steam or tenacity were from all the ranks, Officers, N.C.O.'s and Privates alike. Staying with the centre, those who had the farthest to go, some now had the farthest to get back. My Father's Division and the 34th had virtually lost all their officers and most of their N.C.O.'s. Between them the three Brigades (eleven battalions) of Infantry of the 8th Division according to an authoritative list, had lost 189 Officers and 4719 Other Ranks, of which 1927 men were killed in action. Another list puts the total at 5,121. Assuming each Battalion had fielded 650 men totalling 7150 their losses stood at nearly 70 percent or seven men in every ten! Only three men in ten had survived that day technically unharmed in the strict application of the rules regarding causalities. I am certain that no General would send his soldiers into a battle of this magnitude expecting or believing that this could possibly be the result, and yet many have followed this lie when expressing and publishing their views and accounts, so much so, as to make it a common belief.

A Commanding Officer may exhort his men to supreme sacrifice in many situations. It has happened in every war on both sides of most conflicts, but Commanders want to win, and the excessive losses, such as occurred on the 1st July 1916, were not and never were part of their agenda.

Lieutenant Colonel Edwin Sandys, Dad's C.O., was amongst the eleven battalion commanders from the 8th Division who exhorted their men to give of their finest efforts. He was one of the seven C.O.s who became casualties themselves. Four were killed and three were wounded. Sandys was one of the latter, but he was unable to get over the mental scars that the loss of his men caused. He was only forty years of age, which should have been his prime of life, but he attempted to kill himself whilst at home on leave recovering from his wounds. He left his friends a note confiding to them that he not had any peace since the 1st July in France. He felt so responsible for what had happened during that brave dawn charge. Sadly, he died from his suicide attempt a few days later in hospital, on the 13th September 1916. This hospital, St: Georges, Hyde Park Corner, happened to be the one in which my Father, who had shared that day with him, passed away thirty-six years later.

Despite the circumstances surrounding 2nd Middlesex's C.O.'s death (suicide was a very serious crime), he was laid to rest, quite rightly, at Brompton Road Cemetery in consecrated ground. He now rests amongst another 395 other war heroes who succumbed to their wounds and died back in England. Yet another almost unsung example of the early understanding, benign and sympathetic approach taken by many in authority to the victims so mentally scared and affected by the war.

The official record show that Lt:Col E.T.Sandys, D.S.O., Middlesex Regiment, was one more of the Commonwealth's War Dead, which no doubt he was.

Back in France, the Commanding Officer of the much depleted 2nd Middlesex was now a 1st Lieutenant, acting temporary Captain. He and a seriously pared down 2nd Middlesex were not excused duty by their re-assignment. They were soon back in the line again north of the town of Arras so as not to lose their touch with the reasons for which they were there.

Not so the wounded, as the grey dawn of the 2nd July broke over Picardy's downlands just east of the town of Albert, my gaunt eyed Father was patiently waiting in a queue of similar men hoping to get a brown label tied to his tunic that would mean a spell in Blighty for him again. He looked as if he needed it, the shock of being shot, seeing so many men die, being bombarded for many hours knowing full well the next crump or thud could be his last, these horrors and the exertions of getting back to his own lines, had taken their toll of his reserves of strength.

As darkness had descended over fourteen miles of continuous pity-less battlefields the night before, he, in his own small patch, had reasoned that it was now up to him to get back to those most likely to help him. What help there was or that may become available in no-man's land would or should be directed to those in a much more critical state than he was.

He had stopped his wound from bleeding and kept it reasonably clean by fixing a tight field-dressing around the damaged muscle. The wound hurt, his sock and right foot was caked in blood but he believed that, with an effort, he should attempt to get back to Dorset Street trench, which was near his assembly area and thence to the Regimental

Aid Post situated at the end of Argyll St. The trenches there would be familiar to him. He also longed for a hot drink and a bite to eat which he knew he would not get in no-man's land.

Even the shelling had stopped after nightfall, so it was safe to get above ground again and try to drag one-self back across that field of horror, putting the least weight possible on the wounded leg. As he progressed, he would pass and recognise many of his less fortunate fellow Die-hards who were destined to spend a far too long length of time without proper help. Sadly, because of this, many of their names would be eventually added to that lengthening tally headed "killed in action".

My Father did not want to be one of these. It took him just over the hour to drag himself across Mash Valley into the line now held by the fresh faced men of the 12th Division, very willing to share what they had with their less fortunate comrades. The brotherhood of the trenches, much in evidence, helped him on his way through the system of communication trenches and saps that led to the overworked Medical Officer or orderly at the Regimental Aid Post. Army No 7458 R.J.Reed of the 2nd Battalion Middlesex Regiment, needed that all important brown label fixed to his tunic recording the nature of his wounds and his orders or instructions as to where to proceed next.

Many needed to know what had happened to him. Treatment was a priority, but a set procedure along the chain of command would want to record his whereabouts and condition. Eventually the fact that my Father was a casualty of the assault made on the enemy's lines on 1st

July 1916 would get to the records of the 2nd Middlesex Battalion; the 23th Brigade; the 8th Division, III Corps and 4th Army's H.Q., until finally, it would reach the B.E.F.'s General Head Quarters in Montreuil.

It would have taken several days before this fact included in the total figures of those killed, missing and wounded reached General Rawinson, the Commander of the 4th Army and General Haig, the Commander in Chief. They both would have known already known much of what had happened in broad terms, certainly enough to influence their commands regarding the course of the battle and to let their political masters know the bad news.

In turn, the initial reports that were allowed to filter through the system for the general public's consumption, did not relate to the full and factual situation of that first day of the battle. That gradually and officially emerged from the endless casualty lists that were published on a daily basis quite long after the event. The first reports in the newspapers emphasised the gains achieved on the right where the villages of Mametz and Montauban were captured and held and the overall good morale of the 4th Army.

However, of course, the British public were not spared for long. They expected and received the bad news of their loved ones fighting in Picardy and Flanders generally within a few days of the event; and in a short while, the telegrams, letters and newspaper lists were spelling out the tragic news, both of the personal and national losses, for all to see.

My Father's wife got her second telegram in less than ten months very quickly, informing her that her husband had been wounded again but that he had survived the day. Scarred as he was, the bullet wound he had received was not enough for him to be sent home. He would do his recuperating in a base hospital in France and accordingly, he followed the line set up by the Director of Medical Services that generally worked with an all too practised efficiency.

Search today for actual locations or sites of Advanced Dressing, Casualty Clearing and Main Dressing Stations of the Somme Battles of 1916 and you have to dig deep into the Divisional Diaries of the Assistant Director of Medical Services. They are all carefully recorded with accurate five digit map references like the A.D.S. near Aveluy at Crucifix Corner W11d.9.2. where I am certain my Father got his wound redressed and his tag telling him he was not down for Blighty.

I marvelled at his fortitude as I traced his steps from that Regimental Aid Post situated in the trench named Argyll Street, turning right into Donnet Street and, finally, left into Lancaster Avenue, which was a nearly mile long communication trench descending the crest of the hill at Donnet Post to the relative safety of Crucifix Corner which was well out of sight from the German positions on their side of no-mans-land.

There were and are no signs on the ground I walked that indicate the dramas that were played out on the first day of the battle. There was never a medal clasp struck and issued to indicate that a man had served and, more often than not, spilt some of his blood here. Perhaps a

Tennyson's "Charge" poem was and still is needed as well as that Presidential Address to make the nation and its leaders really appreciate and perpetuate the proper memory of this day of battle and all who served here instead of treating it as some misguided effort concocted by some incompetent Generals.

In spite of that, the one day (1st July) and a mop up to victory, would turn into one hundred and forty days of unprecedented conflict which only the weather was capable of easing half-way through November 1916.

One could almost say with truth that there were to be 'no more mister nice guys'. Whether it was a General, a platoon commander, or a fighting soldier, everyone had to adopt the same ghastly message and attitude. Those who kill the most and cause the most pain will break the other's will and win the war.

One Die-Hard Commanding Officer expresses the approach required in his farewell message, after four months with his battalion on the Somme. He said to his Battalion "--------: *sad, because of the good men and true we have lost in action since July: proud, because of the Battalion's achievements, particularly in Trones Wood and at Thiepval. No failure has spoiled our record since the real business began nearly four months ago, and none is going to. In that period we have begun to learn that the only way to treat the Germans is to kill them, but that message is only half-learned, for we either do not want to kill them enough, or we forget to use that best of weapons, our rifles, to 'down them'. We shout for bombs, instead of shooting with our guns.--------------. Finally, remember that the 12th Die-Hards do (underlined) kill; don't get taken prisoner unless wounded and don't retire. And with these one 'do' and two 'don'ts' I wish all ranks 'Good-bye' and 'God speed'."*

My Dad's efforts for that first day did not account for many dead Germans, none in fact, but he not been de-moralised. He had felt terror for a time at the thought of meeting his German foe 'en- face', but that feeling did not last long as he witnessed his own people slaughtered during the charge. Now he was feeling a lot better as he joined others of his kind waiting the transport of the Bearer Division of 25 Field Ambulance to move him on. He was due to go to the Main Dressing Station at Millencourt, map reference at D.5.a.9.9. which was nearly four miles from the A.D.S. at Crucifix Corner. There were three Field Ambulance units, numbers 24,25 and 26, allocated to deal with the casualties of the 23rd Brigade, each having a Wagon Rendezous Collection Station neatly map referenced before the battle started. Besides stretcher bearing, these Field Ambulance units would use horse and mule drawn wagons, petrol wagons, hand drawn carts and light tramways to get their charges to the help they needed.

It was hard for my Dad to believe that all this had started just a little over twenty-four hours ago, as he patiently waited his turn for the transport in that sheltered disused quarry, hard by the Medics and the road that would take him away from this battle front.

He was by no means fit and out of trouble, only feeling better. The wounded leg needed expert attention and the proper treatment to heal and avoid infection and the likely fever and deterioration that often followed the slightest contamination. He needed that ride to the M.D.S.. Unfortunately, so did so many others.

By early daybreak on the 2nd July, the D.A.D.M.S., Deputy Assistant Director of Medical Services, a blue tab staff officer with a long title and a big job, had toured his area, including 23rd Brigade's front, and the establishments he had set up to deal with the casualties. He had already been to the A.D.S. at Crucifix Corner and it did not take him long to realise that his medical teams were now dealing with an avalanche of wounded men on a scale never previously expected. Each wounded soldier who got to the Regimental Aid Post, became his responsibility and there was, literally, a continuous stream of them coming in from the battlefields. The records show, however, that by the end of the second day, his men and the reinforcements he had patently arranged, had dealt with a total of two thousand seven hundred and fifty four casualties.

My Father was one of these, and, what is more, he had been moved on quickly to the C.C.S. and subsequently to a base hospital set up in the town of Amiens, from where he could still hear the sound of the guns of the battle that was awaiting his return and another much longer contribution.......

When can their glory fade?

O the wild charge they made !

All the world wonder'd.

Honour the charge they made !

Chapter 13

My Father was back on the Somme before the 2nd Battalion Middlesex returned there.

It took barely four weeks for his wound to heal and for him to become fit enough for a spot of leave, return to khaki and get posted to his third and final Die-Hard Battalion on the 27th July1916. This Battalion had started to battle on the Somme on the 15th July before he joined them with sixty-four other men as replacements for their losses sustained in carrying out works under fire around Mametz and High Wood.

A seasoned soldier, he was now in his twenty-eighth year, a man with a wife and three young children dependant on him, he had the substantive rank of Lance Corporal, two war wounds and he had been on active service in the most dangerous of all the theatres of war, France and Belgium, for nearly eighteen months. He had been sent from the 25th Reserve Battalion of XV Corps to join the 18th (Service) Battalion, Middlesex Regiment, 1st Public Works, New Army, that had been serving with the 33rd Division since its arrival in France in November 1915. In fact the whole 33rd Division, known for their double three domino Div: sign, embarked for service on the Western Front at the same time.

Whether he had volunteered to join this unit, attracted by the extra pay, a Private in a Pioneer Battalion received two old pennies a day ($£0.008$ or nearly 6p per week) more than a Private in the infantry, or he was just allocated to them to replace their losses, I do not know. There may have been other reasons. It is probable that whilst he was in hospital, he had palled up with the friend shown in the only photograph his later family had of him in khaki. This man, who I have not been able to identify, may have been already serving with this Battalion. Dad had, no doubt, lost a lot of his friends on the 1st July and so he may have requested to be sent to this particular unit rather than return to the 2nd Middx. This photograph clearly shows the tell-tale chalky dust marks on the men's boots and puttees, which indicates that it was taken in the Somme region behind the forward areas, when the two men were out of the line. A closer examination of insignia on the lapels of their uniforms and the cap badge confirms that the two men belong to one of the Middlesex Regiment's three Public Works Battalions. The cross rifles and picks are the easiest to see, an extra scroll on the cap badge defining the particular Public Works Battalion is harder to recognise. My Father's medal roll records, however, confirms that he did join the 18th Battalion finally, after his service with the 3rd and 2nd Battalions.

The 18th, 19th and 26th Battalions of the Middlesex Regiment were raised in that order by Lt: Col: John Ward, M.P. during 1915 as three Pioneer Battalions for Kitchener's New Armies. The Battalions were formed between January and August 1915 with most of the recruits volunteering from various construction and civil engineering enterprises that worked in the London area. Unlike today, in the first half of the twentieth century, most industry and construction projects were very labour intensive, and whole groups of friends and neighbours from particular areas, streets or firms would be persuaded to join up together to form a particular unit. These units were often referred to as "Pals" Battalions.

My Father would complete his first world war with the 18th Middlesex: a New Army Battalion, which was a part of a New Army division in the 4th New Army. He had now become really one of Kitchener's men, barely a couple of months after the great man's sad death, and tracing Dad's activities in this role, it is hard to believe he could have made a harder choice. Or perhaps he did not have an option of choice?

The infantry was bad enough, but now, in one of the pioneer battalions each and every division had on its strength, he was starting to combine a support role of helping in the construction of all the paraphernalia needed at the front, such as the trenches, dugouts, barbed wire entanglements, roads and drainage systems etc, etc. as well as his infantry activities when there was a shortage of fighting men. These support units were destined to spend far longer times in jeopardy, at the front, than the infantry units. The latter's spells in the trenches were counted in days, where-as the support groups tended to be in the line for weeks on end. There was always so much work to be done. In addition to new work, there was much maintenance and repair needed, caused mostly by shelling, some other enemy action and very often by atrocious weather that made local conditions hardly tenable or sustainable.

He had others to serve now, the primary one being the Commander Royal Engineers. These C.R.E.'s attached to nearly every division of Infantry, were involved in what was virtual siege warfare along an unprecedented distance of just about the worst, wettest, most unhelpful farmland terrain, and for these reasons were unable to cope by employing their normal methods. Up to this war, Royal Engineer field squadrons or companies of skilled artisans of all types did the work necessary to attain and maintain the fighting Armies' needs, with labour provided by the P.B.I. when required. On the Western Front the needs for skilled and structured labour demanded too many men and could not be supplied adequately from the fighting infantrymen.

Accordingly, in every Division's Order of Battle, that up to then had consisted of three or four Brigades of Infantry, perhaps some mounted troops and always a good establishment of artillery, engineers, signals, transport and medics, a pioneer battalion was ordered to be added. Remarkably, by the end of 1915, each of the fifty plus divisions of the British Army in France and Belgium had been allocated such a battalion to be included in its support units under the control of its C.R.E.

To meet this demand most county regiments formed one or more specific pioneer battalion from their newly recruited units or in instances, by asking for volunteers from men already serving as infantry. They became a unique part of the history of the Great War, although more frequently, they were left unsung, when they were all disbanded shortly after the hostilities had finished. Ultimately nearly seventy such battalions were formed to meet this essential and vital need, most doing Trojan service on the Western Front.

The mining operations and massive explosions that had preceded many attacks like the 1st July ones on the Somme and the prelude to Third Ypres in June 1917 at Messines Ridge, just south of the Ypres Salient, comprise two rather spectacular examples of the outstanding efforts contributed by these Pioneering Battalions.

The latter instance was especially conceived by the Commander of the 2nd Army, General Sir Herbert Plumer, to literally blow up a large part of the enemy's front. The tunnelling and preparations went on for many months preceding the offensive. A total of 19 mines were set off at 3.10 am on 7th June 1917, enabling the British Forces to capture a ridge as important as the one at Vimy which went to the Canadians earlier in April of that year and the one between Thiepval and le Transloy during the 1916 Somme battles. This greatest series of detonations took many thousand German soldiers to their deaths contributing more and more to the attritional agenda both sides in the conflict had adopted.

The Messines charges had been primed and fired off, as usual, by the R.E.'s and hence they tended to collect the glory and credit; but the bulk of the million plus lbs of high-explosive that had been placed in position was carried by the worthy men of the Pioneer Battalions. Squads of these men had also dug a great number of the underground saps below the enemy's front line positions, obviously at great risk to themselves; and probably, as important, they had also helped with the distribution and spreading of the great quantities of surplus earth and spoil from the diggings in order not to warn the enemy observers, using aircraft or balloons, of their mole like activities.

Regarding the front at Messines, although nineteen mines exploded at zero hour several others did not. The reasons why were not explained nor resolved during the conflict. Now, I believe the records of the precise locations and sizes of the charges are irretrievably lost, much like the exact location of minefields and the horrors planted there, in various parts of the Third World during recent and more minor conflicts. At Messines to this day, it is still commonly believed that there is at least one large unexploded mine buried below that ridge, between Wytschaete and Ploegsteert in Belgium, perhaps awaiting that phantom R.E.to press the plunger again. One such event did occurred in 1955, more than ten years after the opposing armies of World War 2 had passed over the same ground at least twice, and thirty-eight years later than it was intended to explode!

The German activities in this underground warfare went mostly unrecorded or kept secret. They had no motivation to tell their enemy where they had planted their nasty surprises. One such incident, if it had become known to them, would have been much gloated over. It happened, and caused great loss of life and harm to more than one British battalion while they were out of the line. There were many men occupying an area recaptured during the early Somme fighting. These men were at rest in their temporary Nissen hutted camp that had been located between the villages of Carnoy and Montauban, in the Somme Region. It seems that a group of young officers decided to go on a rat hunt with grenades and terrier dogs in some old German trenches that were within the cantonment and infested with these pests. It is believed that one of the party must have come across an old mine shaft, but by mistake, took it to be a dugout.

Tragically, he tossed in his bomb to flush out the rats, but of course, it tumbled down the deep shaft to trigger and set off a massive unused mine that had been set there, causing another six hundred men to die. The savage eruption left only a steaming deep crater tens of metres wide with no one to tell exactly what had happened. The King's Liverpool Regiment suffered most in this incident, and one may ask, was it a well placed booby-trap, carelessness, bad luck or c'est la guerre? I am inclined to think it is more down to the last, but we shall never know for certain.

It is hard for me to believe that my Father knew the job description of the 18th Middlesex when he joined them. It is true that he was an artisan, defined in the dictionary as a skilled workman, a craftsman, but did he know what these units were expected to do? Building work had been his life, as was his father's, but that was very much on a domestic scale. Here on the Western Front the scale was really Herculean.

Settling into his new unit, by this time in his army career, had not been a difficult or worrying prospect. He had seen enough service not to let joining a different unit bother him. However, I believe, his contribution to the war became more fraught with peril and uncertainty, much more personal effort, frequent re-location, and not much time for a break, or a few days leave, than had he stayed with the infantry.

The official lists of the various men who formed, at any one time, the four companies, (A.B.C and D), that were each divided into four platoons and then four sections of about sixteen men each, have long been

293

missing from the archives. Nevertheless, my Father's activities definitely followed his new Battalion's sterling war efforts, which I have been able to glean from a number of quite reliable primary sources.

Some records suggest that more than eighty percent of the men wounded, returned to service of some type. They were not pensioned off but they did not necessarily return to active service. L/Cpl R.J.Reed did, in what must have been in a fairly record time.

My Dad, as part of the 18th Middlesex, was back on the Somme, the crucible from which the methods to resolve the Great War would be forged.

I suppose, as far as my Father was concerned, his quick return was due to the efficiency of the Medical Services operating out of 4th Army H.Q. back at Querrieu and now they were getting busier as each day passed. Casualties that summer and autumn mounted to an all time high of any war. One remarkable man eventually recovered, not only from two machine gun bullets in his left leg, but thirty five other shrapnel wounds received in the space of a few hours before he was finally removed out of harm's way. There were five wounds to his head, nine to his chest and back and the remainder in his other three limbs! The enemy tried his best, three times, to have done with this soldier, that day on the Somme, but they did not prevail, much due to the efforts of the first aiders, the stretcher bearers, the doctors and nurses and the grit of the man himself. He was a miner from South Wales fighting with the Canadian Black Watch on the day when tanks were first used in battle. He did not return to active service but he was still writing about his story many years later.

Field Marshal Douglas Haig, and the 4th Army's Commander, General Henry Rawlinson did not give up after the 1st July, neither did the French troops on the right of the offensive. Some quite good gains, by Western Front standards, were continuing to be made by heroic, though tragically costly, efforts by the Divisions on the south side of the pivotal Albert to Baupame Road. However, apart from several tries to take German positions north of this road, these had mostly been put on hold after the capture of Ovillers-la-Boisselle, shortly before my Father was back on active duty. Attrition, bite and hold was happening.

The 18th Battalion's C.O. was Lieutentant Colonel H. Storr. He had been with his Battalion since it had become a part of the 33rd Division. One of his Company Commanders would have given my Father his slot in the scheme of things. A Lance Corporal had a particular roll as part of a section and he may well have taken over as a member of a Lewis Gun team, taking into account his previous battle experience. This would have been only part of the duties he would have been expected to perform once he had been integrated into the Battalion.

Those first few days in the village of Ribemont must have been bliss for him. It was the height of summer, parades were being cancelled, because the weather was too hot, between the hours of 10.30am and 4.00pm. The padre arranged a band concert in the village square on Friday, 28th July, his second evening there. Sunday, found the Colonel taking the service after a band had led his men on the normal Church Parade at the wholesome hour of 11.30 am. After Sunday dinner their afternoon was free until 5pm when the Battalion had to be ready to march, smartened up, in drill order, to Divisional Headquarters by 5.30pm to attend an award ceremony. They were not the only Battalion present, but two of their companions were there to receive the ribbon of the Military Medal for gallant conduct in recent operations. A full General made the awards and addressed all the soldiers present, with his thanks for their vital   contribution in the on-going struggle, as well as congratulating the men he had decorated.

In an unusual entry, seldom seen in a Battalion Diary, the two other ranks that were awarded medals, are mentioned by name. They were Acting Sergeant J.Peake (C Coy) and Pte E. Booth (A Coy). Whether these two were the first men from this Battalion to get awards I have not checked, but it is such a pity that there is so little else recorded in this way. 2nd Middlesex's diarist did not mention the "Other Ranks" by name regarding their gallantry medals won in the raid on the enemy's lines in May 1916 just before the battle proper started.

Ribemont sur Ancre, to give the village its full name, was one of a cluster of such places, a reasonably safe distance west of Albert and the fighting zone. A mile from the main road that links Amiens to Albert and then Bapaume; and at the start of the Somme battles it was about six miles from the front. Like all the other villages and farmland in the vast area behind the lines, it was full of soldiers, moving to or from the battle lines, stocked out with their impedimenta and supplies, and witnessing all the bustle and the noises of war. But, there was amongst all this, the odd spot, like the narrow footpath that bordered the slow moving and shaded River Ancre, that had a peaceful and softer tranquillity much as did the meandering River Somme into which it flowed, a short distance downstream. It was here a man could and did collect his thoughts of nicer things; and when I was there with my wife, researching this book, I had little doubt that we were sharing similar scenes of this, more gentle, calmness, as many a British Tommy, including my Father, did, in those more troubled long gone days.

We certainly did not share the same flush of adrenaline that he and his pals would have had, when the orders went up that they were relieving the 51st Highland Division and their 8th Battalion Royal Scots pioneers, in particular, at the front on the 6th August 1916, barely a week after Dad had relocated to active service.

The 8th Royal Scots, was part of the Royal Scots Regiment, which maintains the privileged first position in the Regimental Order of Precedence for infantry regiments, having their place immediately after the Regiments of Guards. The 8th had been part of the Territorial Forces that had come to France in November 1914 to stiffen the much depleted regular British Army. It was one of several Battalions that converted to Pioneers "in toto", detailed, or by choice, in August 1915, to become one of the support units of the 51st Highland Division. They had been at the front with that Division for a much shorter time than normal, fifteen days only, since the 21st July. This was probably due to the bad time their Division had received, as a whole, at Mametz Wood. Although the wood had been finally cleared on the 12th July, the area to the east of it, consisting of a smashed up village and fields with surviving trench systems, all this was still much in dispute and proving very costly to assail.

It was the men of the Double Three Domino sign that was to take the place of those with the famous HD sign, by passing through Mametz Wood via Buire, Dernancourt and the southern skirt of Albert. Each unit of the relieving Division had its timed orders and rendezvous to obey to affect a smooth and efficient transfer.

My Father did not expect to be amongst the muck and bullets quite so soon, but there he was, starting another stint of unknown duration. He was thinking, no doubt, that it could all be over as quickly as the last time when he took that awful run across Mash Valley. Was his name coming up for a third time?

This apprehension could not last, he and his unit were in the line for too long for him to maintain such thoughts. Day after day, for the next three weeks, hardly a moment went by when one could say that he and the men of 18th Middlesex were really at rest.

Not only were the pioneers required to work on front line installations ready for the next attack, there was a need to consolidate the areas from which the Germans had been removed. Too much blood had been invested in that ground for it to be allowed to be retaken. The bite and hold policy was working, but all thoughts of winning a major breakthrough went after the 1st July, and it is fairly obvious that not only the Generals but the troops were also fully aware of this fact.

The 18th Middlesex men, until the end of August, when it was their turn to be relieved, contributed much to the wearing down of their enemy, as, slowly, working with the British infantry of the 33rd Division, they took and held their small gains of French soil, similar to a row of steady steam rollers that go backwards and forwards over freshly laid tarmac constructing a new road. They were not laying tarmac, but their C.O. did make a record of their efforts in this period, between the 7th and 29th August 1916. He noted that his men had dug 12,500 yards (over 7 miles) of trench, constructed five Flammenwerfer emplacements, timbered up 31 dug-out entrances and put out 800 coils of barbed wire and their pickets. They had been working under intermittent shell fire the whole time, and, day by day, night by night, their losses had added up to 18 men killed and another 80 wounded in a constant tally of bloodletting and strong pain.

Along the Somme battle front this style of action would take place throughout the battle's long duration. A number of histories have tended to summarise situations at specific dates and draw arbitrary fresh start lines, as if to emphasise losses relative to ground gained, rather than report it as the only on-going process that really was achievable at that time. This was the reality. The battles were fought with no fixed geographical objectives as was the case before 1st July. It was fought deliberately to engage the enemy in fighting an attritional battle, to wear him down, ease the pressures at Verdun for the French armies and on the Eastern Front for the wilting Russian Tsarist regime. The Generals in command did not expect to make great inroads and recapture miles of occupied France at a stroke. They knew it was not yet possible with the tools they had to hand and the known strength of their enemy.

The Army Council clearly named the fighting taking place on the Somme between July and November 1916. The approved committee named thirteen battles with precise dates of each engagement which took place between 1st July to 18th November 1916. These places had little strategic value but they were of much tactical importance. The line on the 1st July was where the German forces had been stopped in 1914 and whilst the attack on that day sought to roll up that line and win the war, it was afterwards decided that this could not be done without some very serious tactical fighting.

Great Britain was fighting an enemy, that if it was not tackled carefully, could in fact win. Britain had not lost a war since the American Colonies won their independence, but the Central Powers were powerful enough and they still really expected to defeat the Triple Alliance, including the British, and show small mercy having done so.

Neither the Army nor the Navy could forecast when the fighting would end, but the weather was sometimes capable of determining when the clashes would ease. It was only the politicians who could stop the war. Until that happened the conflict had to continue. It was this remit that had been given to the Generals.

Even after November, with a million casualties from both sides in Picardy alone, and when the Germans offered their first serious, albeit disingenuous overtures for peace, there was not one allied politician who offered to negotiate an end. The military certainly did not have the final say in the matter.

Thus it was that my Father would spend the next two long years of his life on the Western Front, hoping and praying like all those in uniform at the sharp end of the war, that their own leaders would not let them down when the war had been finally won. They and their Generals well knew the efforts and sacrifices that would be needed to be made for this to be achieved. Victory would not come cheap and should not be wasted ever again. The politicians had to find a better way to resolve their differences.

The Somme battles, as all of the efforts our forces made in the Great War, should not have the taint of being classed as unnecessary, a failure and an utter waste. It was never those things and does not deserve that reputation.

My Father did not leave this area until long after many histories report that the battle had ended. The soldiers were not aware of this, it was definitely on-going to them and the fighting was beginning to show results that mattered. L/Cpl R.J.Reed and his unit from that second excursion in August served across the length and breadth of this historic battlefield until April 1917, experiencing much of what was occurring there.

He saw active service at Mametz Wood, Bazentin Ridge and High Wood on that first tour. During another four weeks in September and October, he shared the stubborn, but unsuccessful attempts to breach the lines at Hebuterne, Fonquevilliers and Sailly-Aubois on the extreme left of the British attack. The miserable cold months of November, December and January 1917, saw him serving south or to the extreme right; his Division during this tour, taking over from the French at Maurepas, and stiffening the British front after the capture of Guillemont, Ginchy, Morval and Flers. Finally he was, amongst many others places, at le Transloy, Sailly-Saillisel and even Epehy only a stones' throw from Cambrai.

I visited a few of his contemporaries at rest in one of the most isolated but piquant battlefield cemeteries near the latter small town. It is called Pigeon Ravine Cemetery after the long valley in which it is situated. The tiny graveyard sits like a first class postage stamp near the edge of a large sheet of A2 paper, it being so small compared with the surrounding prairie type fields and it contains 135 British war dead. Theirs is a lonely peace, rarely visited, except by their local, dedicated carers. It is seldom on anyone's itinerary, which is a pity, considering its beauty and its honour of being situated in the area furthest east reached by British soldiers in the Somme Department during those 1916-17 battles.

I believe so many of these small towns and villages with their indelibly emotive graveyards deserve to be counted indeed amongst other British battle honours. Sadly, the actions and events were never properly acknowledged in the later accounts of this war that distorted so much of the reality.

To my Father and most of the men of 18th Middlesex and other units of the IVth Army, they meant less visually, than the map references that were more commonly used in their orders and war diaries for location purposes. They were, when my Dad saw them, no longer farming communities consisting of dwellings, barns, lanes, woods with open fields between, those Four Horsemen had seen to that. My dear Father and his like only saw death and destruction on such a scale that was unique in its awfulness. Everything above ground level had been pulverised so as to make it virtually unrecognisable. The buildings had been reduced to hardcore, dust or rubble; the trees in the woods were matchwood and shattered stumps and the fields were a morass of shell holes, debris, filth and pollution. Even the chalky white trench systems were better defined and, of course, aptly named in Tommy's inimitable way as sunken highways to the slow movement eastward of the battle line. In fact some places no longer existed, they could only be located by map references.

So it was that Lance Corporal R.J.Reed served his time fighting in the Somme battles of 1916 through to early 1917, with, that, in turn, leading to the greatest German pullback of the war. All the horror and effort since the 1st July did produce a victory, heralded at the time by the brave men who fought there, virtually ignored ever since.

As during the 2nd Battle of Ypres 1915, when the British had to acknowledge that a tactical retreat was necessary, so the German High Command had to accept that their position in Picardy by November was no longer tenable as it stood. The line would have to be significantly changed by a major withdrawal from French territory.

The man who had deliberately started the type of attritional battle at Verdun and demanded that every inch of ground won by the British on the Somme be contested to the last man, General von Falkenhayen, was dismissed and replaced by Field Marshal Hindenberg and General Ludendorff as Joint Chiefs of the German General Staff. Other very senior people also lost their jobs before the year was out. One was the British Prime Minister, Herbert Asquith, who resigned. Lloyd George took his place on the 4th December. The Commander in Chief of the French Armies, General Joseph Joffre was replaced by General Robert Nivelle on the 12th of that month. General Douglas Haig stayed where he was, no one seriously sought to sack him then. He still commanded all the British Armies in France and Belgium, he was the best man in that job, sharing the full trust and confidence of his men, his colleagues and staff.

By December the Battle of Verdun had been "won" by the French insomuch as the Germans, by then, realised that they could not take the city. They also knew they could not continue to sustain the casualties that they were bearing on the Somme against the British.

General Ludendorff wrote of the situation in Picardy "The decision to retire was not reached without a painful struggle. It implied a confession of weakness bound to raise the morale of the enemy and lower our own. But, as it was necessary for military reasons, we had no choice, it had to be carried out".

The German Chief of Staff ordered that a new front, behind which they would retreat, to be completed and ready by the beginning of March 1917. He records that "it was necessary to shorten our front in order to secure a more favourable grouping of our forces and create larger reserves." Of course, such a reduction in the battle lines served equally for the British and French, but this fact has not been often acknowledged, registered or appreciated.

If possible, the Germans did not want a fighting retreat. They would occupy new positions of massive and impenetrable defensive works, behind which they would stay and be safe, whilst letting the Allies shatter their armies like the waves that pound and spend their energy against the stone and concrete work of a good harbour.

The Germans did not announce their withdrawal, but in a frenzy of wanton destruction pulled back their armies to what they called their Siegfried-Stellung, and which was quickly renamed by the British as their Hindenburg Line. The Germans were giving up many of the square miles of France that they had occupied since October 1914. I have calculated that perhaps more than one thousand square miles of La Belle France was liberated by these moves, a fact, ignored to the great shame of those who have left it almost unrecorded, instead of expounding it as the victory that it was.

Even the reserved and undemonstrative Douglas Haig in his 3rd Despatch, since his appointment as Commander in Chief, to his masters at the War Office and Cabinet, that recorded the activities resulting in this triumph; ends his very long and factual report "The winning back of land by combined Allied Forces resulted in lively satisfaction by all ranks of the British Armies in France". He and his men knew it was a victory even if his later critics did not. It was tough enough fighting anywhere on the Western Front and "the same meat different gravy" syndrome applied, although to them they rightly considered this was a good result for their outstanding efforts.

The 18th Middlesex shared parts of this great advance in and out of the front lines. The winter was very cold and wet for most of the time even as the longer days warned of the approach of spring. They followed the German retreat witnessing the effect of their enemy's withdrawal.

Unlike, after D-day in 1944, there were no rejoicing and thankful French civilians, grateful for their freedom and liberty from the hated Boche, to greet my Dad and his fellow liberators in khaki or azure blue. The hapless and despairing inhabitants, old men, women and children alike, had been brutally forced out of the zone, generally to provide labour for works on fortifications designed to maintain even longer the agony of the occupation of their homeland.

This and the other crime of laying waste to these peoples' lands and property was called "Alberich" by the perpetrators. There was a hint of their later Minister of Propaganda, Doctor Joseph Goebbels, in the use of this word. In Teutonic folklore, Alberich was the king of the dark subterranean world inhabited by malevolent, though skilful dwarves. When these creatures were forced to give up what they thought was theirs against their will, they were capable, and often did, put a curse on the objects which would then bring disasters to the new owners.

This mythical threat was notably disregarded by the British and French Armies, and the pressure on the retreating German troops was keep up much earlier than the scheduled date of 16th March 1917 planned by Hindenburg and his team for the withdrawal..

The German retirement, coaxed by strong allied forces, actually began on the 9th February. However, there was no military excuse to create the utter desolation of the vast area involved and turn it into the same type of terrain that existed about the combatant's trench lines and no-man's-land areas of the static Western Front. Their actions were barbaric. Every dwelling, building, road and rail track was rendered unusable, the trees in orchards and plantations were cut down or burnt, any crops, wells and water services were polluted and mines and booby traps were sown throughout.

All this devastation did not slow the British and French Armies, who were sending out patrols following close on the heels of the retiring enemy, and then advancing in strength to take over and consolidate the areas no longer occupied. There were some pockets of stiff resistance here and there along the very long line of retreat. They had been left purposely, to prevent the main withdrawal becoming a rout, but in every case, they were quickly subdued and the orderly advance continued. After two years of virtual stalemate, for the Allies, it was important that their fronts and flanks were not left in the air, their foe was still quite capable of turning round and attacking in strength and reversing the withdrawal. The British and French Army Commanders knew well that this was not the end of the war and it was vital to maintain good and adequate supply lines and to keep their guard well up.

Much of the work consolidating the lines in the "Devastated Area" fell on the Pioneering Battalions that accompanied the Infantry Divisions. My Father and the 18th Middlesex were there. They always had much to do. There is a record dated 14th March 1917 that, in some long forgotten digging known as Macaroni Lane, a large group of the 18th Pioneers spent the night, waist deep in mud and water, clearing the way for the advancing infantry. Another describes the fate of at least six mules being killed by the shell fire that was a constant danger to man and beast alike. Notes like this one illuminate how so many of these animals were lost doing sterling work in all of the campaigns. They also make such sad reading, the story of their silent endurance and the hard fates that they suffered. My Father and the vast majority of his contemporaries at war were not turned into savages, it was not their nature; compassion for these animals and so many of the unfortunates, was there and can be frequently seen on their faces, frozen in that time, on those black and white or sepia images.

The important towns of Baupame, Peronne and Noyon, together with a host of smaller towns and hamlets became French once more, albeit completely ruined, after two years in enemy hands.

The Kaiser's peace overtures that winter were somewhat like his ungracious retreat. His terms insisted on keeping those parts of France still occupied by his troops and the recovery of his costs for the war to date. These terms were only a part of his price to stop the killing and gave a good indication of his under-lying intentions and motives for war.

In the first two years of the conflict his forces had slaughtered or maimed several million Frenchmen, over one million British and Commonwealth soldiers and sailors, comparatively similar numbers of Belgians and other allies of the Triple Alliance. His submarines had sunk much of the British fleet of merchant shipping and his Imperial Navy was still thought to be quite a threat to the Royal Navy. It is almost impossible to assess the damage that had been afflicted on the Russian people and his demands from that country, at this time, are not easy to ascertain and confirm. However it would not be long before the Kaiser would be turning that screw for all to witness, when the newly established Bolsheviks sued for peace.

He, patently, as the leader of the strongest member of the Central Powers, did not expect to lose the war but he was prepared to stop the hostilities providing that it was made worthwhile for him. The other terms he expected to be agreed included, that the whole of Belgium be left under the total control, both economically and militarily, of Germany; and he expected that the Belgian Congo be ceded to him. The territorial gains demanded continued, much as the bit by bit bid for world supremacy, that was adopted by his later successor, Adolf Hitler, who was still serving as a Corporal in the trenches around Loos. This first bite would also include taking over from the Tsar of Russia the vassal provinces of Poland, Estonia, Latvia and Lithuania. He also wanted an appropriate share of Persia commensurate with his status and with not much regard to his faithful allies in the Ottoman Empire. It was also demanded that the regions of Alsace and Lorraine became permanently recognised as parts of Germany.

These ambitious peace plans were put out despite the Army Chiefs of Staff in Berlin knowing that the German Armies had been seriously weakened on the Somme and Verdun. They would have preferred to stop the fighting on the Western Front as soon as possible. They knew that the Americans would not stay neutral forever, and the threat to extend their submarine warfare to include all shipping in the Atlantic would, most likely, precipitate the United States of America's entry into the conflict.

Woodrow Wilson, in 1916, had won another term as President, on a ticket for peace, and he too was anxious to get the warring factions to discuss an end to the fighting before his country had to take sides.

Fortunately, the final word was not with the President of the U.S.A., nor with the German Generals. Neither was it with General Haig or the recently promoted French Commander General Nivelle. Only Kaiser Wilhelm II held that power and hence the outrageous terms expressed in this first German overture to finish the war.

They, and even the Kaiser, could not have seriously expected that the Triple Alliance would even start to negotiate with such an agenda as a starting point; and of course they didn't.

My Father's efforts would have to continue; the not so distant bugles were already calling him and the war weary British and French soldiers to even tougher battles in their epic fight for freedom and decency. The attritional battles on the Somme and Meuse had been little more than a prelude of what was to come.

Wilfred Owen's Anthem for yet more doomed youth about to be called up by the recent Conscription Act expresses some of the mood:-

No mockeries now for them: no prayers nor bells;

Nor any voice of mourning save the choirs,-

The shrill, demented choirs of wailing shells;

And bugles calling for them from sad shires.

Some corner of a foreign field.

Pigeon Ravine Cemetery, east of Epehy, most eastern battlefield
cemetery on the Somme.

Chapter 14

The new French High Command wanted to set up another battle, this time, guaranteed to bring the final victory. General Robert Nivelle had confidently propounded to the French Government that he knew the way. He stated that he had used his war winning plan on a smaller scale at Verdun, and it had worked there. He promised that it would work again, given that he now had command of all the French armies in the North and North-Easern Sectors. He also had plenty of men in reserve to exploit the forward thrusts and maintain movement.

Nivelle had replaced General Joffre, who had been the French C. in C. since the start of the war, he had the reputation of being the bold and heroic saviour of Verdun on a par with the most popular of French Generals, Henri Petain. He had good credentials, and he also promised to significantly reduce the appalling casualty rates suffered by the French up to now. He would put an immediate stop to the attack, if for whatever reason, the planned break-through was not making itself apparent within the first forty eight hours.

This was exactly what his Government wanted to hear, especially after nearly a year un-characteristically having to defend Verdun as their major contribution to the war. This was not what they had planned, it had been imposed upon them by the enemy's coldblooded strategy to wear down France's Armies to a veritable point of extinction. In the event, both sides had bled too much and it could be argued with conviction from the French side, that the battle for Verdun had been even more costly than any previous attempts to throw out the hated Hun invader, stubbornly and maliciously occupying too much of the beloved homeland.

The French needed a proper victory to bolster the national morale that was now balanced so delicately on a knife edge, after more than two and a half years of constant and savage fighting, without any tangible successes that were likely to bring the war to an acceptable close.

In addition, to his own people, the new French C. in C., was able to convince the new British Prime Minister, David Lloyd George, that his plan of action could not fail. The new broom, Nivelle, to shuffle and mix metaphors, was the prophet in his own country and elsewhere who was being heard loud and clear. There is nothing quite like hearing what you want to hear, particularly when the other alternatives are so unpalatable.

Lloyd George was so thrilled with the prospect, that he was quite prepared to subvert Field Marshal Sir Douglas Haig's Command of British, Commonwealth and Empire Armies and hand control over to the French carte blanche. He only pulled back from that extreme position after Haig voiced his grave misgivings to him and King George V, the latter being patently most concerned. Giving up command of the largest army the British Empire had ever assembled was simply not acceptable to most. Amongst many a nuance, what would become of a soldier's attestation that he made on joining the British Army? It could only be an act of gross political folly and lack of confidence in one's own people to hand over one's fighting forces to some other Nation to command outright. The England National Football team may take on a Scandinavian or Italian manager but surely the British Army should not have a Frenchman as its Supreme Commander. Such a man would not have allegiance to the Sovereign, his loyalty and fealty was elsewhere.

Unlike a scheme favoured for some time by Haig, who wanted a Supremo to be appointed who would have the authority to plan and co-ordinate the Allied resources as a single force, but leave the directives and modus operandi sovereign to each state using their own officer corps; Lloyd George was prepared to forfeit the ultimate command of the B.E.F. in Europe to a French Commander without further ado. Under the British constitution the armed forces obey the King's authority through Parliament and in reality the Prime Minister. Lloyd George as such, wanted to put the French General, Robert Nivelle, in command of these forces which of course included every Commonwealth and Empire contingent.

Fortunately, that did not occur. It was decided that the British Generals would maintain their office and only for a limited period co-operate totally within the plans of General Nivelle.

This compromise meant that my Father would stay in khaki, not switch to the azure blue of the French poilu, nor would he have to take a degree in the French language or join the Foreign Legion. He was, in fact, getting on fine using the cards issued to all the troops in France called

'French Made Easy for our men in the British Expeditionary Force'. He was almost fluent, with his "Voolay voo, fair un promenade avec m'wah sasswah mam-zell? spoken, if an opportunity presented itself, with some aplomb.

However that was not likely to happen very often. He would be too busy, as all the men like him, occupying a new line of B.E.F. responsibility that now stretched from south of the River Somme, northwards as before to Arras, on to the wrong side of Vimy Ridge, whilst still holding Loos, Bethune and Armentieres to just north of the salient at Ypres. Dad would get to see them all, several times over, in a yo-yo existence of attack, desperate defence and then attack again, that was about to start. This war was far from being resolved.

It was an error of judgement for the new British Prime Minister to back the wrong General to win the war. The tragic consequences resounded for a long time. It led, at first, to a far greater burden descending on all Douglas Haig's forces, before he was eventually able to lead them to the ultimate and most convincing win ever achieved by British arms. They were still, even then, under the command of that same, unjustly, much vilified and upbraided soldier.

However, that lay in the process of time. Inexorably, the moving finger had written and could not be erased. The combined offensive under the orders of General Nivelle was scheduled to begin in April 1917 and that attack was not to be influenced, according to its author, even by two other important recent events. One of these was the retreat of the Germans to the strongly fortified

Hindenburg Line. The other was the entry of the United States into the war on the 6th April 1917. The United States of America had finally joined the Alliance, two years and eight months after the war had started. Whilst this was welcomed by the Triple Alliance, it would still take another year before their soldiers would see action in significant numbers. Like Great Britain, the Americans had declared war on Germany with its army as equally unprepared or capable of fighting a major conflict such as the one that was being fought on the Western Front.

French and British troops in action, like my Father, would tend to regard that year waiting for the dough-boys to arrive, as an eternity, far too long to be of much benefit to them personally. They also felt that the German retreat had been an event to celebrate, despite the barbaric way that the retiring army had behaved. They had been trying for two years to move their front forward. However, General Nivelle, to his loss, decided to ignore that major withdrawal and take no account of the fact that the Germans were now standing behind much more formidable trenchworks and strongholds than those the British Tommies had had to face the previous year on the 1st July.

General Nivelle was about to command the largest attack yet mounted by the Allied forces against the German armies in France. It would be greater than Rawlinson's attempted big push. Massive French forces were being deployed and made ready south of St Quentin in the Aisne and Champagne Sectors, whilst the British were required to attack slightly earlier, along a fifteen mile long front running from a few miles north of the ancient city of Arras southwards towards St Quentin. The series of British assaults, which began early on the morning of 9th April, were intended to be in the manner of a feint to draw German units away from the French build up thirty to forty miles to the British right.

In the event, the B.E.F. achieved considerable success. The three battles name after the River Scarpe, the Battle of Arleux, together with the onslaught on Vimy Ridge were the five parts of these Battles of Arras of 1917 that took place between the 9th April and 4th May. Valuable ground was recovered that gave the Allies their first view, since 1914, over the enemy occupied Douai plain and the routes to the French border through Cambrai and Valenciennes into Belgium through the town of Mons.

A motorway speeds the traveller across today's landscape and except for the brilliantly conceived Canadian Memorial on the summit of Vimy Ridge there is not much else to catch the eye concerning the events of the Great War in and around the ancient city of Arras. The River Scarpe flows through the university area to the north of the city and flows east across the plain before branching northwards into Belgium. The city of Arras was never taken by the Germans but they came close enough with their artillery to do much damage to its fine stone buildings. By the time my Father saw it, it was just another Wipers or Albert, but it had one significant and very useful addition. There were many underground galleries that gave every protection to the citizens and the troops that garrisoned them. These caverns or boves, as they are called, originated back many centuries and had been extended over the years, recording continuous troglodytic existences dating from then until the likes of my Father in the 20th Century made full and thankful use of them.

An attack by a battalion of British or French infantry could be adequately concealed underground, virtually unaffected by hostile gunfire, until they went over the top during the 1917 battles on the Eastern fringes of the city; thanks to these boves.

Corporal James Reed, recently promoted one rank and in command of his section of ten men, did not benefit from this advantage. The 33rd Division was in action on the 9th April in the unseasonable cold spring weather, in a blinding hail and snow-storm across that part of the front adjacent to the small village of Boyelles which is a few miles to the south of Arras.

It was the time for them to have a go at the Hindenburg line, trying to make the odd dent in the incomplete fortifications. It turned out to be not much different than the bite and hold tactic that had been developed on the Somme and now the tactic was chewing its acerbic way towards Germany.

My Dad and the men on the Scarpe were not going to share in the glory that was bestowed upon those who took Vimy Ridge at the same time and in the same weather. The capture of this prominence is featured in every account of the Great War and included in most itineries of modern pilgrims to the old front-line. It is an impressive site deserving of its honour and distinction, forever associated with the bravery and sacrifice of the best of the young men from the new and loyal Canadian Dominion, who finally took and consolidated the important and dominating hummock, situated between Lens and Arras. English speaking generations since that time, think of Canada and Canadians whenever Vimy Ridge is mentioned. The lost and damaged souls of those who had tried so hard, but unsuccessfully earlier, to take the ridge, have little or no share of the Canadians' immortality.

Many acres have been preserved each side of the summit as part of the Canadian National Memorial, which enshrines and commemorates that country's sixty six thousand six hundred and fifty five war dead. It also calls a roll by name, the eleven thousand two hundred and eighty five of those men who have no known resting place. In stone, a sorrowing woman depicts the spirit of the young Canadian Nation weeping sad tears for her losses, as she stares at a tomb bearing the helmet and sword of a warrior and the vista of the Douai plain for which her men had fought to command. Fashioned in the same hardy limestone, from an abandoned quarry, that once provided ancient Rome with some of its building materials, other symbolic figures are included around the two massive columns behind her. Erected on the summit of Hill 145, the highest point of Vimy Ridge, and the last piece of ground to be recaptured, these twin towers screams out the location of this fine tribute, for all to still see, for miles around. Once there the visitor can also witness the conserved areas of the heavily shell-cratered landscape, sad trenches and diggings that still betray the ferociousness of the fighting that had occurred here and along all the long miles of the Western Front, most of which has, since 1918, recovered and reverted to proper and civilised use.

Boyelles, Judas and Maison Rouge Farms, St Leger, Henin, Lump and Plum Lane are good examples of the latter and they are all situated to the south of Arras. They have long lost their scars unlike those sections on Vimy Ridge. An inconspicuous diary mentions them and many others, which the enemy did not want to give up and that same document tells me that my Father helped to liberate and return them to their rightful owners. My wife and I, by courtesy of that faded document, shared many a view my Father must have seen in those dramatic distance times.

The view points were the same but not what we saw. Dad witnessed for most of his time at this front, a tortured vile landscape stretching for miles up to yet another fortified barricade, his early glimpses of the central part of the awesome Hindenberg line known to the Germans as the Siegfried Stellung. He saw the streams of wounded, bleeding men, many blinded, groping painfully back towards the casualty clearing stations. He saw the dead, sometimes laid out in groups, sometimes starkly alone. They could be just trunks, without heads or limbs, others without a visible mark but there was always so many dead. He could seldom stop long enough even to offer a silent valediction as he passed by. He certainly knew that he was sharing the same abiding risk and possible fate, that was always present anywhere along his Western Front. Did he think, or could he have thought that he would miss his turn?

Speaking of his experiences, one veteran, approaching the front in the early days of these same Scarpe/Arras battles, recalls watching a group of fresh faced young soldiers staring at a pile of headless corpses, victims of a shrapnel shell not more than a couple of hours earlier. The young men, on this occasion, broke their own immediate horror and tension from coming upon such a grisly scene, with a unified, somewhat abashed "Cor' they've copped it all right, the poor sods!" before proceeding on to maybe an even worse fate or more vile apparitions that would stay to haunt the private moments of their futures. What a valiant, stout-hearted generation of universally brave young men the late Victorians had bred to fight this war.

In stark contrast, my vision was of a wide peaceful agricultural perspective, graced by many rich crops and rebuilt village spires. The land was keeping its involvement in the War to end all Wars a secret, the many and tiny half acre plots with their Portland Stone tablets and registers being half hidden and unobtrusive unless sought. We stopped at just one and "Lest we forget" came very much to my mind whilst enjoying more sophisticated rooty and char than my Dad had perhaps munched, exactly there, so many years earlier.

Dad's Division with their support troops had left behind forever more than their fair share of brave young men in the rich and fertile plains that surround Arras, Vimy Ridge and the River Scarpe. Like most of those who "copped it" the churning explosions left little to bury. Their names are carved on what seem more endless stone panels set as part of the British Military Cemetery and Memorial to the Missing, situated back in the city of Arras. Nearly thirty-six thousand men who served, fought and died in the Battles of Arras between Easter Sunday, 8th April and the fading days of summer 1917, have no known resting place but they are remembered there.

There are also an additional two thousand six hundred graves marking known and unknown warriors spaced out in a separate large graveyard adjacent to the memorials. Finally, the gallant airmen in the British flying services, who were killed in action along their extended range of the Western Front, are remembered here by name, very few having a marked and known resting place.

This significant though less visited piece of ground, which now shares its frontage with part of the city's busy ring road system; together with the small and isolated graveyards of the Commonwealth War Graves Commission, frequently constructed on the sites of long forgotten battlefield cemeteries and casualty clearing stations, bear a telling witness of the efforts made by the B.E.F.. With Douglas Haig at its head. he and his men had more than lived up to his orders from London to support the French efforts of 1917, not only in spirit but in deed as well. The disloyal and untrue spin put on the British actions to help the French, as being less than whole hearted, could not be justified nor should it be sustained.

The British and its Empires' fighting record, especially around Arras, erased that lie forever. Both their Commander in Chief and all his forces had done their very best for the common cause, and strangely their actions there, adopts yet another of those quirks, that tend to dot the true history of the Great War. These battles witnessed the heaviest casualty rates, day on day, than any other period from the war's start to its finish in November 1918, regardless whether the B.E.F. were on the offensive, retreating or just holding the line. Most people if asked which Great War battle sustained the heaviest daily casualties, if prepared to reply, would probably choose The Somme battles of 1916 or Third Ypres 1917 (Passchendaele).

According to the records that I have checked, in the thirty nine days of fighting around Arras, during April and May 1917 over four thousand men as a daily average became casualties. Following close behind that unbearable, grievous and painful total, the British Armies sacrificed another three thousand six hundred and forty five soldiers per day in the 100 odd days from the 8th August 1918 until the ceasefire in November whilst achieving their nearly unreported advances to the final and ultimate victory. Compare the Battles of the Somme in 1916 and Passchendaele (3rd Battle of Ypres 1917), where the average daily losses were nearly three thousand and two thousand, four hundred men respectively, I have long concluded that no type of action on the Western Front was easy or could seriously ameliorate the awful rates of death and mutilation if the war was to be resolved. Certainly blaming the Generals was a fallacy and delusion. The largest majority of their men were well aware of this truth but could do little to prevent the so called pundits and experts recording their own versions in order to distort the facts to suit their own agendas.

Unfortunately, for the Allies, France's own and much sought major offensive of 1917, south of Arras, provided even harsher figures than the ones for the B.E.F.. General Nivelle's performance did not, sadly, live up to expectations, though no fault could be laid at Haig's door, although there were several attempts to blame him. The British Prime Minister of barely five months, Mr Lloyd George had got it desperately wrong. The French

General, he had so completely supported, was finished after just thirty days commanding his armies in battle. He had to be dismissed.

The brave soldiers of the French Army had, in less than that time, lost confidence in their Commander in Chief and the officers serving under him. They made it clear that they were not prepared to go on attacking their enemies in the same way as before, charging an entrenched enemy who mowed them out of existence with machine guns and artillery. Nivelle tactics had proved to be the same as his predecessor and his troops wanted better plans, with better prospects of winning, before they would attack again. The French Divisions, that had started the grand "new" plan along the Chemin de Dames, had been decimated, just as badly as the British had suffered on the 1st July 1916; except that instead of one day, the French attacks had been replicated many times over an exhausting period of nearly two weeks.

Thankfully, the knowledge of these astounding events, never reached the enemy as they were occurring in the late spring and early summer of 1917. It was also not common hearsay amongst the British troops in France, whether they were in action, or just holding their parts of the line.

Unbelievably, the French Army, the largest and strongest element of the Triple Alliance, had mutinied against their officers, in the course of this battle. These soldiers had been ordered, just too many times, to charge and storm into the German fortifications, to such little avail, other than to leave the bulk of their chums and comrades dead or mutilated, sprawled across those tortured fields that lay between their own lines and the enemy's.

These same men of Nivelle's Armies had listened to their officers telling them that this new battle would produce the right results. The slaughter of the past was over and victory was assured. This bold confidence had been repeated to them for as much as four months whilst the battalions had been preparing and assembling along many miles of front stretching from Soissons eastwards nearly to Rheims. The invincible plan initially required the capture of the strategic route known as the Chemin de Dames, a road that had been constructed when France was a Kingdom, two or more centuries earlier, and was sited mostly along the summit of an hog's back ridge some fourteen miles in length.

The memories of the failures of 1915 at this place had been forgotten or most likely lay buried with the three hundred thousand Frenchmen who lay mute and unheard just east of Verdun.

Those surviving veterans of the armies now under Nivelle or Petain, had defended Verdun, on at least one tour of that front. Many had suffered even more than one visit to the horrific agonies of the fighting there. They had not yielded and they had fought their enemy to a bloody stand-still. The euphoria of a sort of victory was still tangible in their minds and that spirit was passed on and accepted by the freshly trained troops with an eager enthusiasm. At least four million French soldiers had come to believe that victory would be theirs that summer. There would be no more mass carnage for a churned up field soon to be retaken and fought for endlessly again and again.

These fine men, veteran and novice alike, went over the top fully believing that their leaders had got it right at last. They were cut down in droves by the same entrenched enemy that had bled them to extinction before. Nothing had changed. Despite the barrage of literally thousands of guns designed to kill or derange their opponents, there were the men in field grey, still wielding that invincible Sword of Damocles that poured red hot metal into the attacking Frenchmen, without any serious consequence to themselves.

The tragedy started on the 16th April 1917 at 6.30am when great armies of Frenchmen left their trenches to advance across no-man's land to gain the high ground of the Chemin de Dames. Twenty divisions of infantry with nearly four thousand artillery pieces giving their support could not dent the enemy's line, let alone, break through. The pitiful survivors could scarcely get back to their own positions before fresh Divisions were pushed into the killing grounds. Nivelle's forty eight hours were gamely and gallantly extended by our French Allies to nearly two weeks of carnage, before the first serious indiscipline took place.

Call it disobeying orders or mutiny, on the 29th April 1917, the 2nd Battalion of the 18th Infantry Regiment refused to fight. They had just sustained fearsome casualties, over two thirds of their numbers, in their first attempt in this battle to break the German's defences. The pitiful survivors, less than two hundred men, were then ordered back to the front in just a matter of days to make another assault using the same recipe as before. A heavy artillery barrage up to zero hour, short sharp whistle blasts, over the parapets, into no-man's land and death.

This was the catalyst that heralded the most dangerous situation for the Entente during the course of the whole war. If the French morale had totally collapsed, with the knowledge being shared by the Germans, then the B.E.F. on the left, would have faced a major outflanking danger from which only another Gallipoli or Dunkirk type of evacuation would have saved them. The B.E.F., with the ailing Italian army and the small contingent from Portugal, but without the French Army, could not have held the ring and as a consequence the war would have been lost in mainland Europe. A far greater disaster than 1871.

By providence, this did not happen. The Germans were kept ignorant and unaware even as the crisis got worse. On the 3rd May a complete Division refused their orders to attack and gradually throughout that month and well into June the same pattern of mutiny overtook nearly all the front line assault units. Despite the dismissal of General Nivelle on the 15th May and General Petain taking his place, up to fifty percent of the French Army made it clear to their officers that they would not go on the offensive, attacking heavily defended fortifications held by the Germans. These French soldiers, stated through their appointed leaders, that they were quite prepared to defend their homeland from further invasion and occupation but they would not take part in further futile charges across a churned up battlefield against an ensconced and heavily armed enemy.

Petain, sensibly, did not take on this rank and file, knowing full well that he had no chance of subduing them by force. Instead, immediately upon taking command, he promised his soldiers that urgent changes and better conditions of service would be implemented. Whilst not bargaining, something a military hierarchy does not do, he couched his orders phlegmatically and with realism, with his first directive stopping the rot. There would be an end to further large scale attacks, there would be improvements in conditions of service affecting pay, home leave and food and drink. The acts of "collective indiscipline" would be properly investigated without summary enforcement. Mutiny had seemingly not occurred nor was it mentioned. The euphemism "collective indiscipline" did not really fit, and this rose by another name, was certainly as dangerous and it was very necessary for the French officers to reinstate their proper authority close to the system that had all but gone to the wall and it had to be done quickly.

One may suppose that during this very same, alarming and perilous period, it was a blessing and boon for western civilization and democracy, that my Father and his khaki clad friends, under their respected Commander, Douglas Haig, were not exactly indulging in a feint but in some very serious fighting that was demanding much attention from the common enemy not only around Arras but also in Flanders.

Haig, besides continuing to test and dent the new Hindenberg line east of Arras; on the 7th June 1917, he ordered his 2nd Army, commanded by another now defamed and sometime lampooned senior officer, to take the town of Messines just to the south of Ypres and the ridge of the same name that dominated the southern flank of the Ypres Salient. The nineteen or so spectacular mines, mentioned earlier, that were exploded there, were only the start of another major assault that had been planned by General Plumer on the Commander in Chief's orders. He was honoured for his role in this battle and after the war became Viscount Plumer of Messines. The honour was bestowed by a grateful nation and it was certainly approved by the vast majority of the soldiers who served under him in the 2nd Army.

My Father's Division, the 33rd, did not join in the engagements to take Messines but for two more months, May and June 1917, saw action south and to the east of Arras. Like every unit in that Division the pioneers were very busy. In and out of the line they saw off enemy aircraft with their Lewis Guns, took casualties, chipped away at the Hindenberg defences, got bombed, got drunk and paid the price, won medals for courageous and selfless acts, endlessly repaired the lines of communications and roads, constructed or reformed dugouts and fire trenches and sometimes marched until they dropped.

When they did the latter, the men paid the penalty in the form of more marching coupled with heavy pack drill for an hour or so. This punishment was standard in the British Army. It took the form of an extra parade under the command of a N.C.O., and supervised by a junior officer, at some inconvenient hour, when the rest of the men in the unit were in their own time and at rest. Discipline was served by having to parade with full packs and equipment, including rifles, sharp at the appointed time and go through another uncomfortable hour or so endlessly repeating drill functions and marching often in double time or at the trot. Repeatedly standing at ease, coming to attention, saluting, sloping arms, coming to port arms, fixing bayonets and many other movements was the medley that was generally adequate to invoke good order and discipline and deal with most breaches or violation of that state. The penalty was not generally recorded against the individual's service record nor did it involve deductions from pay or loss of other privileges.

Meanwhile, for the British and Commonwealth's main Ally on their right, the French Army had to set about resolving the more serious matters that had to be addressed regarding the refusal of men from many units disobeying orders, and refusing to attack their German enemy when ordered. A mutiny if ever there was one.

Exact records of these incidents have not been made available or were not kept. There are no accurate figures of men called to account for their actions. Some histories indicate that approximately three thousand men were found to be guilty of the crime of "collective indiscipline" and, obviously, these very low figures are commensurate, when considering the dramatically kid-gloved attitude taken by both the political and military authorities, who dealt with the matter. Most of the three thousand guilty French soldiers, escaped the firing squad, with less than fifty men called to pay the ultimate price. These unlucky few were sentenced to death and then shot at dawn. The remainder seemed to have been given and served varying terms of imprisonment with hard labour that was mitigated by a built in privilege to return to active service before the full sentence had expired.

Considering the scale of the revolt and what was at stake the velvet touch exercised by the governing parties did much to bring the situation to a tolerable conclusion. Even when the ancient Roman Empire's method of decimation was used within certain units to select miscreants, i.e. by charging every tenth man, it is obvious that General Petain's promise to the army regarding this matter was generously kept. These unlucky tenth men most often did not pay with their lives, which had been the Roman levy for such a crime.

In fact, all the promises given by the commanding Generals were kept, and the need to do so extended far; both politically as well as from the military point of view. More and more of the French populace had begun agitating, attending anti-war demonstrations to make their feelings felt. It was the same in most other contending main land European Nations. Large sections of the civil populations of Germany, Italy, Turkey, the Austrian-Hungarian and Russian Empires, all were finding the demands of service, shortages, death, hunger and loss unacceptable. The war had gone on far too long and they wanted an end put to it.

Farthest along that route was Czarist Russia, the people there had descended into a tragic civil war and Czar Nicholas II and his family were under house arrest and prisoners of the Bolshevik authorities. The new order was anxious and ready to make a separate peace with their main enemy Germany and they were prepared to concede to even more outrageous terms than those the Kaiser and his cronies were offering in the west to France and the British Empire.

The French Government did not want anything similar to this, nor a repeat of their earlier revolution of 1789 that had been in near living memory when my Father and a lot of his French contemporaries had been born. Their Republic was not perfect but the majority of their politicians sensed that a stronger grip would have to be put on the country as a whole, civilian and military agitators alike, if they were to avoid having to negotiate a disastrous peace and settlement that would surely plunder their Nation's assets even more than was about to happen to the Russian nation.

Subversives and agents provocateurs in France, would no longer be allowed on the streets to voice their discontent and opposition to the war; strict discipline would return to the army but improvement and due attention would be paid to the soldiers' conditions and combat 'modus operandi'. Even decimation was much diluted if one was to believe the figure of three thousand men ending up in that benign dock. A relatively small two hundred thousand strong army would have produced twenty thousand culprits by that method and could such numbers have been covered up and hidden from the common foe? Of course not, is the answer to that question. Petain had to limit the disciplinary scourging of his army.

My Father would have to bear the burden of keeping the war going with his fellow soldiers from Great Britain and its Empire as France's political leaders took stock and considered how 'its' war could now be pursued. They would have to take into account that its armed forces were demanding better leadership and planning than had hither-to been given. Blind obedience to their orders could not be taken for granted any longer. The British officers privy to this state of affairs would have prayed that it would not be too long before they could begin to rely on their principal ally with confidence again. The Americans were still a long way off. France needed to act quickly, and, fortunately, their senior political leaders soon realised that there was only one basic policy to pursue above all else. A fervent intention to "wage war" was vital; and any opponents daring to oppose this concept would be put behind bars or where they would be of little or no influence.

An historic and significant change was made at the very top, not unlike the Churchill/Chamberlain switch of nineteen forty. "Tiger" Clemenceau was brought back as Prime Minister after an absence since 1909 and he had the leadership qualities to gain the confidence of many of the British troops as well as his fellow Frenchmen. One veteran from the 18th Die-Hards to whom I spoke during my earlier research, when such men were more available to speak of these times at first hand, mentioned, with much warmth, of the time when Monsieur Clemenceau visited his part of the front and the sight of the distinctive white moustached seventy six year old Frenchman showed to him how apt was the little man's soubriquet. He, if anyone, would pull his nation out of the impasse caused by the French Army's "collective Indiscipline", was this veteran's strong opinion.

Nevertheless, for the present, Clemenceau acknowledged, with many others, that it was the British that had to front the enemy and keep that pot or is it cauldron boiling?

Dad, would be going back to the damper climes and gluey polder around that other fated city, ravaged and pulverised, sad old Wipers. Still in British hands with its 1915 salient virtually as my Father had left it, and the place where his Commander in Chief now wanted to concentrate his forces in another major battle-plan to achieve at least three objectives. Of course, as always, the first was to break the deadlock by destroying and outflanking the Germans' trench lines; he also wanted his forces to receive all or at least maximum attention from the enemy in order to take as much pressure off the French sectors as possible. Finally he wanted to recapture and secure the occupied Belgium coastal installations to prevent the German Navy using them as bases from which to launch his much expanded U-boat attacks on Allied shipping in the Atlantic and Western Approaches. Quite a "call", it could be said, for an ill led Expeditionary Force not trained or used to fighting continental wars?

Haig's already prepared plans to advance and retake the parts of Belgium towards the towns and ports of Ostend, Zeebrugge and Antwerp had been kept very hush-hush. They are not much mentioned or written about even now. The plan was a forerunner of that famous World War 2 event, Operation- Market Garden, that occurred in the autumn of 1944, and was aimed at ending that war by Christmas. The surprise assault behind the enemy's lines in 1917 was designed to use ships instead of aircraft and airborne troops. The Navy would land on shore a strong force of heavily armed and well supported Tommies to capture and hold a vital area of the Belgium coast-line until the main forces advancing out of the trenches of the Ypres salient could link up with them and permanently secure the gains.

If successful, these moves would outflank the German right on the Western Front and create the beginnings of movement again and hopefully put an end to the attritional siege stalemate that had not changed for more than two and a half years.

Much work was done for the amphibious assault. Massive pontoons six hundred feet long and thirty feet wide were constructed capable of landing a full Division of heavily armed soldiers on the beaches very quickly. Each pontoon was fastened between two heavily armoured shallow draft warships (monitors), with most of the landing deck projecting for'ard from the ship so that it would run up the chosen beaches across low sea walls to deposit the assault troops with tanks and artillery ashore ready for action. The monitors with their heavy batteries of naval guns would keep the enemy's heads down as they steered for the landing grounds. The initial training for the top secret operation continued well into 1917 even after General Haig's political masters had vetoed these operations in favour of what proved to be the 'Nivelle' debacle.

In early June 1917, as part of the revised strategy to deflect German attention from the French, it was decided to resurrect the British Commander's original plans for a serious offensive in Flanders, which was later to become another neglected and unsung battle honour for my Father to remember in his quiet and private moments.

He and his Divisional friends were chosen to contribute their part in the series of actions now known to history as the Battles of Ypres 1917, alternatively as 3rd Ypres or more emotively as "Passchendaele". The Die-

Hard element moved up to the outskirts of Dunkirk by train at the beginning of August, before coming to grips with the Germans again where Dad had first been in action, two years and three months earlier.

Prior to this, the 18th Middlesex as part of the 33rd Division were ordered to move out of the Arras sector on the 3rd July 1917, and relocate for a well earned break in a holding area, nearly fifty miles away.

It took the Battalion four days of tough marches during the height of the French summer to get there. After a one night stay in each of the villages of Arqueves, Villers Bocage and St: Sauveur and many renditions of "Pack up your troubles in your old kit bag" , "Tipperary" and "There's a Long Long Trail A-winding" they marched into one of the many transit camps which had serviced the Somme offensives since the beginning of 1916. The camp was set around the village of Le Mesge which is midway between the city of Amiens and Abbeville, close to the Atlantic coast. It was well away from any battle front, and the rest and exercise periods for nearly four weeks suited everyone after such a hard tour of service on the Arras sector of the front.

In fact, Dad and quite a number of the other ranks and officers were selected for something even better whilst there. They got seven day leave passes to Blighty. My Father had not seen his family for more than a year and this time he did not have to travel amongst the dying and sick, and nursing a wound and feeling a bit delicate.

He was a man who expected to enjoy this leave. It is a pity it did not turn out exactly as he would have liked it.

He had saved a tidy sum of money in back pay to take with him, after the many weeks not needing real money or even the odd French franc or sou. Relatively flush with the cash that he had been handed at the pay parade, together with the essential pass and travel documents, he smartly saluted and was quickly on his way.

I am sure that he managed to buy a generous selection of nice gifts from the shops that had been established in the port areas on either side of the Channel, and which he would bring back to his wife and each of his three young children. The latter, two boys and a girl would have grown much since he was last in Wimbledon. Leaving the communal military life of the battalion for a spot of leave, was no hardship, even when out of the line, and it would be a tonic that he really intended to make the most of and enjoy.

My Father knew all too well that the modest home and family to which he was returning was what he had been fighting for; putting his life on the line too many times for it not to register, but also shrugged off with the inbuilt natural modesty of his kind. Like probably eighty to ninety percent of his peers in uniform, he did not have a massive stake in his country, no riches in the practical sense to defend, and definitely not the collateral or prospects even to be considered for a mortgage. But he could work, and he had done so since his early teens, and his efforts had provided him with his home and later a compact family that was perhaps, unknowingly to him, his raison d'être.

He did not want his life changed by some foreign power, alien to his British ways. He had seen at first hand in the liberated areas on the Somme, towns like Baupame and its surrounding farms and villages, just how the French people and their property and estates had been suppressed and taken over by the Germans, eventually only to be totally destroyed when they were pushed out. He knew that his enemy was no better than the Hun barbarians were when they were at their height of power and attacking parts of Europe in the same way fifteen centuries earlier. He had been told in his history lessons of their vile behaviour, and now he had helped to dislodge their successors from territory that was not theirs, and he certainly did not want his England succumbing in the same way.

Whilst he and the nation, as a whole, had done much to prevent this from happening, after his year long absence, things at home were not the same as when he was last there. He was saddened to see that his own immediate family, as well as various relatives and friends he had left behind, were now suffering their share of the country's hardships brought about by this world war. The homeland he knew seemed to be blighted in many ways. There was a pervading anxiety for the future that extended in many cases to what the very next day would bring. More than generally, it would take the form of a dreaded telegram, one of the several thousand delivered daily throughout the country by young adolescents wearing a blue pill-box hat marked G.P.O., a leather belt with pouch around the waist and riding a red bicycle. They could appear at any time and all seemingly heralded the death or mutilation of a loved one or friend, that would be plunge yet another family into deep mourning or desperate worry.

Besides this universal grief, there were extensive shortages and rationing of foodstuffs and an apprehension of what could happen next. Even after three years of war, parts of my Father's homeland were receiving reminders from the authorities, regarding what to do, in the event of an invasion by enemy soldiers landing from the sea. As it was, the Germans were regularly and indiscriminately bombing cities, towns and even the odd village, adding civilians, women and children to the spiralling casualty lists. The German Fleet operating out of their lairs on its North Sea coast-line, from moorings like those in Wihelmshaven, had shelled several east coast towns, of which Sunderland and Lowestoft were but examples. My Father's "sceptred isle set in a silver sea, against infection and the hand of war" had gone forever. War was not only happening on the battlefield, every civilian was affected across every age range and each gender.

What would it take to end the war? The question was being asked as Dad did his rounds of the family, neighbours and pre-war friends who were still there to be asked. Nobody was sure.

Dad had tried hard these past two and a half years, but he still pondered the answer.

Precious little ground had been given up whilst he had been in France or Flanders. In fact, he had helped to take more land than had been given up; that tally showed him to be in credit.

He also knew that it needed to be a lot more before victory could be even thought to be close.

He certainly longed to be out of uniform, and with his wife and young children, to resume his life where he had left it; but he also knew that there was no chance of that until he and his kind on the Western Front had driven the enemy out of France and Belgium.

This leave with its fake laughter, genuine love, the overhanging anxiety, shortages in essential food supplies and the apprehension for the future confirmed the scene that total war was not a game, and it would not be over, even by this Christmas of 1917. "Keeping the home fires burning" as the song went, was not the half of it. He was not just following the drum, he knew he was fighting for his way of life, his freedom and independence. He and his like had fully matured on the Western Front, in the hardest theatre life had ever had to offer. If they kept their nerve they knew that they would win and afterwards their betters of the future would be resolved never to let the same thing happen to another generation once that victory had been secured.

I think, these thoughts were the mainspring that prompted my Father and his fellow soldiers not to challenge their officers as many a Frenchman had done. It allowed my Father, weighed down with his full kit and rifle, to kiss goodbye to his beloved wife and children, yet again, on that busy and sad station platform and be taken back to that base camp in Picardy with a certain unruffled fortitude and courage to fight on. It is, though, paradoxical that he could also join in to the chorus of a well known hymn adapted to suit every Tommy's yearnings:-

When this ruddy war is over

O, how happy I shall be,

I shall tell the Sergeant Major

No more soldiering for me.......

Chapter 15

"I'll be making this same trip across the briny when I'm ninety!" my father half quipped to his mates as the troopship lurched out of Newhaven on to the dark rolling channel swell, bound for the harbour of Dieppe in Northern France. Dad was just one soldier amongst many returning to their units from a standard seven day leave. They were mixed up with small draughts of new men replacing casualties from many of the regiments serving with the B.E.F. There was also a full battalion of freshly trained infantry that was destined to stiffen a weakened Brigade after it had done its acclimatisation to service on the Western Front at the largest British base camp that had been established at Etaples.

These soldiers were the human manifest of this steam vessel on its five hour long sea crossing. Twelve hundred men, each one facing an unknown future in a foreign land, that was really quite close by and from which the sound of heavy gunfire could be often heard, spelling out that good reason for their departure. The Defence of the Realm was the proper cause and at the heart of why these and many other British, Commonwealth and Empire soldiers made this journey cheerfully, but with much inward apprehension.

The ship, only one of a veritable fleet of troop-transports and cargo vessels which plied, mostly at night, escorted by Royal Navy warships, that fed the five armies of the British Expeditionary Forces in France and Belgium in 1917. They operated out of four main ports on the British side of the English Channel; Folkestone, Newhaven, Southampton and Portsmouth, destined generally for the French ports of Boulogne, Dieppe or Le Havre. Five armies at war; needed a lot of men, munitions, food, equipage and forage to keep up the endless conflict in which they were engaged.

Unlike the supply routes of Napoleon's "Grand Armee" of 1810-1812 that were forever lengthening or spreading across all points east of Prussia and into the Imperial Russian Empire, the B.E.F.'s were still virtually the same in 1917 as they were in August 1914, when it all started. That was when, just over half of the British regular army, less than eighty thousand men, (the Old Contemptibles), crossed over to the continent to fight an enemy whose armies' soldiers were counted in millions. Only the magnitude of the operation had changed in the three years that had passed since that hot summer. These supply routes had become industries in themselves and were vital to sustain and maintain the nation's fighting forces who were still occupying almost the same churned up fields opposite the German forces, along a tragic line that divided freedom from tyranny.

Corporal Robert James Reed was, like so many born in the decade that roughly centred around that fated year of 1895. He, like them, had volunteered and joined the army for the duration of the war. Now well into his third year on active service he could see no end to it. He was experiencing war unendingly, whether he was on leave, at the front or travelling, in how he dressed, in what he ate and what he said. There was nothing else and it seemed it could go on until the very last recruit or conscript of service age had crossed over to France.

Although he was confident that the war was not lost, morale was a bit low and the thought that had definitely occurred to him and many others was, "could it really go on forever?"

Tipperary and its promise of home and a return to normal living did not seem to be getting any nearer, only that short term rest and training camp at le Mesge in Picardy was.

Once there, he knew that he would not be waiting very long, before another battle plan would emerge. This would involve him and his Division in another change of prospect and, most likely, some even more gruelling activities than can be thought up for the men in the haven of the "rest" areas. Together they had been away from the front for a whole nice month. He had had his seven day leave and he knew that it was time for that to change.

Indeed, five days after returning to France on the 31st July, he and his Battalion were ordered to entrain at the small rail junction at Pont Remy, for an unspecified destination, but of course knowing that all trains only pointed one way, northwards, towards Dunkirk and the Flanders' plain. Flander's pain was more appropriate, my Father would have thought, fully intending the Freudian slip, although that definition of such a thought, had barely yet been mooted. Psychology was in its infancy.

In a similar way to the countless Roman Legions, during much of the first millennium, who had criss-crossed Gaul, keeping the hordes from the East at bay, less than a century from the end of the second, such marching brought 18th Middlesex and the cohorts of the

33rd Division to the railway junction at Pont Remy. This important hamlet with its river bridge over the widening Somme that flowed westward, towards Abbeville became well known to the British. Like the Roman volunteers and levies; a thousand years later, these men too, were engaged in much the same role. They were fighting to retain a more civilised and better society and using the same roads, where only the names, and in some places the pave, had changed. These particular routes are now called the D936 and D901 on the standard Michelin 236 square, a map that actually covers all areas of the old front line in Flanders, Artois and Picardy, for which the British Armies were responsible. Both these roads were and are still in place, straight as arrows as when the Romans set them out; and still offering little shade during the hot and dusty mid-summer slog along their full twenty kilometre length that had to be tramped.

Loaded as they were with their kit, for a number of the Middlesex men, there was not much enthusiasm for the intended move and quite a few behaved in a unacceptable and certainly un-soldierly fashion. A total of twenty eight men fell out during the tiring and sweaty march. The cause, quite simply, that they had drunk too much wine or beer and were incapable of marching.

This breach of discipline was serious and dealt with quickly by the Commanding Officer. He did not delegate the matter. He decided that the whole Battalion would have to be held to account. First, all officers and men on that march would have to do a good one hour pack drill before boarding the train. Only a soldier certified as unfit by the Battalion's Medical Officer in writing would be excused the sanction. Next, he ordered that all bars or estaminets were out of bounds to the men under his command until further notice. The drunken miscreants would have their names taken but he decided that the Battalion was too busy and on the move to pursue and impose individual punishments. There were more important matters afoot.

It was, and remains, not an unusual practice for a C.O. to tighten a unit's discipline and performance in this manner, and 18th Middlesex's current Commanding Officer, Lt: Col: P.D. Ionides, was no exception. He took the view that in their situation everyone had some responsibility for the behaviour of the man next to him. Where there is a serious failure or indiscipline, the blame must be shared and like it or not, all ranks would accept his ruling. Certainly, there would be no mutiny, not even a hint of it, and his orders and punishments were borne perhaps with grumpy resignation and probably more likely, a stoical good grace.

My father, holding the rank as he did as a full corporal, together with the rest of 18th Middlesex did just that. He also had to do his own fair share to liven up the men in his section to the realities of their situation. A drunken and undisciplined rabble, in his expert opinion, would never beat their German enemies and beat them they must. It was the basic and only reason for them being there and having to march those god-forsaken roads.

For now, courtesy the dear C.O., it would be without a glass of Vin Rouge or oeuf avec pomme frits; that was really the hardest to take or think about. Even a glass of weak French beer provided a modest but welcome change from these soldiers' usual diet of bully and two veg or other army food often dolloped into their metal mess tins to be consumed as best they could.

The off-limits order was tough but, nevertheless, initially, the ban would have but minor effect. There was a train ride next on the agenda, and the rolling stock for that journey was never going to be Pullman or wagons-lits. There would not be even a corridor or a buffet car on my father's train to take him and the rest of 18th Middlesex elsewhere to fight. The Battalion Quartermaster would provide his customary fare on the way, which would not differ, menu- wise, from the countless days before. Using the culinary jargon of the Western Front he served variously :- plain old burgoo, sometimes, for their sins, called porridge, rooty with plum and apple, (bread and jam) a wad and a mug of char and perhaps a ration of M and V. with duff for afters. These items were not for the gourmet exactly, nor if calorie counting was important. Even as the modern Prince of Wales is still apt to say, when dispensing his dietetic advice "you are what you eat", there is little doubt, that, the British Tommy of the Great War was, regarding stamina and fitness, without equal; thanks in many ways, to that burgoo etc.

The Great War period was in a time before the wholesale packaging of every type of food, when even biscuits and milk were sold loose. Feeding several armies, amounting to nearly two million hungry men, was far from easy. It had never been done before, but it was achieved by well organised Staff work and requisition. There is certainly little or no evidence that the British Army ever went short of food for any extended periods.

The Battalion Quartermasters got the decreed daily rations for the men in his unit in bulk. This food allocation followed a strict, wordy and precise form of application and subsequent distribution, that involved even the Generals at Divisional and Corps Headquarters knowing the exact daily eating strength of each unit under their command.

Most often the meat would be supplied as animal carcasses or in large tins. The bread would be baked from loose ingredients stored in tins or sacks, whilst the vegetables, mainly potatoes, onions, carrots and cabbage would also come in sacks. Smoked bacon would come as animal sides, to be jointed and sliced by the unit cooks; jams, tea, sugar and condensed milk were provided in smaller cans to suit a section or platoon. Small tins of corned beef (bully), sardines and loose hard tack biscuits were often issued individually. Cigarettes and tobacco and the all important lucifers or vestas were made available and there was an occasional free issue.

By this time, there was always enough food and drink to go round; cooking and distribution was well organised, but the freedom and ability to chose a cup and something to eat from the Salvation Army's stall or local bistro was very popular as shown by the enthusiastic patronage these and similar establishments always received. For a time my father would not enjoy these pleasures.

Although he did not know it, the train journey that took him from the Somme area of Picardy to the Nord-Pas-de-Calais region and on to Dunkirk would not be his last trip on the French railway system whilst he was on active service. Many such pleasures were still in store for him. However, Shanks' pony was also scheduled to take him far. Initially, he would be ordered to march another seven miles eastwards, crossing into Belgium at Westhoek and savouring the smell of the sea, the fine sandy dunes and beaches that continued well past his destination of De Panne. There were no drunks or drop-outs on that march.

My Father and his pals had no idea, that these same areas, in which they were about to do another stint of dogged soldiering, would witness, just over twenty years later, tragic scenes of thousands of khaki clad, tired and dishevelled young men, waiting patiently, to be rescued by warships of the Royal Navy and flotillas of smaller pleasure craft, often manned by civilian crews. More cruelly, he would not have believed it, even if the Archangel Michael had appeared and told him that the same German Corporal, that he had been trying to dislodge from Flanders and France for nearly three years, would be responsible for this rout.

I was too young to ask him in 1940, what his thoughts were, as the news of the evacuation of the B.E.F. from the beaches of Dunkirk was unfolding. Reported at the time as a miracle, was he thinking of the price he and his soldier mates had once paid, close by, for a so called lasting peace?

When he was there, his B.E.F. had left very many more khaki clad young men, such as those that were plucked from the sands in 1940, in the horror-soaked mud between Ypres and Passchendaele. Sadly, he must have known that at least twice as many of his contemporaries never made it home. I expect it seemed to him, that the men of his time had, unknowingly, paid a frighteningly high price, not for a lasting and permanent peace with freedom, as they had been led to believe; they had in fact paid very dearly for what amounted to a worthless twenty year politically ill managed adjournment. A second round that his successors, could not hope to win; matched as they were against an enemy allowed to massively rearm, by the careless, incompetent and culpable wit of their elected representatives.

In those far off days of 1940, he also would have been able to tell me, that as parts of the 33rd Division disembarked from their numerous trains around the rear areas west of Nieuport, the coastal termination of the Western Front throughout the war, that this was where the Belgian Army, well backed by forces from the B.E.F., defended the tiny remnants that were left of their own free homeland. He was now in another war zone with different Divisional, Corps and Army boundaries. My Father's division was now a neighbour of a part of the 2nd Army's 1st Division. It had been in this coastal area for some time. It had been active alongside the small Belgian army holding back the Germans at Nieuport, sustaining, at times, heavy casualties in fighting that did not warrant the high profile attention given to the more major engagements either at the time they were played out, or in later histories and accounts of the Great War.

That state of affairs might have been about to change. The 1st Division had been removed from the front and subsequently ordered by Haig's General Headquarters to set up a top secret training area complete with secure fences and boundaries that would prevent loose talk, observation and mixing with other units and civilians in the vicinity.

As mentioned earlier, the men of the 1st Division were going to spearhead a daring amphibious attack along the German held coastline of Belgium between Middelkerke and Ostend that was designed to shorten the war and hopefully end it before Christmas 1917.

Commander in Chief Douglas Haig, saw an assault in Belgium as the most likely place to achieve a war winning victory. It was nearer to the German homeland, the salient at Ypres should not be allowed to remain as it was, and, not least in a list of good reasons, the Royal Navy could be involved, bringing its powerful resources to bear and add weight to the offensive. A combined operation indeed, destined to be tried on an even greater scale twenty-seven years later, over much the same ground, as an airborne operation.

All it needed was some decent weather and a break out from the trenches that had not been achieved through three long and heart breaking years.

The previous attempts had not been solely of Haig's making, more, they had been visited upon him by his political masters exercising their authority and decisions to go with their most important ally, France. Finally, after the terrible outcome of the Nievelle offensive in April 1917 and the uncertain length of time it would take to get the French Army back on track, the British Commander was ordered to get on with it, as long as it did not involve the French and had the intention to ease pressure away from them.

Haig had worked on this scheme for some time with General Plummer before it had to be shelved in favour of the dictate to fight at Arras. Finally, for the first time since becoming Commander in Chief, Haig would pursue the fighting on the Western Front in an order of battle that was mostly of his own making, notwithstanding, that he had still to take full account of any unpredictable actions and manoeuvres of his principal enemy, the powerful German army.

Part of his strategy had put my Father on that discredited march from le Mesge, the train from Pont Remy to the north coast of France and subsequently his participation in training for the 2nd Army's proposed assault behind enemy lines. An attack that was intended to be linked with a major offensive and breakout from the Ypres salient. 18th Middlesex pioneers, as part of the whole of 33rd Division needed proper and secret rehearsals for the landing and onslaught across those sandy beaches and promenades a few miles to the east, in enemy occupied Belgium, which was to be carried out in conjunction with large capital ships of the Royal Navy.

The two weeks training for this action, on the friendly beaches close to De Panne, was almost a tonic for my father and the rest of his unit. Notwithstanding the fact that they were kept incommunicado from the adjacent military camps and civvy establishments, an extra benefit was that they were located much too far from the front lines to be given that extra night time rack of carrying duties. A bonus much appreciated by all who had suffered the drain on the stamina that these activities always caused. The weather happened to be very wet and unseasonable but that did not bother them too much.

They were used to it. It was the type of weather expected and usual on the few high days or holidays many of them had spent at the seaside in peacetime. Part of their island race psyche gave them a natural liking for the sea and actually being on the beach was what really mattered, not the quality of the weather. These men got to grips with their training, whilst enjoying the sand dunes and briny, and they would save their worrying for if, or when, they were embarking on those enormous armoured pontoons for real and there was that whiff of battle in the air.

It turned out to be the right attitude to take, for after that unexpected fortnight on the beach, with not a trench in sight, there was no wide scale break out by the other B.E.F. forces from the glutinous conditions of the Wipers' Salient. Enemy resistance and the weather made it impossible, and this failure meant that there could be no attack behind the German lines along the Belgium coastline, and all the benefits of getting the enemy on the run would have to wait. The well planned operation had to be cancelled and the Battles of Third Ypres 1917 were destined to develop into the same bite and hold tactics that had been learnt and developed so well, first on the Somme and then at Arras.

My father, his unit, and the whole of the 33rd Division were sucked into these battles just three weeks after the initial attack, which had begun on the 31st July 1917. In fact, Corporal R.J.Reed slowly advanced over the same ground that he had given up just after he had first arrived in Belgium in May 1915. Then it had taken just one night to withdraw and since that time countless shells and bullets had been exchanged to leave the salient's disputed areas even more undrained, evil smelling and corpse strewn than when it had been given up. The same place names existed and were targeted, but the advances were exceedingly painful both for them, the British, and their foe alike. It took nearly four months, well into a cold November, to recover what had been conceded on that one night more than two years earlier, both sides now using a fuller inventory of death that included contraptions spraying liquid fire and shells emitting blinding or suffocating gas. Nothing in this war, however, became a quick fix, even the early tanks were not invincible, and I have thought and wondered, just how many men, now engaged in this fighting, were back in this same place for a second time. Quite a few I wager, my father being just one of them; and how I wish I had had the precognition to ask him, just how he felt about this horrific example of déjà vu.

Knowing him, his reply would have been that of a soldier who had learnt how to serve and fight and also knew how to win or lose. He would have said "You don't have any choice, you do as you are told and follow orders, just as everyone else does, and it does not matter where you are, it's always 'same meat, different gravy'."

When that high ground on the Passchendaele ridge was in Allied or British hands again, the war did not end. It certainly answered a query regarding the effect and efficacy of introducing poisonous gas, flame throwing tactics and tanks, into warfare. They too, did not win wars, any more than the machine gun had done, they only made the fighting more lethal. Leaders of nations as well as their armies, have to be at high risk, before they sue for peace, and until that occurs, the fighting is invariably sanctioned to continue.

Two atomic bombs stopped the Second World War in its tracks, after six very long and difficult years. Emperor Hirohito had to survive and these bombs had proved to be very indiscriminate, well capable of treating a sushi bar in down town or emperor's palace in uptown Tokyo, alike.

A strategy of mutual nuclear destruction prevented a third world war, that had been lined up between the Nato and Warsaw Pact political alliances for more than forty years, for very much the same reasons.

These are, however, the only two examples to date, where political leaders have been forced by weapons of mass destruction to avoid conflict between different creeds or regimes. Even despite the United Nations' prodigious and perhaps sincere efforts, the plain facts are that bloody wars continue to this day, in some form, on most continents, instigated and controlled by politicians. Without the ingredient of threat to the highest orders in the hierarchy, fighting and killing goes on, exactly as it did for the obliterated town of Ypres and its salient in my father's time, when he was young.

Personally, I never tire of being in this part of Belgium. It is not the landscape or the buildings that causes this feeling. It is the imagery that does for me. I think how my father and the legions of men in khaki came here to fight, hold the ring, and eventually win.

They lived in this, for them, heartless, uncompromising and awful land for what must have seemed eternity. For many it became just that. For my father, he was destined to remain there for another full year after disembarking from that train just a little east of Dunkirk. A year, full of the most extreme dangers and horrors, serving most of that time, in a God forsaken and desolate landscape devoid of the slightest form of hospitality or comfort. Many of the towns and villages had kept their names but they no longer existed. They had been obliterated by nearly three years of constant shellfire. The roads and tracks were mere impressions in a feature-less dreary landscape, which was incapable of providing and sustaining even the most modest forms of comfort to the troops, fighting, working, or resting there. The very ground had been virtually lost and contaminated by unspoken, stinking and perilous abominations. For men to move across this region or plot it generally meant a progress, each step of which, could leave one beyond hope, trapped and sinking in an enormous midden, more evil by far even than Dartmoor's Grimpen mire, a place of much ill repute earned by its association with the monstrous hound in the Conan Doyle story. Step off the corduroy track or duct-board footway in the defended salient beyond the pitiful town of Ypres, and every effort made by your comrades to get you out, would often fail. Many are the men, who suffered the horror of being permanently stuck, some for hours or even days and nights on end, before a mental madness put paid to their torture and nightmare. This was the extreme of Rupert Brook's "some foreign field", and it took much time and hard effort to redeem and make it fit to visit, or occupy, in a civilised way again.

During my father's long stay it started badly and got worse. The maps used to send men to fight or support the attacking Battalions indicated the places by name but to locate properly only a map reference accurately observed in relation to a known location, would work in the tortured prospect of the Third Ypres battlefields of 1917. My father's Battalion's diary records the place where his presence was needed as variously N.5.c.9.6. : H.33.c.5.6. or X.16.d.8.9.etc etc. He probably knew, but did not care much, that he was helping to re-secure the vicinities he used to know as St Jean, Kitchener's wood, Clapham Junction, Frezenberg, Zonnebeck, Broodseinde and Passchendeale. It was, and still is, the strangest of ironies that this priceless real estate, rendered and ground into an open sewer, was so coveted by both sides alike.

The 33rd or lucky double three domino division with fifty others, contributed towards a series of advances the like of which had been, hitherto, unprecedented, in such bad weather and over such hostile and unforgiving terrain. The Somme was bad, this was foul. Over the months of August and September into October and November of 1917, these men sustained a painful advance against a tenacious enemy, that deserved proper recognition, far greater than "Third Ypres" or "Passchendaele" has yet been accorded. To the politicians, after the war, it did not rate even a combat clasp on the ribbon of the British War Medal. Several hundreds of thousands would have needed to be cast and perhaps that is one of the reasons they were never issued.

This remarkable force of British and Commonwealth soldiers managed to achieve the tenure of that low ridge with the tiny village of Passchendaele on its summit, by pushing the German stranglehold on the salient in front of Ypres five or six miles back to where it was, and slightly beyond, before the first gas attack in April 1915. It was a battle that was purposely fought for a number of reasons. In no particular order of importance, it was a continuation of the mighty efforts to break the German Army and substantially weaken its ability to fight. It was intended to draw the enemy's attention away from the French Army, whilst it was re-establishing proper discipline and control through its officer corps, after the mutinies. It was to recover occupied territory. It was to gain some of the higher ground forming the salient and of course break the German front and send them reeling back towards their homeland.

An analysis of the facts and figures involved, I think, demonstrates in a special way, this unique event, that has often been neglected and where the emphasis has concentrated only on the negative aspects.

Over a period totalling one hundred and three days from start to finish, eight separate battles took place involving thirty-nine of those days in very violent but not continuous fighting. The remaining sixty-three days could be described as ones of lulls or diminished activity but, hardly as "getting one's breathe back". Wherever you were in that Salient, it was definitely Sisyphean, and there was always shellfire churning up the ground on both sides of the front, day and night.

For the Entente, more than a million men were assembled and played their part, fighting a more than equally balanced foe. The defenders had the natural advantage of cover and high ground that had to be overcome, and their troop and division numbers (at least eighty) were well tipped in their favour.

On the Allied side, forty-one of the divisions used were British, and an extra infantry brigade fought in the first two engagements. The French Army deployed one Corps from their forces that were serving with the army of Belgium, holding the allied line from the north edge of the salient to the sea at Nieuwpoort. All ten divisions sent to France or Belgium from the British Commonwealth were variously deployed. Five of these came from Australia, four from Canada and one had travelled from far away New Zealand. It is a fact that nearly two-thirds of men from Britain, and all the Commonwealth contingent on the Western Front, served time in this series of battles, and that brotherhood of those trenches became a very strong bond between that exceptional band of men. Passchendaele to King George's men was as Agincourt to King Harry's.

The Battle of Pilckem started the fearful struggle on the 31st July and lasted three days. At least two hundred and sixteen thousand men from twelve British divisions and a French Army Corps on their right, where involved, and their efforts were successful along about one half of the seventeen miles of front that was assaulted. This distance included the line formed after the successful Battle of Messines that had been fought early in June, and which effectively cancelled the old salient into just a curve in the front line's northerly direction.

The powerful German Army Group, led by Crown Prince Rupprecht of Bavaria, that garrisoned this section of the Western Front, was pushed back an average of two miles from the part of the front that crossed the Menin Road just over two miles east of Ypres' Menin Gate and the Salient's British left extremity at Boesinghe. On the right of the Menin Road, virtually due south to that part of the front just east of Ploegsteert only minor gains measured in a few hundred yards were made. These types of actions set the pattern for the next three months, varying to suit the enemy's response and the weather. It was exceptionally wet for most of the time, and the land did not improve, but got progressively worse. I also think it can be reasonably stated, that despite the horrendous conditions, the resolve of the British, Commonwealth and French troops never faltered.

There was a lull of nearly two weeks, after this first engagement, waiting for the weather to change, and when it did, slightly for the better on the 16th August, a total of fourteen divisions were ordered into action and undertook three more days of savage fighting during the Battle of Langemarck. Nine fresh divisions took part, supporting the 8th, 15th, 24th, 38th and 39th divisions who had seen action in the earlier engagement. All the various units of the fourteen divisions, plus the French, were deployed along a much shorter front, less than seven miles long, having found that the enemy's resistance on the right, centred on village of Gheluvelt, very difficult, costly and needing to be tackled separately. The attacks were concentrated from the extreme left of the sector near the village of Steenstraat to just opposite St Julien, a larger village complete with a ruin that was once a pretty church.

The two substantial villages of St Julian and Langemarck and the countryside beyond were the objectives in this particular bite and hold tactic, which was designed to force the enemy backwards, taking his substantial defences in the process. Unfortunately, the reality was that, after each and every advance, achieved in the most trying conditions, even the taking of the two target villages in this instant, there were always more enemy, with in depth fortifications on the horizon, that would have to be assailed. Certainly, the invader intended to keep this land and in the two years plus of his occupation, he had made it, in many peoples' eyes, impregnable.

Despite all this, the soldiers of the Entente did advance and consolidate another two miles across this muddy and fanatically defended Flanders polder, only to wait for their next orders. Meanwhile, in the comfort of history, it is clear by careful study of the maps, that the shape and topography of the salient was gradually improving to the advantage of the forces of the Alliance.

Tanks were used in this battle, quite successfully, in terms of taking a number of dangerous pill-boxes and saving the PBI (poor bloody infantry) infinitely more casualties than when they had to attack without them. Generally most histories of these events depict the early tank as a rather sad and forlorn relic stuck in the morass of this battlefield, serving little purpose in their deployment. Of course the ground of 3rd Ypres was not ideal for the tank, (one may say, it was not ideal for anything of a military nature) but against the German fortifications, they were the best thing available and had to be tried. In fact, a very early member of the Tank Corps, cynically recorded that although his tank could not swim or even float very far, he and others did have a very successful battle against a number of difficult enemy pillboxes designed to defend and hold the villages of St Julian and Langemarck. They had quickly learnt to manoeuvre their tanks to the rear of the pill box and, depending on the gender of the tank they were using, they would send a shell or burst of machine gun fire through its only sizable aperture, the one through which the German soldiers had entered. This action neutralized any resistance and enabled the attacking infantry to occupy the position to their own advantage.

Unfortunately, the ground got worse as the "summer" progressed and after the Battle of Langemarck ended, it was not possible to use the tanks again in the salient as much as would have had a significant influence on the B.E.F.'s casualty rates. They were used, but they were really destined to make their mark elsewhere along the Western Front shortly after "3rd Ypres" had finished. Their unavoidable absence in numbers here, inevitably contributed to there being many more names added to those already too long casualty lists.

The enemy, who garrisoned the defences of 1917 saw to that. Their concrete block houses or pill boxes, which they had built and sited with such great tactical skill, could also generally withstand hits from almost any artillery piece. Without those clumsy ungainly looking tanks, they had to be taken out by the infantry. Obviously these brave men, although so few survived, had to get in much closer and the drill was then to use flame throwers, gas, grenades or bursts of fire from automatic weapons that were injected into the narrow firing slits.

Due to the nature of the war that they were fighting, mainly one of attack to recover lost ground, the British and French armies did not have any pill-boxes sited along their side of the front lines until 1918. They introduced the use of a few prefabricated ones then, but at the time of Third Ypres, "pill box" was not even a common term in the English language, nor was it much used in the military sense.

In correspondence that I have seen, the Sovereign, King George V, expressed his dislike for this word, used to describe these almost impregnable fortifications. Much valour was shown in their taking, but the King did not think it proper to use the expression "pill box" in citations that would be read out at investitures and that would appear eventually in the London Gazette. However, despite this early Royal disapproval, the name has stuck, and generally, it is now almost the only way to describe these heavily reinforced concrete emplacements. In fact today, well into the twenty-first century, I believe it is the intention of English Heritage to put "preservation orders" on many "pillboxes" that were sited in the early nineteen forties to defend this still sceptred isle.

Continuing my analysis of the battle, there were more pill-boxes to take when the Battle of Menin Road started before dawn on Thursday, the 20th September, after a lull of just over one month after the Battle of Langemarck had ended. Field Marshal Haig was raising the anti, and certainly that month of comparative inactivity was vital to put together the resources needed to push the offensive forward. As many as nineteen divisions, a third of a million men were ordered to take part during the course of this six day struggle, including five Australian divisions, brought from the Somme battle area to join the fourteen British divisions chosen to take part.

My Father was there as a member of the 33rd Division, and the account written by the officer commanding the division's, 100th Infantry Brigade's Machine Gun Company, linked with other documents of the period that I have examined, brings to life a lot of his service during these valiant though distant times.

By 1917, each of the B.E.F.'s sixty four divisions on the Western Front, as I have written before, had the same Order of Battle and, of course, the nineteen divisions destined to take part in this particular battle were no exception. Dad and each one of those eighteen thousand men with the lucky double three domino sign on their shoulders, had to be instructed, provisioned and deployed via a chain of command that started with its Divisional Commander, Major-General R.J.Pinney. He had over eighty separate entities, each needing special consideration to enable them to carry out their separate tasks. Amongst the staff helping him in these matters, it is worth mentioning, a certain Captain Bernard Law Montgomery, D.S.O. of the Royal Warwickshire Regiment. This future British Field Marshal, Montgomery of El- Alamein, who successfully fought Generalfeldmarschal Erwin Rommel and his Afrika Corps out of North Africa in the Second World War, as well as accepting the unconditional surrender of all German forces on Luneberg Heath in 1945; was learning the details of high command as one of General Pinney's three G.S.O.s (General Staff Officers). He was working with, amongst others, the A.A. & Q.M.G., the Adjutant-General's and Quartermaster General; the A.D.M.S. or Assistant Director of Medical Services; the Ditto Ordnance Services; Ditto Veterinary Service, and the Assistant Provost Marshal.

It was from this Headquarters that all orders for the 33rd Division actions were initiated. This part of the military structure, in turn received their orders through another well tried hierarchy that had been expanded very quickly since hostilities had started.

In ascending order, every four divisions, out of a total of approximately eighty, were controlled by one of twenty separate Corps establishments, and every four of these Corps H.Q's, then had one of the five Army H.Q's directing them. Finally, there was General Headquarters at the head of the British Expeditionary Force. This had been established in the small town of St Omer, near the port of Calais, in Northern France, by the first Commander in Chief of the B.E.F., Field Marshal Sir John French. It was moved in March 1916 to the larger town of Montreuil, not far from Boulogne, when Douglas Haig replaced John French as C.in C.. It was here that this G.H.Q. remained until sometime after the war ended (April 1919), with Haig in command throughout the whole period.

Of course, even the top general had his various masters in Whitehall in London, and they had to take their orders from the politicians in Parliament. This was the seat of all power and thus responsible to the nation for the conduct of the war. The system of command worked well. It still does, but with much more emphasis on combined services and, obviously, a much smaller army than the one of 1917. Those vast and unparalleled forces of the B.E.F., established in France and Belgium, during the Great War, certainly did not flounder not knowing what to do, as some would have it. In truth, it was run with precision through its hierarchy of command and finally achieved what could be described as one the greatest of all victories of British arms.

My Father and the rest of the 18th Middlesex Battalion, as per their orders, were back on the battlefields of Ypres, at the beginning of September 1917, more than two weeks before the Battle of Menin Road was due to start. They did not pass through what was left of the town they called Wipers, but having marched the thirty odd miles from the coastal dunes between Dunkirk and Nieuport, which took a couple of days; on the third day they skirted south of those awful ruins to enter the salient through the village of Vierstraat and then on to Zillebeke, quite close to the front, from which that third part of the offensive, would be launched.

As usual, my Dad never mentioned the heroic service he rendered with his pals in the British army in this most epic of First World War battles. The records indicate that he remained in this part of the Western Front until long after the various battles ended, with only very short relief periods a few miles march away in the rear areas. He never mentioned that Monty was part of his team, even when the General's name became a household word after 1942 on account of his victories in the North African Deserts and Northern Europe. To be fair, he probably did not know that himself, and I have had to research this and all the other facts in my narrative, mostly from original documents in the Nation's archives.

These documents often published as they occurred give many facts and are very reliable. Two such items, amongst many, are Divisional "Location of Units" and "Order of Battle". These important documents were

367

produced regularly in meticulous detail and fortunately kept within the records available, and in turn they have told me so much about this war, the way it was fought and how my Father was involved.

As far as this battle is concerned, I have been able to confirm his contribution to the massive efforts, first, in helping to set up the prodigious supply requirements of three hundred thousand troops attacking an enemy along a six to seven mile long front, and subsequently helping to sustain the efforts as sections of the occupied territory were recovered.

He could have told me that he and his kind, at one stage, helped to carry something like seven hundred thousand rounds of machine gun ammunition, under enemy fire, using pack mules, across the most atrocious and ill treated of landscapes, as part of the preparations for the attack. These vital supplies had to be transported to precise locations defined and marked out by the O.C. of the 100th Infantry Brigade's Machine Gun company, who had no doubt attended both the Divisional and his Brigade's plan of action conferences. Parts of this officer's comments regarding the terrain and nature of these endeavours, that were written whilst clear in his memory, reflect much that my Father could have expressed, if only I had asked, taking for granted, that his methods of expression, would not have been quite those of a lieutenant colonel. A small sample of what the colonel wrote says a lot:- "…. but it was a victory with no sweets." "The enemy gave only a crumbling mud honeycomb filled with sticky gaseous slime." "God knows what cynical wit christened those splintered stumps Inverness Copse or Sanctuary Wood, and who ordained that those treacherous heaps of fifth should be known as Stirling Castle or Northampton Farm? " "At no stage in this or any other war were the courage and endurance of man tried more highly."

My Father never said a word about his but his service continued. He was ordered to assist in the building of roads, rail-tracks and troop platforms across the salient, essential for any movement forward. He helped to repair those that were destroyed by enemy gun-fire. The battalion diaries set out the efforts made to secure areas that were recovered. This was carried out by the digging and forming of new trench lines and barbed-wire entanglements. His section, no doubt, spent long periods helping to form fresh communication trenches and quite often they had to stand to, if needed, to repel attempts by the German forces to take back the British gains.

One such note in the 18th Middlesex Battalion's records, mentions an incident, when on the first day proper of the Battle of the Menin Road, 20th September 1917, no less than eleven fierce counter-attacks were mounted against a section of higher ground, captured by the British. It recalls the determined German intention to recover every yard of retaken Belgium ground regardless of the loss of life. Despite these tactics the slow advance went on, ground was recovered and both sides shared, often very un-equally, the heavy burden of dead or wounded and shattered soldiers.

The tactics in the attacks were not set in stone. The commonly held view, that all fighting on the Western Front took the form of a heavy bombardment, followed by mass ranks of infantry, going over the top, to be slaughtered by an enemy peering over parapets and from pill boxes is hardly correct. This certainly changed after 1st July 1916 for the British, if not quite as quickly for the French. The attacks ordered by Douglas Haig and his generals were developed from lessons learnt subsequently on the Somme, then at Arras, Vimy Ridge and Messines. They still involved heavy loss of life and much pain, but this was due to the fortitude and endurance of the opponents on both sides of the trench systems. It is a truth, that when nations, choose to fight each other, their Generals cannot only fight the battles they know they can win easily.

Changes in tactics were still occurring as the Battles of 3rd Ypres progressed. One such is a good example, and explodes the myth, again, that the top brass sat in their safe and ivory towers, unaware of what was happening on the battlefield.

The German forces quickly realised that the co-ordination between the British artillery and the subsequent infantry attack was working too well when the bulk of their forces were deployed in the front line trenches. The accuracy of the guns had improved so much by this stage that it was causing heavy losses long before the infantry arrived.

As a consequence, the Germans decided to leave their front lines lightly defended, with the second and third lines housing the best of their forces ready for the counter-attack.

This ploy was not a lasting success. The British answer was to stop after taking the first line German trenches only, await the enemy to advance from his second and third lines and then rain down the wrath of his artillery, whilst they were in the open and well exposed. No, this did not prove to be the panacea to win the war but it is yet another example of how the various stages of command, did, on a whole, respond to the circumstances at a given time and adjust the tactics accordingly and as necessary.

My dear Father experienced all this and so much more as his service with the men of the 18th Middlesex took him to many of the places so synonymous with Third Ypres 1917.

He knew The Culvert on the Ypres-Menin Road, the splintered trees of Inverness Copse and Sanctuary Wood, passed Hellfire Corner more than once, and came back to the railway dugouts and Dickebusch for a cleanup and perhaps a plate of decent food and a much needed rest. The Battalion records mention so many names and map references where their men were required and I suspect that my Dad spent time in them all. Sites like Clapham Junction, Polygon Wood, Poelcappelle, Blackwatch Tower, Battersea Farm and Observatory Ridge, St Jean, Frezenberg, Broodeseinde and what was left of Passchendaele village. Most of these names of immortal memory, were tortured sites that he had first fought across in 1915, and here he was, back again, after more than two years, fighting, soldiering and serving King and country elsewhere.

The six day Battle of Menin Road, which officially ended on the 25th September 1917, was very successful by Western Front standards. Despite very hard fighting and achieving the main aims of this action, the Commander in Chief decided that it was appropriate to try to keep the enemy moving backwards to the relatively higher ground towards that summit on which the village of Passchendaele was situated.

The Battles of Polygon Wood, Broodseinde, Poelcappelle and the First Battle of Passchendaele continued straight on. The first lasting eight days, the others each of one day duration and ended on the 12th October 1917, with both sides panting for breath and less than one thousand yards or metres from where the salient stood before the withdrawal in May 1915.

Haig put sixteen divisions into the field to fight for Poloygon Wood. They were my Father's Double Three Domino division with nine others who had seen service in the previous battle plus an additional six fresh divisions making the full count. The New Zealander's, at 3rd Ypres for the first time, were part of the latter.

They, the New Zealanders, stayed on for the next one day battle for Broodseinde which was fought with thirteen divisions on the 4th October. They missed the next one day fight at Poelcappelle on the 9th October, but their close neighbours from down under, the Australian 1st and 2nd Divisions, were part of the thirteen divisions that were chosen for this action.

The advances made in the four battles that started on the 20th September went very well with, for once, help from more clement weather, in particular a drying wind. The attacking forces recovered many small village sites as well as the town of Zonnebeke followed shortly by

Broodseinde, both important locations that were heavily defended. These attacks recovered significant areas of land when judged by World War 1 standards. However, the one day engagements on the 9th and 12th October, the Battle of Poelcappelle, and the 1st Battle of Passchendaele respectively, both fought with thirteen divisions each, left the allies' line less than satisfactory.

Passchendaele and its summit was still slightly uphill, still in the enemy's possession and still nearly three thousand yards, almost two miles or three kilometres out of reach. Poelcappelle was uncompromisingly shared by both sides. The Germans knew what both were worth, and their commanders were quite determined to press their troops to fight for every centimetre of ground regardless of the cost in men's lives, which were now far exceeding those of the Alliance. Equally so, the British Command wanted and needed the very top of that hill that would allow them to look eastwards towards Brussels and the actual German frontier and added to this, following their victory at Messines in June, their salient would then not be over-looked from any direction by the enemy.

Despite the appalling weather that had set in again and the impending on-set of winter, I believe that Douglas Haig had every reason to order a final attack, although, of course, he had to ignore his own mental traumas, caused by knowing the conditions in which his men would have to fight. He decided to use twenty three divisions, nearly four hundred and fifty thousand men to climb and capture the hill, my Father being one of them.

The Commander in Chief decreed that there would be a two week building up period for this final assault and every resource available would be used. By this stage he knew that it was unlikely that the Germans would crack and allow a break out. The bite and hold progress since Messines in early June had gained much, but the actions had not developed into a war winning advance as he had hoped and planned. If the breakthrough had occurred, if it had become possible to launch those large armoured pontoons and monitors to turn his enemy's right flank, "Passchendaele" would not have happened, the war would have been over.

However, "if's" do not count in the grim job of fighting wars and the B.E.F.'s Commander knew that it was essential to take Passchendaele before winter, and before the Germans had time to stiffen their defences there any more than they were already.

Sixteen British, three Australian and four Canadian Divisions, made up the total of the twenty three divisions, that were put in the field to make the final assault before winter. The four divisions from Canada were fighting at 3rd Ypres 1917 for the first time, as were three that were from Britain. The others were veterans of this campaign having fought variously in up to two, three, four, five or six of the individual seven battles to date. In addition, it must not be forgotten that the French Corps would also provide contingents of fighting men on the extreme left once more.

The line from which the Entente's final attack would start extended from the retaken ruins of Broodseinde on their right, then turned or wound in the direction north, north west for nearly ten miles to the old front line which had been held by the French and Belgians since December 1914.

This new line now provided a much larger salient for the British, but they still needed that slightly elevated ground rising gently along this ten mile stretch for no more than two or three thousand yards, so as to be at a better advantage to the enemy.

However, only another sixteen days of savage fighting, added to the twenty three already fought, would achieve these vital prizes, and enable the Commander in Chief to put an end to the offensive that had really started when those nineteen mines exploded at Messines on the 7th June.

The Canadians finally took the ruins forming the village of Passchendaele on the 7th November, their part of the struggle lasting two days. Many other units including the 1st, 2nd and 5th Australian Divisions had tried during the preceding eleven days but were unable to hold this particular spot on the top of the hill. Nevertheless, it should never be forgotten that this village was not the only objective that had to be recovered. It was the same for all the ground that was won. The important village of Poelcapelle needed three tries, Veldhoek much the same. Many units, several miles to the left of the Passchendaele ridge and the village of Poelcappelle, advanced well over a full mile past the villages of Madonna and Veldhoek up to the heavily defended Forest of Houthulst, all the time extending their grip on this must hold salient. They entered the dangerous forest zone, but they were unable to hold the ground littered as it was with stumps or apologies for trees.

Whilst my Father's division as a whole had been taken out of the line after the Battle of Polygon Wood, 18th Middlesex with many other pioneer battalions had to remain in the expanding salient, with elements of their C.R.E. masters, to cope with essential needs required to fortify and sustain the expanding front line defences. My Dad was fighting in all these subsequent battles and well after that dust had settled.

A famous and well respected war correspondent, who was there at the time, and saw the conditions etc, reiterates a number of the views that I have expressed. He, actually witnessed the enormous numbers of enemy prisoners that were led into captivity during and after much of the fighting. He knew that the pathetic ruins of the village of Passchendaele was not the be all, or end all, of the Battles that were fought to enlarge the salient in front of Ypres. He certainly knew that these actions produced a considerable defeat that the Germans had done their uppermost to avoid and did not expect. It was not, and should not be, held as a hollow victory for the allied cause.

Three days after the capture of Passchendaele had been consolidated and further attacks from the German Eleventh Prussian Division, to recover lost ground, had ceased, Douglas Haig called a halt to the offensive.

He ordered that a new front be established and held along a line that had significantly extended the former salient. The Allied Front, under his command, would then revert to trench warfare, at least until the spring of 1918.

I believe it is worth remembering here, why there was a salient protecting the ruins of Ypres. It was, primarily, because the French and British politicians back in 1915, had ordered their military to do all in their power to hold that ground. The two governments had, in their wisdom, decided that it was essential to keep the only notable city left in Belgium unoccupied by the enemy. The place, certainly, did not count with the British Generals as one of strategic importance, a straightened front line would have been more appropriate for their purposes.

However, regardless of this, the Battles of Ypres, 1917 were over without anyone ever really knowing the actual costs, in all aspects, to both sides. Official and unofficial histories have neglected to provide accurate accounts. My searches have not revealed enough reliable data that would assist a proper audited account, whilst experts and historiographers have, either buried deep, or put their own particular incomplete spin on these events.

My incomplete records show that two British armies, with eight Corps and fifty one divisions provided the men to fight this series of eight separate battles that lasted a total of thirty-nine days over a period that started on the 31st July 1917 and finished one hundred and three days later on the 10th November 1917. A group at varying times of one million men took their share of the fight towards the enemy, whether they were in the support lines, as artillery men, medics, pioneers or engineers or at the cutting edge as infantrymen. Each and every-ones' contribution was vital and necessary. It was the latter group that took the worse casualties, although all the other units were much at risk.

A typical Infantry Brigade in 1917, consisted of four battalions of infantry, a machine gun company and a trench mortar battery and each battalion would field an average of not more than six to seven hundred men in an offensive assault. There were three infantry Brigades in a Division.

I believe these fifty one divisions, between them, secured a very good result, inflicting enormous losses on the German defenders, far in excess of their own as acknowledged by their enemy, as well as recovering not less than 39.52 square miles, or nearly 53 square miles, if the ground won in the slightly earlier battle of Messines that occurred between 6th and 10th June 1917, is included. These gains were unprecedented by Western Front standards and the Ypres Salient was now nearly four times larger than it had been since 1915.

It was the hardest battle ever fought by the British and German armies to that date, the weather creating much of the agony, but I do not believe that either of the armies involved came near to giving up, as has been suggested in some quarters and accounts. The evidence for this is not substantiated or validated.

My Father certainly did not break his contract made when he volunteered to fight for his King and Country three years earlier, nor did anyone else of the slightest significance. The million men of Passchendaele, did not falter, each acted out the "Die Hard" tradition, as my Dad had done. The men of the 33rd Division were on call for fourteen long days and nights, nearing the average of those who served in the series of actions.

The analysis also shows that the time an individual served at the front did not necessarily follow the actual time his Division was detailed for action. The 49th and 66th Divisions took part in one battle (The Battle of Poelcappelle) which lasted for one day, whilst the 37th and 39th Divisions fought in six and five battles each respectively. The 37th's battles took in thirty-three days of hard fighting, whilst the 39th took in a bare three days less than the overall period of thirty-nine battle days for the whole campaign, which actually came to an end on the 10th November 1917.

My research has indicated that an individual infantryman, attacking the enemy at some time during the eight various actions of 3rd Ypres, probably did not spend more than two to three days forcing the pace forward before being relieved at best, or at worst, being wounded or killed in action. Of course, that length of time was more than enough, but the visions of unrelenting, day after day, never ending slogging over the tortured landscape of Passchendaele is apt to be mis-leading. The soldiers of the British armies were not expected to do that, particularly during offensive operations.

An infantryman was a member of a nominal sixteen man section, four of which formed a platoon, four platoons making up a company of about two hundred men. Each of these three units having one or more officers or N.C.O.'s (non-commissioned officers) controlling their actions in a battle. There were four companies forming a infantry battalion and nominally at least four of these battalions provided the pool from which was made up the front line attacking elements. A meticulous study of each battalion's war diaries would provide the proof of my assessments.

My main interest has been my Father's contribution, which continued long after the savage fighting to recover land, try to affect a break-through, and kill Germans, had been ordered to stop by Field Marshal Haig. The 18th Middlesex men including my Dad had lots to do that cold Sunday morning after the heavy sounds of battle had faded. Unlike in most previous wars, for many there was no return to more congenial "winter quarters". There was a new front line to build and make secure amongst so many other tasks that needed attention. Any surviving wounded had to be collected, the dead had to be properly laid to rest wherever they were found; roads, tracks, trenches and command posts had to be established, with so much more, to bring some sort of order to the chaos of this awesome battle-ground that now stretched several miles deep along a new front line more than twelve miles long.

There were no fast food solutions for these hungry men, no Colonel Sander's K.F.C., Big Mac or Pizza Hut to satisfy the taste buds of this generation of unsung heroes. They were lucky to get an occasional lukewarm mug of tea and slice of bully-beef stuck between a chunk of bread, in the horrendous conditions of the 3rd Ypres battlegrounds. Certainly, it was no place for a picnic and it must have been a nightmare to just try to feed and water the thousands of men that had to continue soldiering there. Of course this was done, just as every survivor, got thanked for his efforts by a senior Commander.

After his visit however their work had to go on, the war had still to be won and I believe the general approach taken by my dear Father and the legions like him was put very succinctly in the poem titled "The Burning Question". I found it in an old copy of the "Wipers Times" dated around the same time as that battle ended. It certainly refutes the spin that the British Army was close to breaking. The whole five verses are worth a read(see appendices), but I hope just three, much longer than I usually include, will be forgiven:-

1. Three Tommies sat in a trench one day,

Discussing the war, in the usual way,

They talked of the mud, and they talked of the Hun,

Of what was to do, and what had been done,

They talked about rum, and – 'tis hard to believe—

They even found time to speak about leave,

But the point which they argued from post back to pillar

Was whether Notts County could beat Aston Villa.

++++++++++++++++++++++

3. *The earth shook and swayed, and the barrage was on*

   As they leapt o'er the top with a rush, and were gone

   Away into Hunland, through mud and through wire,

   Stabbing and dragging themselves through the mire,

   No time to heed those who are falling en route

   Till, stopped by a strong point, they lay down to shoot,

   Then through the din came a voice: "Say, Jack Miller!

   I tell yer Notts County can beat Aston Villa."

   ++++++++++++++++++++

5. *Two "Blighties", a struggle through mud to get back*

   To the old A.D.S. down a rough duck-board track,

   A hasty field dressing, a ride in a car,

   A wait in a C.C.S., then there they are:

   Packed side by side in a clean Red Cross train,

   Happy in hopes to see Blighty again,

   Still, through the bandages, muffled, "Jack Miller,

   I bet you Notts County can beat Aston Villa!"

What an Army!!

Chapter 16

Besides not being quite certain that Notts County could beat Aston Villa, no one knew that, when the Battles of Third Ypres stopped on the 10th November 1917, the Great War would end and the guns would fall silent, and the killing would stop, exactly one year later. The brutal war on the Western Front still had another full year to run and my Father, yet another year of hard soldiering, in every sense of that word.

He, his Battalion and Division, missed the Battle of Cambrai, which was fought over eighteen days from the 20th November to the 7th December 1917. It had been planned long before Third Ypres had ended. Field Marshal Haig was determined to keep as much pressure as possible on the enemy, for the reasons given previously. He ordered the use of twenty three divisions and the strongest force of tanks ever assembled, to attempt to breach a ten mile stretch of the Hindenberg Line. The experience and limited success of this new weapon in the Battles of Third Ypres and the Somme, convinced him that tanks could only have a significant effect, when operating in great numbers over land that could take their weight. Accordingly, he chose the well drained chalk downland, where the Hindenburg Line centred on the village of Ribecourt, about six miles, to the south west, from the outskirts of the large town of Cambrai.

Briefly, the initial success caused church bells to be rung in the British homeland, with the news that advances of up to six miles, across a wide front, had been achieved.

However, the premature euphoria was very short lived. The determined German counter attacks proved to be more than could be dealt with and resisted successfully and, within a few days, most of the gains were back in enemy hands. Another new weapon, whilst saving many an infantry-man's life, was proved not to be a war winner in itself.

At the same time, the war on the Eastern Front was about to conclude with a significant victory for the Germans and Austrians/Hungarians against the Russians and their Serbian allies. Brest-Litovsk, situated as part of Belarus now, but, in 1917, just another small Russian town located a short distance within the Ukrainian territory captured by the Germans, gave its name to the Treaty that was about to be negotiated between the Central Powers and the "Red" Bolsheviks led by Vladimir Lenin and Leo Trotsky. These new rulers of Russia conceded much to their enemies in this treaty, and this ultimately meant that early in 1918, the German and Austrian-Hungarian Empires would have a distinct advantage over the French, Italian and British Allies fighting or holding the line in the West. Their Russian allies had given up, accepting the harshest of terms, dictated by their enemies.

The Central Powers, also at the same time nearly repeated their stunning victory over the Bolsheviks, when they came very close to wiping out the Italian element of the Alliance. Fortunately, for the Entente, the Austrian and German considerable success took their own High Commands by surprise. Their somewhat half-hearted offensive along the River Isonzo, close to the Austrian Italian border, broke through the Italian defences like a knife through butter. The attack, which happened to be the twelfth attempt in this area, all but routed two Italian armies, advanced a good sixty miles across a very wide front and finally came within artillery range of Venice.

All this was achieved between the 24th October and 12th November 1917 and became known as the Battle of Caporetto, named after a tiny alpine village located at the centre of the initial attack. This historical site is no longer shown under that name on the average Michelin of the area, the 1917 place names have changed following the subsequent boundary adjustments ratified after the conflict.

Notwithstanding, this serious setback for the Alliance, I believe that it can be speculated, that if the German army had not had to contend with the massive drain on their resources, that had been sucked into the Battles of Third Ypres and Cambrai, they would have been able to move much stronger forces to take advantage of the debacle the Austrians had caused across the whole Italian front. These combined forces of the Central Powers would not have stopped at the reformed front along the River Piave, they would have, in all likelihood, swept Italy out of the fight altogether. It was a tragedy waiting to happen. The Italians had long been fighting a more powerful enemy and, it could have resulted in a totally different and infinitely more difficult and unfavourable treaty for the Allies, than the one that was signed in Versailles a couple of years later. With two Allied Powers gone and more than half of the French Army not obeying every order, could the forces of the British Empire hold the ring was a speculation that did not have to be answered.

Nevertheless, the un-expected defeats and massive losses in arms and men inflicted on the Italian forces required urgent help from the French and British holding the common enemy at bay in France and Flanders. Two full Corps, one British and one French, totalling more than two hundred thousand men, with all their arms and equipment, were dispatched with speed and were quickly in place, backing up their Ally, along the stabilised front behind the Piave, creating an even greater lack of reserves on the Western Front. Having so many men taken out of the roll calls of the British and French armies was to lead to all sorts of difficulties in the very near future, just as their enemy was shedding his burdens in Russia, and consequently having many divisions, previously in action there, free for service on the Western Front.

Yet a third very worrying factor for the British at the end of their third year of war, was the unrestricted U-Boat campaign, set against any ship supplying Britain's needs, regardless of the flag, under which it sailed. This policy had been launched by the German Navy at the beginning of 1917 and they certainly appeared to have the means to carry it out. The Royal Navy, up to that time, had been unable to cope fully with the large numbers of submarines operating in the vital supply lanes so essential to the British. Rationing of essentials had reached such a peak by Christmas 1917, that, if not resolved, it would not take long to become another adverse influence on the likely outcome of the war.

However, with all these woes, it would be wrong to indicate that all was doom and gloom, even for the most pessimistic of the nation. The British Army had more than held the line throughout the year on the

Western Front and had had singular success fighting for an approach to the soft under-belly of Europe from the Middle East.

General Edmund Allenby's forces were advancing to occupy large parts of the Turkish Empire in Palestine, Syria, Arabia and Persia, before attacking the Turkish home-land proper. Baghdad in Persia had been occupied earlier in the year, whilst hard fighting in October and November led to the capture of Gaza, Beersheba and on the 11ᵗʰ December, General Allenby formally accepted the surrender of Jerusalem.

The first Englishman to be offered the keys of the Holy City, by its mayor, after the Turkish and German troops had left, happened to be an army cook. He did not want them. He had turned up in the city, via the Jaffa Gate, by mistake. He had been looking for eggs to buy, for his officer's breakfast, and doggedly proceeded with his task. Patently, he did not want to stay there any longer than he had to. However, returning to his master and telling his tale, it soon led to several senior officers racing off to have a hand in this most historical event, each of them being superseded by a more senior rank, up to the Commander in Chief himself. Indeed this, was truly the start to the demise of at least one member of the Central Powers.

Just before this expected capture of Jerusalem by a Christian power, after so many centuries, on the 6ᵗʰ November 1917, Arhur Balfour, the ex Prime Minister and then Foreign Secretary, made his, still much quoted, "declaration" recognizing that Palestine was the "national home" for Jews, a people, who had been for generations dispossessed and scattered from their "promised land". It was and still is, a matter of my Father's war to end all wars, that as yet, defies a proper solution.

Maybe that cook should have taken the keys proffered by the mayor?

My Dad was too busy to contemplate these things, as were all members of his Battalion. He and 18th Middlesex would spend the whole of the next five months in and out of the line established along the Passchendaele ridge. It was to be a long, cold and hard winter followed by a very dangerous spring.

At first there was a two day break on the 16th and 17th November, spent at rest in the French town of Bailleul, sixteen miles from Passchendaele.It would have been hard enough at first, to realise that there was still a civilised world out there, not affected by the horror in which they had lived without relief for more than three months. It was here that the men of 18th Middlesex could get clean again, brush off much of the all invasive slime and mud and eat, drink and sleep as normal human beings once again. I believe, Bailleul would have been the source of many fond memories that my Father could have recounted to me, had I had the foresight to have asked him. I am sure he would have preferred to talk of the good times he had, rather than those that were about to follow.

The 18th November 1917 found him back in the Ypres salient having marched from Bailleul to a place he was getting to know quite well, namely the much fought over village of St Jean, a couple of miles east of the battered Menin Gate. Corporal Robert James Reed was destined to be in the area of the latter, plus his old friends Frezenberg, Savill Road, Zonnebeck and Passchendaele until the 18th Middlesex were relieved by the 7th Battalion Durham Light Infantry Pioneers, on 27th January 1918, a period of seven weeks and one day in all. That one day was probably Christmas Day 1917. It was their only proper break, because the Corps Commander decided to grant it as a holiday to nearly every man serving in the salient. Of course, a careful guard had to be kept up and those, given that task, had to be the exceptions.

There were certainly no "New Year" celebrations for the Sassenachs, from south of the border. Each day was hard work, and my Father's rank, meant that he was continually directing his section, often at night, on tasks allocated by his company commander. There was so much to do, and just a sample of their activities, during this seven week stint, using a single day's precise record, indicates not only my Father's, but most of this British Army's, best endeavours in Flanders' fields, most of the time being under enemy fire and taking casualties. The 14th January 1918 sets a typical verbatim example:- " 'C' Company was given a day in camp. 'A' and 'C' Companies were to have dug by night a trench leading to an O.P. near PASSCHENDAELE but owing to a fall of snow in the morning this had to be cancelled as the position would have been shown up. 'A' Company were sent out to repair six direct hits on the plank track near Devil's Crossing. 2 platoons 'B' Company continued work on "pill boxes!" Remainder of 'B' Coy and 'D' COY were employed pushing planks on tracks from KANSAS CROSS to SEINE."

Take a pick of any one of those tasks that were performed under intermittent shellfire, with that steady drip of casualties, and combine them or their likes, over periods lasting several weeks, and it is not difficult to deduce the excellent calibre of the men fighting this war for their King and Country.

The C.O. of 18th Middlesex, Lt:Col: Storr, needed the short leave that he started on the 21st January 1918, knowing that the battalion would be relieved very shortly. He left Major W.H. Coles in command to keep up their vital work, being aware that any men entitled to normal leave would get theirs when the unit was taken out of the line.

On the 27th January 1918, the 7th Battalion Durham Light Infantry Pioneers took over the battalion's duties at the front, and for the umpteenth time, my Father, now accompanied by all four companies of the 18th Middlesex Diehards, marched out of the salient in battle line or single file. They stayed in that order, as they tramped into Ypres, via the Menin Gate, and on past the ruins of the Grand Place and then on to the makeshift railway terminal, set up by the Royal Engineers, amongst the shelled ruins of that city's western outskirts..

The train waiting there was to take them to the large military camp that had been gradually built up, around the important town of St Omer, in Northern France. Wizernes, one of many small villages in the area, was where the Battalion had been ordered to detrain.

Most of the Tommies did not have any maps of Belgium or France, and still did not know where they were going until they got there. It was no exception, in this case, but having the sun on their backs in the morning, or in their eyes, towards evening, gave them a good idea that they were moving away from the Western Front's battle lines. My Dad would have known that there was every prospect for having a good clean, perhaps even a bath, maybe some Blighty leave, certainly more training and a visit from a General or two.

The three hours that it took to travel the thirty plus miles from Wipers, did not worry the men of the18th Middlesex, nor did the fact that their final destination would be just another map reference, namely F4.a.5.1., on one of the many detailed survey maps produced and used by the British Army. They most likely, would have found it hard to believe, that mainly thanks to them, ninety years later, it would be possible to take a high speed train passing quite close to the old site of their billets near Wizernes, to travel from St Pancras station in London to the Gare De Nord station in Paris in less than two hours.

There are several cemeteries and memorials maintained by the Commonwealth War Graves Commission, together with a few original features, that are now the only evidence remaining of my Father's and his pals' four week stay in this area. They have quite a lot to say.

They commemorate, amongst many things, the birth of today's Royal Air Force, that occurred there, only six weeks after my Dad left. This new and separate branch of the British armed services was established within all the other military sections, that had been built up around the town of St Omer. It was at the Aerodrome de St Omer, three miles south of the main town, that the Royal Flying Corps and Royal Naval Air Service combined to become the R.A.F. on the 1st April 1918.

My Father and his mates would have witnessed, with much interest, the intense flying activities of the early warplanes, of all types, that were coming and going from the airfield a short distance from their quarters. In the time they had been in France or Belgium, this historic site had become the main headquarters and base for yet another, rapidly developed, instrument of war. Under various names or initials, including R.F.C. and R.N.A.S. it had cut its teeth, with great distinction, along all sections of the British part of the Western Front. However, up to this time, this arm of the services had never been quite so close to these Diehards.

My Father and most men who had been in action, had witnessed various dogfights between the early planes which had been originally designed basically for reconnaissance purposes. These men in the trenches had also suffered the strain of a couple of other tactics that had been quickly developed by the pilots of friend and foe alike, that of strafing or bombing, even though in each case, little account was taken of their effect. The artillery was always more deadly. The early flying machines however were being constantly redesigned to become more efficient killers, and by the end of the third year of the war, serious bombing by both sides was causing great hurt behind the front line, as well as at the cutting edge of the Great War.

Examples of these types of attack occurred shortly before and after 18th Middlesex's stay in the St Omer area.

Military establishments including the hospitals, casualty clearing stations and aerodrome were all badly bombed by a heavy force of German raiders, which resulted not only in much damage to buildings and installations, but caused many deaths and injuries to people both military and civilian personnel alike.

So the increasing horror of total conflict continued, but for my dear father, for nearly four weeks, it could not get much better. At map reference F4.a.5.1., he was actually sleeping dry, eating proper food regularly, his tea was hot, he was not having to share a furtive drag on a soggy last woodbine, or thinking or even praying that so many life threatening whizz-bangs did not have his name on them. Anywhere had to be better than the salient and the Passchendaele ridge, and these new fangled planes would not stop him sleeping; generally, they did not fly at night.

Four weeks out of the line was not really long enough for 18th Middlesex and my Father. They and he received thanks for their endeavours and service from the Generals, who came to see them; several men were publicly decorated with their well deserved awards and some had a few days leave at home in England. I do not know for certain, if Dad, in his expression, "clicked for a Blighty Pass", I somehow expect that he did. I do know however, that he was not awarded a medal for gallantry and having got cleaned up, his days in the camp, were filled with soldiering and training with a few hours of free time each day, during which he could rest and perhaps write a brief letter to his dear wife and family.

On Wednessday 20th February 1918, my Father knew for certain that he was going back to active service in the Wipers salient. Orders posted that day set out the details of their return. He and the rest of the Battalion, fully kitted up, were required to parade in time to march the comparatively short distance to Wizernes railway station and board the train for departure by 10.15 am the next day, Thursday 21st February. These orders also included precise details for ensuring that the temporary quarters were left properly cleaned and tidy, ready for the next intake, and that all personal bedding and other general items be returned to the Quartermaster's stores, leaving their billets the same as when they found them, empty, in the time honoured way of the British Army.

The four companies of 18th Middlesex detrained at Ypres station at 1.10 pm after a slow ride lasting nearly three hours. My Dad and I wager, quite a few more, did not mind however long it took. There were not many in the battalion in a desperate hurry to resume the activities, so gratefully passed over to the 7th D.L.I.'s nearly four week ago.

At any rate they were soon back where they were most required for another indefinite period. My Father knew the way, it had been well trod by him, many times since his initial visit nearly three very long years ago.. A sacred way indeed to me, as I envisage in my mind's eye his march, as a section leader, in open order, from that make-shift station. The route took him and all the others along the main road eastwards, now flanked on both sides, only by the pulverized relics of a once proud burgh, through the ruins of the Grand Place and on from there, to exit the city, as always, via the Menin Gate and out into the salient.

The whole journey from Wizernes was really, from one map reference to another. The 1 to 20,000 Map Sheet used by the Battalion's guides, had changed for the one used in that area, and the new five figure reference I.3.c.1.3., which pin pointed their destination, indicated that it was about two and a half miles from the station in Ypres.

As these small groups followed the road that turned north-east, towards Zonnebeke and Passchendaele, instead of taking the main road to Menin, they had about a mile to go. They all hoped that the Quartermaster and cooks, already ensconced at their next base, would have a decent meal ready for them, and by the time, all four companies of the battalion had arrived, and had been allocated their various quarters, it was at least time for tea.

Nothing could have prepared them for what the Kaiser and his senior Commander, General Erich Ludendorff, were setting in store for them at this very time. Of course, it was prudent for the British to strengthen their defensives within reason, but not to make them into lasting and impregnable lines as static boundaries. The continuing brief of the Entente, depleted though it was, by the absence of the Russian Empire and the exertions of nineteen seventeen, was still to reclaim all enemy occupied territory in France and Belgium, and go on to make the German nation agree to a peace settlement, strictly on the Allies' terms.

The fresh divisions, trained and available in Britain and requested by Field Marshal Haig to make up his losses, were denied by Prime Minister Lloyd George. They would be kept in Britain. This veto, as well as leaving the British part of the Western Front insufficiently manned and protected, certainly affected the periods that my Father and his Battalion had to be deployed. The politicians, especially those charged with winning the war, when they made this denial, had taken little or no account of the fact that Germany was no longer having to fight its war on two fronts.

It would be a full calendar month from the time that my Father returned to the Ypres salient and the start of the series of attacks, often referred to as the Kaiser's Battles. It had taken the German ruler and his Generals just short of three years to launch another serious aggressive initiative against the British and Commonwealth armies on the Western Front, but what a launch it would turn out to be.

All of that time, my Father had been in the thick of the offensive activities carried out by British Army, excepting only the short, heaven sent, relief when he returned to Blighty, to recover from his wounds, or to rejoin his beloved family in their modest home in South London, for a few days leave.

It is so often the case, but a fallacy, to imply that the Western Front was a series of static trench lines that never moved from the time the race to the sea ended in October 1914, until the battles of 1918 that led finally to victory for the Allies. I believe my Dad and most of the men who fought in this most difficult of wars, would have said that this was not really correct. These men were aware that they had fought their battles throughout 1915, 1916 and 1917 for a number of important reasons; but amongst them all, it was a fact that every yard recovered from the enemy was very worthwhile, something to be pleased about, and one less yard to restore to its rightful owner. The actual tally was quite impressive and significant. Extending southwards from the much enlarged Ypres salient, it included the gains at Loos, across Vimy Ridge, on to a wide front east and south of Arras, on to the extensive gains in Picardy where British responsibility was taken over by the French army.

My Father had given his true best and now thought he was helping to secure the new gains at Passchendaele by making his contribution towards a better and more sustainable and stable front.

One might say it was all a waste of time. The German Army, with incredible speed was about to retake all the ground it had lost in Picardy and Belgium with much interest. In fact their gains were so impressive that, for a time, the Kaiser and his forces believed they had won the war and began to let it be known what their rather harsh terms would be, even to discuss an armistice.

Meanwhile, before all this happened, my Father, on Friday, 22nd February 1918, marched his section out of Middlesex Camp or map reference 1.3.c.1.3. on the trench map, to assist in the construction of a tramway that was planned to pass near Crest Farm a short distance behind the consolidated front line protecting the hard won village of Passchendaele.

The ground across the salient had not improved much, despite all the work since 18th Middlesex had left and 7th D.L.I. pioneers had taken over from them. Now that the former were back, the same difficult work went on ceaselessly. Dad and his section, after completing the tramway, went on to get their full share of moving supplies, repairing and forming other roads, footpaths and narrow gauge tracks; filling in shell craters, strengthening trenches and burying the dead. For the pioneers, this type of work went on for yet another six weeks, until the beginning of April.

My research has shown that the captured German pillboxes retained in Tyne Cot Cemetery, the largest of the Commonweath War Graves Commission's cemeteries for both world wars, had been repaired and converted from fortified blockhouses to A.D.S.'s (Advanced Dressing Stations) by the British Army after their capture in 1917. These were, and still are, situated a half a mile or so from the summit of the Passchendaele ridge and within less than two hundred yards from where Corporal R.J.Reed first joined the front back in nineteen fifteen.

My Father's unit helped to carry out this work and also had to assist with the unenviable task of interring the less fortunate casualties who did not make it. They had to be buried close by in the hastily sanctified ground, near to the A.D.S. that had been converted from the German pillboxes. Inevitably some of the dead were from the A.D.S. itself, brought in too badly wounded to survive, whilst others would have been discovered near-by having lain where they fell during earlier engagements. The C.W.G.C. records indicate that there were over three hundred and fifty burials in this place by the end of March 1918, just about the time that my Father left for the last time.

Now, that once modest, somewhat makeshift ex-military strong-point, turned icon, by a King's suggestion, has become for me, a part of yet another place, so special, as I ponder, where I am able to follow Dad's footsteps and speculate that amongst the twelve thousand soldiers at rest there now, which ones did he and his small section know and together with their Padre, reverently lay to rest.

It is yet another unanswered question, like so many, but I do know that the 5th Army's Commander visited the 18th Middlesex Battalion's camp and quarters on 27th February 1918 to express his thanks to the men working out in the difficult conditions of the salient. General Sir W.R. Birdwood, at fifty three years of age, had been recently promoted to command the 5th Army after spending most of the war with the Anzac Corps, both at Gallipoli and on the Western Front.

He was another very popular General but patently, he was not privy to the Kaiser's plans due to erupt shortly, else I believe, he would have been trying to make every effort to stand and hold the salient as it stood. The initial blow would be elsewhere and the subsequent attack in his area would outflank the British lines holding Passchendaele.

So it was that on the 21st March 1918, three fully revitalized German armies, the 2nd, 17th and 18th, started their all out attack on the 5th British Army, along a fifty to sixty mile front centred on the important town of St Quentin. It was certainly a hammer blow, on part of the front, that took the British Command by surprise and off its guard.

The German Armies had been reinforced by up to a third, by the men relieved from the Russian front. The British troops had been sent to this "quiet" sector as a relief from their exertions the previous year and they were comparatively thin on the ground and not expecting any attacks. The location was well chosen. The German aim was to drive a wedge between the French and British in Picardy, pushing the latter back to the Channel coastline with their backs to the sea and probably seeking an evacuation by the Royal Navy. This strategy, if successful, would also isolate the Allied forces in Belgium and extend their right flank from their front at Arras to unmanageable lengths and the obvious dangers of encirclement.

Regarding my Father's battalion, the fighting and retreats in Picardy were of little account according to its diary of that time. No reference is made of them.18th Middlesex were charged to continue their works of strengthening the British front line installations across the Passchendaele ridge, and this they did, until the 4th April 1918, when they were relieved by their old friends the 6th/ 7th Royal Scot Fusiliers.

Although no mention is made of the setbacks on the Somme in the diary entries, I am sure, the events, that were un-doing all the efforts of nineteen sixteen and more, were common knowledge to the troops all along the Western Front.

Regarding this, I have asked myself, how did the men in the British army, men like my Father and his brother, in every rank, take these savage and disastrous repulses and carry on serving? Not only did they continue to serve, they continued to obey their orders and put up fighting retreats, involving staggering losses, but which, in the end, prevented their enemy achieving a total victory.

I have thought that this attitude could have been an earlier and similar example of the one that later held the line during the dark days of the early nineteen forties, when Great Britain and its Commonwealth and Empire stood alone against Nazi Germany. A stubborn resolve of an island race believing in their cause, against a far more powerful Adolf Hitler, than the one who, as a corporal, had from time to time, faced my Dad over the trenches of the salient.

Maybe ...., but whatever is the true explanation, never once, during those dark times when I was young, did I get the slightest impression from the adults I knew, such as parents, relatives, teachers and shop-keepers, that the second war with Germany, could be lost.

Back in my Great War mode, I can imagine my Dad thinking, "oh well so what", "san fairy ann" or "c'est la guerre" and "it ain't my problem".

In truth, it was Field Marshal Haig's. He had to ask again for help and fresh troops from Prime Minister Lloyd George. He did and they were, again, promptly refused. It is possible that the latter wanted to keep his reserves in Britain to protect the homeland from possible invasion, although this is not the only explanation that has been expressed regarding his attitude.

Haig and his team of staff officers however, had no time to debate this to them political issue. They found it necessary only to resort to a more daring and risky strategy. In the shortest length of time they managed to pitch over two thirds of the B.E.F.'s forces against the three enemy armies, that were intent on winning the war. It is obvious that this tactic left the remainder of the British part of the Western Front inadequately defended but, when needs must, the devil rides.

As the efficient Commander he was, Haig did not leave it there. After more repeated pleas for help, he managed to persuade the French Army to throw in some of their substantial forces, in spite of its mutinous behaviour of nineteen seventeen. The poilus, and their leaders, had already agreed with their officers that they would always be prepared to fight in order to stop further encroachments of their land by the German Army. Therefore, sharing command with the British, Marshal Foch, the newly appointed French Commander in Chief, was able to quickly take over the defence of many miles on the right flank of the British forces in Picardy. It was more a shared take over than a positive separation of British and French units. The men from both armies were fighting side by side, slowing down and eventually stopping the enemy advance.

It took less than two weeks for all this to happen. The British and French Commands, working at breakneck speed, established a substantial new defensive front capable of halting the enemy and ending a possible debacle that was initially in danger of becoming a rout.

In fact, just fifteen days after the Kaiser and his Generals had started the operation, that they had named Michael, the combined British and French newly fortified line, some ninety miles in length, centred just in front of the village of Villiers Bretonneux, about ten miles short of the all important town of Amiens, effectively held firm and halted the Germans despite their repeated attempts to break through it.

However, their old friend, but much destroyed town of Albert, with its hanging Madonna, so much associated with the British efforts of 1916, was now back in German hands, as was every yard that had been so expensively   recovered in that period.

In spite of all this, by the 5th April, operation Michael came to a halt and although it was a welcome change for the two allies not to be continuously on the back foot, bearing in mind, that they had stopped their enemy's doom laden advance, there was still a lot more very bad news on its way.

For my father, his Kaiser's Battle was about to start. Although he had come out of the line in the Ypres salient a day before German offensive operations had come to a halt in front of Amiens in the south, he, as well as the High Command, were not certain of this fact. It certainly was not going to prevent him from becoming much involved. The lucky double three domino 33rd Division, which included 18th Middlesex, had been ordered to proceed west and there was a lot of marching to do. Map reference B26.c.7.2. their first destination out of the salient was just over five miles away. It was a holding area for various units on the move about a half of a mile north west of the village of Vlamertinghe.

They were not there very long. In two days, just sufficient time to properly clean up and receive replacements for missing kit, before moving southwards towards the extreme right of the Michael operations being fought by the German 17th Army. Late on Saturday evening 6th April the men of 18th Middlesex marched nearly six miles to Hopoutre, near Poperinghe to entrain for Aubigny a tiny halt on the railway line connecting St Pol and Arras.

It was towards Arras that the Kaiser and his Generals made their final efforts in operation Michael, and probably prompted the British High Command to risk taking more troops out of Belgium as reinforcements for the forty-eight divisions already holding that long line in Picardy. There was, of course, no way that Haig and his staff could have known that, at this date the offensive operation Michael was over. The German armies involved were exhausted and would need to be much reinforced before they would be able to resume their offensive. Besides, the German High Command had other fish to fry.

Regardless of this, the sixty or so miles train journey that my Father took to Aubigny was completed in time for the Diehards of the 18th Battalion to establish themselves, a four mile march away, in the village of Lattre St Quentin by the 8th April. It was a suitable location to support the front line protecting the all important city of Arras.

It turned out for my Father and the rest of the 33rd Division to be another march to the top of the hill and down again. This was not, in my opinion, unusual. Nothing is quite certain in any particular battle, or series of battles and it follows that, every senior Commander has his bad, as well as his good days. I suppose, another case of "c'est la guerre".

In this case, the Kaiser's actions determined that there was a more urgent need for my Father's services, back north. With a punishing vengeance, just as he was expecting to go into battle near Arras, what would become known as the Battles of the Lys by the British, and Operation Georgette by the Kaiser and von Ludendorff, erupted with a volcanic magnitude on Tuesday, 9th April at 4.15am.

Later that same day, my Father's battalion was ordered to move early on the 10th April back to Aubigny and hence by train to Caestre, which they had passed through two days ago. They were going back close to the southern end of the salient, still in France but with the Belgium border less than five miles to the east.

Corporal Reed could have been forgiven if he believed that it was the 2nd May 1915 all over again and a kingly cry from Harfleur was ringing in his ears:~

Once more unto the breach, dear friends, once more;

Or close the wall up with our English Dead!

Shakespeare's King Henry V.

Act III, Scene I. Line I.

Chapter 17

It was not really King Harry's exhortation that induced or encouraged my Father and the rest of the British Army to fight and stop the massive German offensive efforts, known as the Kaiser's Battles, which took place in the spring of 1918 between the 21st March and 6th June. These powerful assaults were expected to win the war for the Central Powers. They were:- in Picardy, (named by the British, First Battles of the Somme 1918, or Operation Michael by the Germans), in Flanders (Battles of the Lys or Operation Georgette), and in Champagne (Battle of the Aisne or Operation Blucher).

As far as the Tommies were concerned, it was their Commander in Chief's rallying call or special order of the day to all ranks of the British Armies in France and Belgium, on Thursday, the 11th April 1918, that settled it for them. This moving appeal, the full text of which I set out earlier, in Chapter 10, has become known as Haig's "backs to the wall" message; although it was much more than that to the men of the B.E.F. They were already fighting with their backs to the wall, long before Douglas Haig's famous appeal.

Characteristic and typical examples of the spirit and fortitude of the men of the British Army from the earliest days of the conflict existed long before his call. They can still be found scattered along the whole line of the Western Front. I will cite here, just two instances to make my point. They concern the men of one of my Father's previous battalions in which he served. This unit, the 2nd

Battalion of the Middlesex Regiment, in fact, gave their all so many times, that I sincerely believe that Dad's transfer to another battalion in July 1916, contributed much to his ultimate survival of the war.

He was with them, in my first example, when they went over the top on the Somme on the 1st July 1916 and that experience, certainly did nothing to change the quality of their gallant service. The second example, that I have chosen, occurred nearly two years later. During Operation Michael offensive on the Somme, from the 21st March 1918, this unit stood up to overwhelming odds from massed infantry, tanks, strafing aircraft and heavy artillery to buy time to form a stable line. In one day's action alone, on the 25th March, one man, Capt. A.M.Toye, won a Victoria Cross, whilst the battalion lost, during its savage resistance, the equivalent of eleven platoons, spread across its four companies, a total of more than five hundred men. As the regimental history recalls "all perished in accordance with the order of no retirement and resistance at all costs", and the battalion's O.C. ends his comments of that day, "not once had an officer to reprimand a man. The fighting spirit was perfect and worthy of the traditions of the 77th. Only at Inkerman had they fought against such odds."

Haig's special order of the day was a read out to my Dad and all the officers and men of 18th Middlesex on detraining at the town of Caestre a few miles east of Bailleul a town in northern France, close to the border with Belgium.

It followed in the same vein, as the plea made by Marshal Joffre, when he rallied the French troops in the

First Battle of the Marne in nineteen fourteen. Haig told his men the stark facts of the situation, their enemy's intentions and spoke of their fanatical losses. He praised the efforts made so far, in the brunt of the attack and promised that much more help was on the way from the French. Finally, it was a rallying cry, in which he earnestly implored his tired forces that theirs and everyone's way of life and freedom depended on their efforts and unwavering refusal to give up any more ground from then onwards.

It was the sole reason that the whole of the 33rd Division had been turned back from their approach to the front in Picardy, and were now heading the same way as my Dad.

Meanwhile, in another place, slightly earlier in April, the Kaiser and his senior adviser General von Ludendorff had reached the conclusion that, for the time being, they were unable to achieve their aims on the Somme, in front of Amiens. The German armies' supply lines there had been extended too far for their transport to be able to cope adequately and more importantly, its strength had been much depleted and now needed urgent renewal.

Both men therefore decided to up the stakes and turn their attention to the Channel ports of Dunkirk, Calais and Boulogne again, whilst also, keeping as much pressure on the front in Picardy, as was readily available. They ordered their pre-planned attempt to break through to the English Channel to start on the 9th April on a twelve mile front extending from La Bassee northwards to Armentieres with forces ten times stronger than the much weakened British and Portuguese units left in place after their comrades had been sent off to the crisis on the Somme. A second or double blow was then scheduled to start the day after the first attack against the Messines ridge at the south western end of the Ypres salient. The early spring weather had been unusually dry along the whole of both of the fronts chosen for the assaults, which was in stark contrast to that endured by the B.E.F. for much of the time they were fighting the battles of 3rdYpres. This improvement in the weather conditions also had a considerable bearing on the German High Command's decision.

A complete German Army would be used for each thrust. It was, as usual, a very well planned offensive with fresh troops and they met instant, spectacular and worrying success as far as the Allies were concerned. As well as the Channel ports, the important railway junction for the British Armies in Flanders, situated at Hazebrouck, was the first objective for General Ferdinand von Quast's 6th Army, whilst the 4th German Army under General Sixt von Arnim hoped to take Ypres early in his offensive.

Neither of these two first phase targets were ever taken, despite the overwhelming forces set to achieve them.

Why, one may ask? Was it Haig's cri de coeur?? We shall never know. Most pundits are sceptical; but we do know, that there were a lot of English dead piled up at the breaches and deserving to be still much honoured, as does their Commander, to this very day.

It is not hard to imagine the flow rate of aminohydroxphenyipropionic acid expended, as the C in C's order of the day, was read out to more than a million men on the Western Front. My Father's own adrenaline and that of all the men of his battalion would certainly have taken another leap, on being told they were needed at the unheard of French village of Meteren, just a mile or so east of Bailleul, a town they all thought to be miles from any fighting front.

They were informed, to the contrary, that this place, a mere four mile march away from Caestre, was in imminent danger from a powerful German army advancing towards them. As pioneering infantry, they were initially, required to picket the town that night and hopefully as more elements of the 33rd Division arrived, they would be relieved the next day, April 12th, to carry out their proper function. If there was still time, a new switch line trench was critically needed between map references X 23 a 8 4 and X 18 c 8 2, on Sheet 27 of the 1/10,000 trench maps that the battalion was now using. I have not studied a copy of this particular sheet mentioned in the diary, I have relied on other maps of the area for my research purposes. However, as all trench maps use the same system for map referencing, it is quite easy to use a similar 1/10,000, that I happen to have, to confidently work out the distance between the two points mentioned. It was quite a way and my Father and his section had to play their part in digging a zig zagging trench that had been planned to connect two defence systems that had been planned in a hurry at staff headquarters. Actually there were eleven hundred metres or well over two thirds of a mile between the two references; and there is little doubt that the whole battalion was needed for this vital task. This was the most efficient way to send reinforcements to the front line trenches or offer a safer means of escape and retreat in a Western Front battle. A steam powered excavator, such as one that helped to cut the Panama Canal, would have been very useful, had the enemy not been so close, whilst today's machines such as the back-actor Hymacs or J.C.B.s did not come into common use until well after the Second World War. No, this long trench had to be dug in a hurry by men with strong backs using standard issue picks and shovels.

The Generals obviously wanted to hold the lines that existed where-ever possible, but a plan B or even C had to be ready or up and coming. So it was. Another in depth defensive front was being rapidly planned by the B.E.F.'s General Headquarters in Montreuil, who were also co-ordinating the military efforts needed to check this additional offensive, using any units that were locally available to them.

In the high echelons of command, moves were also afoot, to achieve a more unified command of the Allied Armies. Most senior officers in Montreuil and the French G.H.Q. knew that in the short term, it was certain, that there would be more war-winning efforts from their main enemy. He had already beaten the Russian Empire and of course, it was logic that they would go all out in this offensive before the Americans could field their own armies against them. On this account and much to the approval of Field Marshal Douglas Haig, on the 14th April, General Ferdinand Foch, soon to become a Marshal of France, was appointed Supreme Commander of the Allied Armies in France. The most important aspect of this appointment was to improve and properly integrate the various activities of the French, British and Belgian armies on the Western Front.

Three days before this event, on the 11th April, down the vast chain of command, Corporal Robert James Reed, Middlesex Regiment knew exactly what was expected of him; his orders had been explicit. He was in charge of a sixteen man section, who were kitted up in battle order with their Short Muzzle Lee Enfield rifles with bayonets fixed. They had been posted out along the road to Bailleul, looking out for the first signs of enemy troops approaching the town of Meteren with hostile intent.

The history of "The Diehards in the Great War" published in the middle of the nineteen twenties, describes his and his battalions' duties in just eighteen words. It states that on the 11th April, "the 18th Middlesex were at Meteren where they picqueted the southern and south-eastern exits of the town."

The former of these two roads went to Doulieu, just over four miles away and then on to the large town of Estaires on the river Lys, after which the British Army Council later named this major offensive of the Germans. The road to the south-east was barely two miles from Bailleul and not much more than that, to the small town of Steenwerck. It was through this two mile stretch of the thinly defended, forty mile long, hastily formed makeshift line, that the enemy were intending to advance. It was to achieve Operation Georgette's primary objective, to seize or outflank the large and vital town of Hazebrouck. If the attack was successful it would have also outflanked the heavily fortified Forest of Nieppe, that was the final British bastion guarding that city from the south. It would have also achieved probably, the most important advance of their war, a chance to separate the British from the French.

Once again my Father was at the very heart of the cutting edge of the various actions on the Western Front, events historically of much importance, but never mentioned to the generations that followed. Perhaps it needed a Tennyson to give them the same significance that the famous charge deserved?

English dictionaries of today have changed the spelling of picquet to picket without reference to the earlier version. They define that the word can mean the same as the duty my Father was carrying out on the night of 11th April 1918, but it also has an industrial meaning as well. It can describe "an individual or group, who stand outside an establishment to make a protest and prevent or persuade others from entering." I, in turn, have conjectured the thought, "how often do those pickets of today, spare 'a thank you thought' to the picquets of 1918 and the later conflict of the second world war. These men, patently bestowed and much extended the privilege to picket to the future generations, whilst they did their stint and were prepared even to die rather than allow their enemy to pass through."

The German advance did not show up near Meteren during the night of the 11th April. That thin khaki line, four miles away, was still slowing down the enemy in field grey. The picquets of the 18th Middlesex had no occasion to set off any alarms or shots in anger, despite the on-going and unmistakeable noise of battle that seemed to them to be getting closer.

Early on the morning of the 12th the digging of the switch line became the main activity for my Father and the men of the 18th Middlesex. Whilst they had been engaged in their vital work as picquets during the night, more infantry from 100th Infantry Brigade of his 33rd Division had arrived to man the new front line trenches. Now my Father and his men were pioneers again; and he would ensure that his section's allocated target length of trench was properly dug, along the switch line that had been decided at G.H.Q. It is such an excellent example of the British army's chain of command.

The work went on all day and continued as it got dark until the men had to be rested and fed. All this time, the sounds of the advancing enemy increased, his shellfire becoming more dangerous and intense. Added to this was the sad spectacle of the remnants of the retreating forces as they were allowed to pass through the new line to get some much needed sleep or at least a brief respite and a reviving mug of char.

The first time I saw the name Meteren carved in stone was on the Ploegsteert Memorial to the missing. This impressive temple of remembrance in the classic style, guarded by two great British lions, carved by Sir Gilbert Ledward, registers 11,447 debts of gratitude that are owed to men who fought in an area of Flanders, that is not nearly as much frequented as many other more well known sites. Places such as Albert, with its basilica, whose shell-torn tower once hosted a hanging Madonna; the near-by Lochnagar crater that was created on the 1st July

1916, Vimy Ridge, Ypres and its Menin Gate, Verdun with its Mort Homme Hill and so much more. The men named here, have no known grave and most of them do not even have a standard grave-stone, inscribed with Kipling's words "Known unto God". They never received a proper burial.

Quite a number of these eleven thousand plus men, fought and died, defending or attacking the ground within a couple of miles radius of the small village of Meteren. Hence it follows, that place name is properly included amongst the other battle honours that are recorded, with eminent dedication, around the perimeter of this monument. The endless lists of names, chiselled with such care on the tablets, within the temple, include those men who were killed in action from my Dad's regiment and, more particularly from my point of view, several who were no doubt, from his own section, platoon or company and known to him personally.

The British Expeditionary Force fought four actions in all, around the vicinity of Meteren, during the Great War. In nineteen fourteen, even at that early date, it was a part of the British strategy to retain their hold on the important town of Hazebrouck and its vital rail links. This policy led to an unsuccessful defending action that saw the village over-run and lost for a short while. Even Hazebrouck fell then, but within a brief period, both places were retaken and the Germans pushed back to the line that they held until the Kaiser's battles of April nineteen eighteen.

In nineteen eighteen, it was now time for my Father to add his contribution. G.H.Q. had determined that Meteren would be the farthest that the enemy would be allowed to advance, amongst many other somewhat insignificant villages along a new system of trenches now planned to be more than fifty miles in length. This new line was linked with the old front line at Givenchy, in the south, on the extreme right for the British and where the German offensive had begun. From there it described a massive bulge north eastwards of captured land, up to twelve miles deep, that ended just east of Ypres. This line had to be held at all costs or the war could be lost.

This decision determined other actions of the High Command in the crisis, who were continually denied reinforcements from the homeland, by the politicians in Westminister. The Generals knew they did not have the capacity to hold the high ground of the Passchendaele ridge as well as ensuring that the enemy was stopped in front of Hazebrouck. These hard facts, meant that they had no alternative, but to literally remove all their men from that hallowed ridge, that had been more than sanctified, by the losses in 1917. It was a difficult decision for Haig and his army commander, General Plumer to make, but due to the acute shortage of troops, the right strategy was to shorten their lines back against Ypres, yet another vital part of their Western Front; and then use as many of the relieved units as they dared, against the might of the Georgette Offensive. Although much land in front of Wipers was lost, like the French at Verdun, that city would remain firmly in British hands.

There were no fresh divisions within the B.E.F.'s command, to deal with the critical situation on the continent. There were only those in Britain, made up of men who had finished their training and were in camps spread over many homeland counties, but kept there by their political masters. These men were being denied to Field Marshal Haig, who desperately needed them for his armies that were fighting on the only fronts that would eventually determine the outcome of this lengthy conflict. Holding back these reinforcements from the hard pressed Tommies and valiant Commonwealth veterans was yet another culpable act that would have, no doubt, led to endangering these men even more, bearing in mind the modicum of support that the French and Belgian forces were able to provide.

The quickly dug defences, just to the west of Meteren, part of that new British line, were being defended by men of the 33rd Division, including my Father's battalion, obeying the order to hold their ground at all costs. The Germans never got farther west than this point in nineteen eighteen, although it was a tough fight.

My Dad's section was still pioneering on the 13th April, when they, as all of 18th Middlesex, were ordered to pick up their arms and make up the numbers in the front line as fighting infantry. The enemy had advanced to this new line, from which there was to be no retreat. He and the rest of his battalion, stayed in this mode for the next eight days until they were finally relieved on the 21st of that month.

As a corporal, my Father would have been trained to use the now ubiquitous Lewis machine gun, amongst a number of other army skills, learnt during his time on active service. It was a fact that he had become a hardened veteran, with nearly three years of active service on the Western Front, that had certainly honed his prowess as a soldier.

These skills of soldiering would have certainly helped to keep him alive, although I suspect providence also had everything to do with it. It is also a positive fact that he would have taken the lead as his small section, one of so many, who faced the German forces set against them. They were in action seeing off men in field grey with deadly fire from their Lewis guns, rifles and grenades for what must have seemed an eternity. It was actually from that Saturday morning on the 13th April 1918 until they were relieved on Tuesday, the16th. They were then sent to hold a line elsewhere, where they were repelling or killing the attacking German forces right up to their own barbed wire.

It was trench warfare at its worst. Mowing down men in the open with small arms and artillery fire until there were none left standing. Taking their own casualties, mostly from shellfire, while waiting for the next attack, a true pandemonium from hell.

The contemporary records describe their actions as fighting their enemy to a standstill, and after doing much the same whilst in the line at the Mont de Cats at the elevation of 518 feet(158m) for ten more days up to the 29th April, when their efforts and the Battle of the Lys came to an end.

It was the same apt description given for all the B.E.F.'s units who fought in the three week battle that ended on the 29th April. My father was there along its front line area for all but three days rest in the town of

419

Staple between the 21ˢᵗ and 23ʳᵈ of that month. I have included his abortive journey time to Lattre St Quentin, as justification of his virtual, as well as actual presence in the last great German offensive to take place in Flanders during the Great War.

At the end of their first unexpected three day stint as infantry, 18ᵗʰ Middlesex had lost eleven men killed and forty nine men wounded, according to one published tally. I believe up to the 29ᵗʰ April, many more names were added. One or two of the eleven have a proper grave, the remainder are remembered, by name only, at Ploegsteert.

The small village of Staple situated ten miles west of Meteren and less than four from Hazebrouck, is where, I believe, my Dad may have met or at least seen the French Prime Minister "Tiger" Clemenceau. The battalion diary records that this well liked Frenchman inspected elements of the 33ʳᵈ Division, including the C.O., two officers and fifty other ranks from the 18ᵗʰ Middlesex battalion. This French leader certainly knew the importance of what was happening as the B.E.F. strove to hold the line and whittle down the strength of the German Armies on his homeland. He knew, more than ever before, the essential need for the French and British armies to fight together as co-operating forces, in order to beat their common enemy. He knew also that the Americans would eventually come to believe in that necessity as well.

Accordingly, it was not a bad idea to make himself known and visible, all seventy seven years and snowy white bristling moustacheos of him, to as many men as possible from his staunchest ally. It was also a good memory for these men themselves, at least someone appreciated what they were doing, unlike the politicians in Westminster.

The three days, out of the range of most artillery and all small arms fire, was a much needed blessing that could not last. There were not enough of them to be spared from the front for longer. The whole battalion returned on the 24th April and remained east of Meteren serving on a long section of line that was finally putting a stop to any further gains. Much had been lost including the strategic heights of Mount Kemmel, the fair town of Bailleul, now a smoking, shell cratered ruin, Hill 60 and of course Messines and its famous and much disputed ridge.

In spite of these and many more losses, what mattered most to the Allied cause was that the German Armies, apropos both of their major offensives, Michael and Georgette, had failed to reach and occupy any of their essential targets. Checking their advance was all important; taking the breath out of the enemy's armies was equally important. The British Command, now masters in a war of attrition, knew that their enemy had suffered irreplaceable losses of men killed and wounded from which it would be difficult to fully recover. How long it would take to win could not be speculated, the Germans still had more divisions on the Western Front than the Allies. Nevertheless, on the result of these two major battles they also knew that the Kaiser's and General Ludendorff's balance sheet was very much in the red. It was not enough, however, to make them sue for peace yet, and my Father had to remain in Flanders dodging bullets and shrapnel for the rest of spring nineteen eighteen and well into summer until his services were required again on the Somme.

This period was certainly not without its perils. Helping to build sounder, in depth, trench lines was dangerous and that is what the British Army was doing all along the revised fronts both in Picardy and Flanders. The thin red line of old, that often kept an empire in check, could never hold back the might of an industrial power, if set against it. The generals, particularly the Commander in Chief, had learnt that lesson, but it was still one that the politicians again tried to duck, even now, after four years of a land war that had been fought on an unprecedented scale.

Corporal Reed had seen the same need, time and again and here he was ordering his small unit to strengthen this trench's parapet or parados, dig out a collapsed section of that trench, put aside the bodies of the half buried casualties for the padre's attention; increase the depth of picket and barbed-wire barriers stretching into what might become another part of no-mans-land. There was so much to do. Early in May every man in the battalion was used to dig another switch line near the French Belgian border by the village of Abeele, less than two miles south west of Poperinghe.

General Sir Herbert Plumer the 2nd Army's commander wanted an in-depth line to defend a virtual, thus far and no further position, knowing full well that all would be lost should it fall. He was fifty seven years old when the war started, an accomplished soldier, with the rank of a Lieutenant General. He was promoted to General to become Commander of the 2nd Army in nineteen fifteen and like his C in C, Field Marshal Haig, he was much loved by his men. They had been through so much together. He had persistently led them well, when either holding the line, advancing, or as now in retreat, or at least on the back foot. Later in the year, he would receive the ultimate accolade and the satisfaction of seeing his men crossing the River Rhine in order to occupy the city of Cologne as part of the British zone of those parts of Germany, that were to be controlled by the Allies.

Much earlier in May 1918, the General and his staff, shared the dangers of a new, awkwardly shaped, much longer front, caused by the land grab of the German offensive Georgette. He had to see for himself the new lie of the land that only a short time ago, had been a holding area well away from any fighting. He wanted to see the quality and demeanour of his troops who had survived the fighting retreat and, importantly, if the advantages gained by the enemy could be diminished in any way. Of course, the ability to defend and hold the new line, currently being improved and strengthened in depth, also had to be reviewed. The vital work, being carried out by the pioneer battalions of every division in the area, more than justified his attention and in my Dad's battalion's case, no doubt an appreciated "thank you" from their most senior commander, short of the Field Marshal himself, on that 20th day of May.

Spurred on by all this, the hard work went on endlessly, just as the shelling and aerial strafing took their toll. The German infantry were taking a breather, but the other arms like artillery and the odd probe across the wire, continued to make everyone's life a lottery. More so, my father must have thought, as his unit returned to the awful area a few miles west, behind the tortured town of Wipers, yet again on the 7th June 1918.

Unlike the men of the Infantry Brigades, who generally spent three or four days in the front line trenches and then a similar time slightly further back in the reserve lines; repeating this process for two or three weeks, until they were ultimately marched out on relief to a depot well away from the battle area. That system of service, had been my father's lot, whilst he was part of the 3rd and 2nd Middlesex battalions serving in the 85th and 23th Infantry Brigades respectively. In the pioneering units it could be all so different. Such was the case after the offensive Georgette had been fought to a standstill. The pioneers of 18th Middlesex were continuously in this battle area, throughout the months of May, June, July and well into August 1918, when they were given orders to move with the rest of the 33rd Division down to their other "favourite" the dear old Somme.

All this time, in the middle months of nineteen eighteen, my Father's battalion were just one of many similar units, that were engaged, strengthening, or expanding, a new line of fortifications from which there would be no retreat. However, as this time passed and there was little aggressive activity from the German armies, their work took on a new significance. Instead of waiting for their enemy to attack, G.H.Q. now working with the new Supreme Commander, Marshal Foch, decided that the reinforcements that had been building up to protect the line, should be used instead for yet another Allied offensive.

My father observed all this from his vantage point at the five figure map reference on Trench Sheet number 28, G.12.b.6.3. or a very precise location just outside the small village of Brandhoek. This particular camp was a very convenient base for his battalion's final ten week stay in Flanders. It was situated between Pop and Wipers, to him, Poperinghe and Ypres to the map-makers and just a few miles march to the new lines, that they were helping to construct in as much haste as possible.

This section of new front was over four miles in length. It lay in a fairly straight line, from just west of Zillebeke, Hill 60 and Vourmezeele. Places that were once, not so long ago, to the likes of my Father and his type, since the 2nd Ypres battles of 1915, at least two or three miles behind the British front and comparatively safe. As a result of the Kaiser's offensive Georgette, these same places were now alive with enemy troops and their forward artillery. The fighting may have subsided, but it was still very dangerous to be there. For friend and foe, regardless of which side you were on, life was very cheap and even to show oneself for the shortest of time, was to invite instant death from a sniper's bullet.

It was during this period that my Father with the rest of the battalion became acquainted with men from the last Ally to join their cause. Quite contrary to a number of histories, soldiers from the United States did join English troops on the battlefields. The American forces under General John Pershing did diversify and did not only take responsibility for sections of the Western Front exclusively under their sole command. An instance, as far as my Father was concerned, occurred whilst his battalion were working on the in depth, colour coded, Blue, Green and Yellow lines of the new front, in the months of late June, July and August nineteen eighteen.

The first indication of this, that I have seen, records that Pioneer Platoons of the 119th and 120th American Infantry Regiments were attached to various Companies of the 18th Middlesex, to take instructions and then eventually take over the works required on that Green line. Later during August, when things were improving all round for the Allied cause, their unfinished tasks were handed over to officers of the 2nd Battalion, 105th American Regiment of Engineers. Obviously these events were not the only ones, regarding the mixing of the armies. It had happened earlier between the French, British and Commonwealth, Italian and Portuguese forces. Now with the whole group of Allies, their combined efforts, were being co-ordinated under Marshal Foch and it was the right and proper action to take.

The American regiments that certainly served with my Father's 33rd Division were also the very first units to enter Belgium in the Great War. During July and early August 1918, they made good use of all the various training facilities of the British Army in Flanders, to learn the unique skills of trench life and warfare. They needed to acquire quickly a technical knowledge relating to the use of gas, automatic weapons, bayonet fighting, defensive systems as well as modes of attack. Finally, selected officers and other ranks were put in the front line trenches alongside their British counterparts to experience the actual cutting edge. By all accounts they were quick to learn and come the 15th August 1918, under various orders from the hierarchy of the American Expeditionary

Forces in France, they relieved the British 33rd Division to enable them to serve elsewhere. Those orders included Field Order No 14 of the U.S.119th Infantry Regiment and this particular order, in fact, relieved the Lucky Three Domino (33rd) Division's 98th Infantry Brigade and of course, included the part of the front in which the 18th Die-Hards were serving.

For Corporal Robert James Reed it meant that he would be on the move again. Although he was still unaware of it, as was everyone else up to Marshal Foch himself, the final phase of this dreadful war had started. He was seeing Flanders for the last time and at last there were others to take up the quarrel that he and his like had borne so long.

A week earlier, on the 8th August 1918, whilst he and all those serving near Ypres were bracing themselves for another imminent German offensive, the British and French Armies in Picardy struck back with a massive assault of their own. Since then the blood soaked land of the Somme was being re-taken again with a vengeance and the lucky Double Three Domino Division was required to add their prowess to the Entente's efforts yet again. It was the start of another epic journey for my Father.

On the 17th August, after a day's rest at his camp near Brandhoek, a light railway took him with the rest of his battalion to a hutted camp near Proven to get tidied up, re-kitted as necessary, and spend a final last couple of days in Belgium.

He was back in France by the 19th to spend
another week training in more carefree circumstances
than had been his lot in the salient. The battalion was
billeted about seven miles north of St Omer, well out of
the range and noise of battle, but, all the same, subjected
to the ever increasing risks of air attack. By 1918 strafing
and bombing attacks were occurring almost daily in the
garrisoned areas around this important town of the Pas de
Calais Department. They had become common-place and
procedures to take shelter or man defences etc, became
routine and second nature to the men and women on the
ground. The art of self preservation is quickly heeded and
learnt in circumstances such as these and, due to much
political inaptitude, on a much greater and riskier scale,
these same lessons had to quickly comprehended by the
populations of great cities like Warsaw, London and
Berlin just two generations later.

Compared with life at the front, my Father would
have taken these events in his stride. Equally in truth, it
can be said, that he felt and did much the same in
nineteen forty and forty-one, during the long months of
the London blitz and finally in Hitler's "V" rockets attack
of nineteen forty-four. Currently, he was well aware, that
he and his unit would be in much greater jeopardy when
they were back in Picardy.

This fact made all the training worthwhile; and for
me, the fitness of the men of the British Army or B.E.F.
never cease to amaze. This was especially pertinent after I
had analysed, just one man's activities, over the next ten
weeks. The final ten weeks of the Great War, when the
German army gave up virtually all their gains in La Belle
France and much of Belgium, all under a force of arms

that did not achieve an actual rout nor even a stand-off. It was, in fact, for the German army, a continuous fighting retreat and of giving up territory, that would most likely have gone on well into the German homeland, had their Government, not requested and then signed up to an armistice that accepted the terms of the Allies in full.

My Dad's own perpetual movement, in the course of ten consecutive weeks, took him to at least twenty two separate towns or villages spread across a landscape some ninety miles in distance from where he started. He and his platoon would have marched all of that distance in a fighting advance that involved being in action in three of the eleven principal battles named by the Battle Nomenclature Committee under their heading "The Advance to Victory".

The Battles of the Hindenburg Line were the first of these three. They were fought for nearly a month from 12th September until the 9th October across a front more than fifty miles in length, stretching from just east of the city of Arras to five miles east of Soissons on the River Aisne. In that time these awesome barriers, that were unlike any previous defensive wire and trench system of the Great War, had been completely breached and the opposing armies were engaging in the open countryside as the Germans tried to establish a stable line. It was the toughest and longest of the eleven engagements of the advance to victory. It took forty-three divisions or two thirds of the B.E.F.'s fighting forces, with help from the French to interdict these formidable deep barriers intended to retain an irresistible, Teutonic hold on substantial parts of mainland France. The actions took place over a very wide front with my Father's unit

429

providing close pioneering support to the attacking infantry brigades until the end of September.

By that time the Double Three Domino Division was ordered further to the south to join the forces advancing towards the French, Belgian border and the town of Mons that was situated just a few miles beyond.

Whilst the British Armies' onward thrusts were virtually continuous, the enemy was not giving up without a fight on any particular part of the Western front, both in France and Belgium. He was disputing ownership, particularly, as far as my Father was concerned, at the rivers that crossed the British lines of attack beyond the Somme area of Picardy. The final battles my Father had to fight were both named after rivers and in both he assisted in their bridging.

It was quite hard for me to find the River Selle on my much used copy of Michelin 236, France Nord, Flandre-Artois Picardie, but the locations of the British and Commonwealth Wargrave cemeteries poignantly mark his progress. It was a journey that I followed, so many years after him, that enabled me to understand so vividly his massive contribution to this war. What efforts were needed to keep an enemy on a retreat such as this, over so many weeks, is difficult to describe. The journey has to be made to appreciate, that in spite of the political inaptitude, what awesome power the British Army Command staff had managed to put together, against the much larger German forces, to achieve such a change of fortune in such a short time. It certainly, yet again, puts into context, the nonsense fabrications propounded by the "lions led by donkeys" brigade.

The Battle of the Selle started seven days after the Battles of the Hindenberg Line ended. It was fought over nine days between the 17th and 25th October. It proved to be the last major operation the Lucky Three Domino Division had to fight in the Great War. The division was one of twenty-four that were engaged in just a few miles of an extremely wide front of advance, that was now over three hundred miles in length and which had left the old Western Front trench systems well behind them. The allies were moving eastwards with a vengeance, persistently pushing the Germans back towards their homeland.

The British had started their offensives in July and now the whole five armies of the B.E.F. were simultaneously engaging enemy forces and causing him to retreat along about half of that line. On their immediate right the French also had eight of their armies moving eastwards along a similar length. They had held the British flank initially and done their bit helping to destroy the fearsome and formidable Hindenberg Line. Finally, on the River Meuse the American First Army had been deployed, since the 22nd September, with the French Second and were advancing towards Sedan on the River Meuse. Further south the American Second Army attacked on the 12th October making good progress recovering ground between Verdun and Metz until the armistice had been signed.

I believe during this time, the feelings of my Father and most of his contemporaries in the B.E.F. must have been very mixed. On one hand it was good to be moving and liberating parts of France on a scale that had not been experienced previously. On the other hand, it was also very apparent, that every unit attacking the enemy was suffering massive casualties. If anything, they were even more excessive than they were on those days on the Somme in nineteen sixteen and at Arras and Passchendaele a year later. Whilst there was a lot of new blood in the divisions, there were still many veterans like my father, who had seen it all before, although there had never been quite so much sustained movement as there was now. They were not totally confident, but maybe, dare they think, they were at last on their way home. They certainly still had plenty to do.

The small section commanded by Corporal Reed, besides helping with the approaches to a small tank bridge the Divisional Engineers had built over the River Selle, they were continually stiffening temporary trench lines and pickets as the infantry advanced, as well as repairing the shell damaged tracks along which the tanks advanced. There was certainly not much time for rest and although the brigades of infantry were relieved after the Battle of the Selle ended, the divisional support units were required to stay in the field. My Dad's small team, with the whole of the 18th Middlesex Battalion were attached to the 38th (Welsh) Division, to fight the very last battle of the Great War. Just another accolade he left unsaid.

The River Sambre is a much broader affair than the River Selle and its crossing at the small town of Berlaimont, ten miles from the Belgium border, was where my Father ended his part in the Great War. The river gives its name to this very last assault ordered by

Field Marshal Haig from his General Head Quarters in Montreuil. It is called the "Battle of the Sambre" and was ordered to start on the 4th November 1918 and as events turned out, officially ended after the peace treaty was signed in Versailles in 1919. It had been put on hold at 11 o'clock on the 11th day of November and never resumed.

In the seven days before the somewhat unexpected cease-fire of the 11th there was constant activity for the seventeen divisions involved. At least half of these divisions were keeping the utmost pressure on the German forces that still had elements of resistance to be over-come. As along the remainder of the Western Front from Belgium to Lorraine the German Armies did not give up ground on their own account. They too were continually engaged in serious fighting that forced them to retreat.

In this constant bustle, I have little doubt that the men of 18th Middlesex did not have sufficient time to change their div: signs from the double three domino to a very fierce looking Dragon of Wales in red on a black square; the 38th Division's own emblem. They were part of this advance and provided considerable help in constructing a pontoon bridge across the River Sambre in the town of Berlaimont just two days into the battle on th 6th November. Their approach was through of Forest of Mormal that lay several miles in depth across their part of the direction of the advance.

My wife and I stopped in this forest, that did not seem to have significantly changed since my Dad had been there. Whilst enjoying our al-fresco lunch, just off the same track he had marched along, we savoured the feel of the final part of my Father's long and dangerous journey. We had now travelled the alpha and omega of his path of glory. Like I knew, his boots had felt those cobbles in the Grand Place in Ypres, so they had been worn down as he had proceeded towards that river crossing in Berlaimont, that he was helping to construct.

It was certainly a significant contribution, surely more worthy than which he and the legions like him, were, in reality, to receive. In their jargon, sweet Fanny Adams.

In his poem "They"[*], Siegfried Sassoon set it right:-

'.............. for they'll have fought

In a just cause: they lead the last attack

On Anti-Christ; their comrades' blood has bought

New right to breed an honourable race,

They have challenged Death and dared him face to face.'

Epilogue

The Kaiser Wilhelm who had fundamentally engineered the start of the Great War, which led to Great Britain's involvement, caused by his invasion of Belgium, abdicated on the 10th November 1918 and went to live in Holland. Germany and Prussia then became a Republic and its political representatives requested an armistice, agreed its terms and signed the document on the 11th November 1918.

Oberschutze or Lance-Corporal Adolf Hitler on that same date, was recovering in a hospital in Berlin, after being temporarily blinded by mustard gas on the 14th October 1918 in Flanders. He was vowing to himself, to un-do any armistice or capitulation and lead Germany back to be the most dominant force in Europe, if not the world, under his leadership.

Corporal Robert James Reed wanted to get back to his family which he expected should now be able to live in a peaceful, free, benevolent and sympathetic society. It was for this that the war had been fought. He certainly knew only too well that only freedom and decency had been disputed and he had contributed much to that victory.

He believed that it had been worth volunteering and giving four years and four-three days of his life to King and Country as a soldier in the British Army. He had been on active service on the Western Front in France or Belgium, for all but fifteen of a total of two hundred and fifteen weeks. The history of the Middlesex Regiment's service in this theatre of war records that its various battalions were involved in sixty two named separate actions. My Dad had seen service and had been in peril, in at least thirty of these, between May 1915 and November 1918. He had seen action whilst serving, first in the 3rd Battalion for six months, then eight months with the 2nd Battalion, followed by nearly two and a half years with the 18th. He had suffered wounds twice on the battlefield. The first during the Battle of Loos during nineteen fifteen, then on the Somme on the 1st July 1916.

Even in the fifteen weeks that he had to remain in France after the armistice, whilst his battalion was helping to clear the battlefields of the Somme etc, his unit recorded a number of deaths and injuries caused by unexploded bombs, shells and other dangerous items, dumped as the opponents went back and forth across this most unfortunate terrain.

The brief particulars of his service, issued by The War Office after the Munich crisis of nineteen thirty-eight, shows that his service with the colours ended on the 26th February 1919. It conveniently matches an entry in the 18th Middlesex Battalion's diary that states that twenty six O.R's were demobilized on that day. My Father was one of them. It was a long day for him that started in the small village of Aumale to the west of Amiens, where one of many holding camps was situated to accommodate the thousands of soldiers awaiting their last trip back to Blighty. Corporal Reed had been there for three weeks and very glad that his turn had come at last.

The long journey to the demob centre situated on Wimbledon Common was in four legs. Aumale to Dieppe, a sea crossing to Newhaven or Folkestone, a train journey to a London Terminal and hence back to the suburbs and Wimbledon Common, where his service with the colours ended. He was not however, quite finished with the army. Since he had volunteered, a law had been passed that required him to serve another year, on unpaid reserve, which would make his discharge from the army absolute on the 31st March 1920.

Hereafter his story should have been one of joy, happiness and prosperity. But for all his "san fairy ann" attitude, it proved to be almost the exact opposite. The politicians failed their conquering heroes once the peace treaty had been signed.

The nineteen twenties and most of the thirties saw the land fit for heroes rife with hardship, hunger and unemployment, for a great many of the men who had served their country so well. Means testing was exercised by authorities to a degree that shamed or degraded many of those who were more than justified to apply just for basic necessities. Many men, often veterans, seeking a job, were told that they were too old, at forty, to work. There were far too many decorated ex-service men with fine records, selling matches on the streets. The victors of the war to end wars had become worse off than the vanquished.

The conditions set out in the Treaty of Versailles in 1919 were, to a large extent, disregarded both by the same Corporal who had opposed my Father across the trenches of the Western Front, as well as its authors from the winning alliance. Well thought out, and legally binding safeguards, designed by the same treaty, to prevent rearmament by Germany, were allowed to lapse by negligent political leaders who must, or should have known, of the dangers.

As a consequence, Germany and the German nation simply thrived under its new totalitarian leadership and became the most powerful and domineering nation on earth again. This went on whilst their resident Jews and many other foreign nationals went to the wall, without any significant outcry from their fellow Europeans.

These extraordinary circumstances continued, or got worse throughout the remainder of the thirties. The disregard of Versailles and a number of other complicated pacts and alliances, finally led to a British Prime Minister, to his abiding shame going, cap in hand, to the Fuhrer, to bargain away, for the latter's worthless scrap of paper promising peace in our time; the new European State of Czechoslovakia, which had been created by the victors of World War 1.

It was not enough, as tragically only a few less gullible politicians knew at that time; Herr Hitler wanted more. He also felt certain he could take it. The Polish people would be his next victim. However, this brutal attack did cause Britain and its old friend France, to declare war on the nation they had forced to capitulate, just two decades previously. The two Allies went to a war, with Britain totally unprepared and France relatively the same, against a nation known to have the most powerful forces to pitch against them.

My Father did not volunteer his service a second time. He may have thought, Parliament, totally unprepared for the fight, declaring war on a bullying and militarily superior nation once and then overcoming that disadvantage eventually at enormous cost and suffering was acceptable in one lifetime. Doing the same thing twice within twenty-five years; were they careless or did they intend to lose?

That is my speculation of course. It was more likely that he felt he was too old to join the army again. In any case he had to endure another six years of total war as a civilian, with his second family, consisting of his new wife, three boys at school and two young daughters, the youngest, a mere babe in arms. He bore it with the same fortitude as he had done as the characteristic British Tommy twenty years earlier.

The initial shock of watching his previous adversary getting off to such a flying start by conquering all that mattered in mainland Europe in a few short months perhaps made him think, "good job Kaiser Bill never promoted him." It became less obvious after his clash with the R.A.F. over Britain to secure mastership of its airspace, although he and his wife were made to suffer eight-teen months of separation from their three boys. It turned out to be a good decision. During that time he, his wife and their two young girls were bombed out of their homes twice, and great swathes of London and other major towns were reduced to rubble in the Blitz, defined in the dictionary as "the systematic night-time bombing of the British in 1940-41 by the German Luftwaffe".

The German failure to press Britain into submission whilst fighting the war alone, led to the Fuhrer's attack on Soviet Russia in June 1941, despite an understanding and non-aggression pact agreed with Russia in September 1939. This, and a concentration on British interests in North Africa and its possessions east of Suez enabled my Father, in August 1941, to unite the whole of his family back in his new accommodation, still in war scarred Wimbledon, but a slightly larger rented house.

The rest of his war was spent repairing bomb damaged houses, very often repeating the same process more than once. It was called first-aid repairs, as no serious rebuilding could be undertaken.

Finally, despite the fact that parts of mainland Europe were at last being liberated, in the fifth year of his second war, his long term adversary managed to blow out the doors and windows of his family's house yet again. One of Adolf Hitler's V. weapons also brought parts of his ceilings crashing down. A couple of large patches landed on the top of the family shelter he had erected in one of his ground floor living rooms, where his loved ones were trying to rest or feel more secure.

This second close call for him and his family, that was just one incident of a lengthy, full scale assault, aimed at the British and Empires' capital city in 1944. It prompted my Father and Mother to send their youngest three children to a safer place in the country. They remained there until the end of the war, which came shortly after the Fuhrer shot himself at the end of April 1945.

The incident map for the Borough of Wimbledon 1939 to 1945, shows how Hitler's armed forces caused damage to every home in his Borough. The town, noted for its tennis championships, was deliberately attacked by high explosive, oil, petrol and clusters of incendiary bombs, dropped from aircraft, as well as many unguided flying bombs that happened to switch off their engines over the town. Many of its people were killed or injured. Even its famous windmill on the common, used by Baden-Powell, whilst writing "Scouting for Boys", did not escape the attacks, although the bombs and incendiaries dropped there were badly aimed. The first bombs were dropped on the 16th August 1940 and the last, four years later on the 28th August 1944.

This date really brought my Father's dangerous and diverse experiences with a hostile Germany to a close. It had affected most of his life since the day he volunteered to fight for his country early in January 1915, until he celebrated, with me, cheering his King, who was waving to him and many others from the balcony of Buckingham Palace on V.E. day 1945. His Majesty too had seen service in the war to end wars, and then had to lead an empire against an evil regime which had been allowed to become, an unbridled bully.

Epilogue

Appendices

Photographs, War Office Records

and

Other Documents of Interest

The author's father Robert James Reed, on right, with an unknown friend, somewhere in the area of the Somme battle-front, Northern France during the period between August 1916 to December 1918, serving with the 18th Battalion of the Middlesex Regiment.

The author's father, James Robert Reed and unknown friend, somewhere in the area of the Somme battle-front, Northern France, during the period between August 1915 to December 1918.

"It's a long way to Tipperary"
by
J.C. Dollman
(1851 – 1934)

A captivating image, considered to epitomise the soldiers of the Great War. (picture first published 1915)

Tipperary.
"It's a long, long way to Tipperary."
From the painting by J.C. Dollman R.I.

445

COL. F. H. FAIRTLOUGH, Royal West Surrey Regt. A Deputy Lieutenant for Surrey.

LT.-COL. H. C. SMITH, Hampshire Regt. Served in the Nile Expedition.

LT.-COL. A. L. ANDERSON, Bhopal Infantry. He was killed in action.

COLONEL A. P. BIRCHALL, Canadian Infantry. He was killed at Ypres.

COLONEL E. H. MONTRESSOR, Royal Sussex Regiment. Killed Battle of the Aisne.

COL. SIR E. R. BRADFORD, Bart., Seaforth Highlanders.

COL. C. S. CHAPLIN, King's Royal Rifles. Killed August, 1915.

COLONEL R. J. MARKER, D.S.O., Coldstream Guards. Died of wounds at Boulogne.

LT.-COL. E. R. A. SHEARMAN, 10th Hussars. Fatally wounded near Ypres.

LT.-COL. R. ALEXANDER, Rifle Brigade. Had distinguished South African record.

LT.-COL. E. W. R. STEPHENSON. 3rd Middlesex Regiment.

LT.-COL. HON. P. C. EVANS-FREKE, Leicester Yeomanry. Secretary of the Cottesmore Hunt.

LT.-COL. A. FRASER, Cameron Highlanders. He rejoined from the Territorial Reserve.

MAJOR HON. SIR S. McDONNELL, Cameron Highlanders.

LT.-COL. W. T. GAISFORD. Fell while leading a charge.

LT.-COL. W. M. BLISS, Cameronians. Fell in action at Neuve Chapelle.

Photographs of just 16 Battalion Commanders of the 150+ Killed in Action during the 1st Year of the War. In addition to Lt-Col.E.W.R.Stephenson (3rd row 3rd left) the Middlesex Regiment lost 2 more of its Battalion Commanders during this period. They were B.E.Ward killed at Neuve Chapelle and G.H.Neale killed at Loos.

Instructions regarding War Diaries and Intelligence Summaries are contained in F. S. Regs., Part II. and the Staff Manual respectively. Title pages will be prepared in manuscript.

WAR DIARY
or
INTELLIGENCE SUMMARY
(Erase heading not required.)

Army Form C.2...

Hour, Date, Place	Summary of Events and Information	Remarks and references to Appe...
May 1st Trenches	*[handwritten entry, largely illegible]*	
" 2nd Trenches	*[handwritten entry, largely illegible]*	
" 3rd Trenches	*[handwritten entry, largely illegible]*	

A page from the War Diaries of the 3rd Battalion, Middlesex Regiment for the 1st-3rd May 1915, recording my Father's arrival in the trenches of the Western Front on the 2nd May, during the Battle of St. Julien which was the second of four battles which made up the of the Battles of Ypres, 1915, (2nd Ypres). (Last sentence for 2nd May: 'Draft of 1 officer and 30 men arrived'...

DEBT OF HONOUR REGISTER

In Memory of

JOHN KIPLING

Lieutenant
2nd Bn., Irish Guards

who died on
Monday 27 September 1915 . Age 18 .

Additional Information:	Only son of Rudyard and Carrie Kipling, of Batemans, Burwash, Sussex.
Cemetery:	ST. MARY'S A.D.S. CEMETERY, HAISNESPas de Calais, France
Grave or Reference Panel Number:	VII. D. 2.
Location:	St Mary's cemetery is located in the vicinity of Haisnes which lies between the towns of Lens and La Bassee in the Pas-de-Calais. Although the Cemetery lies in open farmland, there are neighbouring towns of Vermelles, Loos-en-Gohelle and Hulluch. The Cemetery can be reached from the D947, Lens to La Bassee road, and a CWGC signpost is visible on this road. The Cemetery is to be found on the D39, Hulluch to Vermelles road.
Historical Information:	The village was reached, or nearly reached, by the 9th (Scottish) and 7th Divisions on the 25th September, 1915, the first day of the Battle of Loos; and parts of the commune were the scene of desperate fighting in the Actions of the Hohenzollern Redoubt (13th-15th October, 1915). No further advance was made in this sector until October, 1918, when the enemy withdrew his line. "St. Mary's Advanced Dressing Station" was established, during the Battle of Loos, and the cemetery named from it is at the same place. The cemetery was made after the Armistice, by the concentration of graves from the battlefield of Loos; the great majority of the graves are those of men who fell in September and October, 1915. There are now nearly 2,000, 1914-18 war casualties commemorated in this cemetery. Of these, over two-thirds are unidentified and Special Memorials are erected to 23 soldiers from the United Kingdom, known or believed to be buried among them.

In Memory of

The Hon. FERGUS BOWES-LYON

Captain
6th Bn., Black Watch (Royal Highlanders)

who died on
Monday 27 September 1915 . Age 26 .

Son of 14th Earl of Strathmore and Kinghorne, of Glamis Castle, Forfarshire; husband of Lady Christian Bowes-Lyon (now Lady Christian Martin). Educated at Eton. Previously served with 2nd Bn. in India.
LOOS MEMORIALPas de Calais, France
Panel 78 to 83

DEBT OF HONOUR REGISTER

In Memory of

ARTHUR WICKENS

Private
G/7448
3rd Bn., Middlesex Regiment

who died on
Monday 27 September 1915 .

LOOS MEMORIALPas de Calais, France
Panel 99 to 101

Loos-en-Gohelle is a village about 5 kilometres north-west of Lens. The Loos Memorial forms the side and back of Dud Corner Cemetery where over 1,700 officers and men are buried, the great majority of whom fell in the Battle of Loos. Dud Corner Cemetery, which stands almost on the site of a German strong point, the Lens Road Redoubt, captured by the 15th (Scottish) Division on the first day of the battle, is located about 1 kilometre west of the village, on the N43, the main Lens to Bethune road. The Loos Memorial commemorates over 20,000 officers and men who fell in the area from the River Lys to the old southern boundary of the First Army, east and west of Grenay, and who have no known grave. It covers the period from the first day of the Battle of Loos to the date of the Armistice. On either side of the cemetery is a wall 15 feet high, to which are fixed tablets on which are carved the names of those commemorated. At the back are four small circular courts, open to the sky, in which the lines of tablets are continued, and between these courts are three semicircular walls or apses, two of which carry tablets, while on the centre apse is erected the Cross of Sacrifice.

HERBERT STANDERWICK

Private
G/7449
3rd Bn., Middlesex Regiment

who died on
Monday 27 September 1915 .

LOOS MEMORIALPas de Calais, France
Panel 99 to 101

GEORGE EDWARD KEARLEY

Private
G/7465
3rd Bn., Middlesex Regiment

who died on
Monday 27 September 1915 . Age 22 .

Son of Elizabeth Emily Kearley, of 55, Burlington Rd., Fulham, London, and the late Joseph Kearley.
LOOS MEMORIALPas de Calais, France
Panel 99 to 101

Just five of the names on the Debt of Honour for the Battle of Loos, 27th September 1915.

A small sample of Men from the Middlesex Regiment as listed chronologically by their Regimental Numbers in the Medal Rolls for the British War and Victory Medals 1914/1918 and their survival rate.

G7447 Private Stevens, Gilbert Thomas. 3rd and 18th Battalion (Sergeant) Killed in Action (KiA.)--19-4-18.

G7448	"	Wickens, Arthur.	3rd Battalion.	KiA.--27-9-15.
G7449	"	Standerwick, Herbert.	3rd Battalion.	KiA.--27.9.15.
G7450	"	Munday, William Edward.	3rd Battalion.	Survived.
G7451	"	Carter, Harry Hezekiah.	3rd and 20th Battalion. Survived.	
G7452	"	Shepherd, Harold.	3rd Battalion.	Survived.
G7453	"	Kerby, Alfred Henry.	2nd Battalion.	KiA.--14-3-15.
G7455	"	Blunt, Fredrick Frank.	3rd Battalion.	KiA.--13-5-15.
G7456	"	Jupp, William.	3rd Battalion.	KiA.--8-5-15.
G7457	"	Uren, William.	3rd Battalion.	Survived.
G7458	"	Reed, Robert James.	3rd, 2nd and 18th Battalion. Survived.	
G7459	"	King, Charles.	3rd Battalion.	Survived.
G7461	"	Collins, Frank.	1st, 12th, 11th and 7th Battalion. KiA.--3-5-17.	
G7462	"	Tween, Charles Henry.	3rd Battalion.	KiA.--13-5-15.
G7465	"	Kearley, George Edward.	3rd Battalion.	KiA.--27-9-15.
G7466	"	Buck, James Thomas.	2nd Battalion.	KiA.--14-3-15.
G7467	"	Blomfield, Albert Edward.	2nd Battalion.	KiA.-- 1-7-16.
G7468	"	Walters, Frederick.	3rd Battalion.	KiA.-- 14-3-15.
G7469	"	Cross, Henry.	3rd Battalion.	KiA.--28-7-15.
G7470	"	Meager, Henry Albert.	4th Battalion.	KiA.--29-9-15.
G7471	"	Skinner, Henry Josiah.	2nd Battalion.	KiA.--1-7-16.

Of these 21 men who volunteered and joined the Regiment early in January 1915,

15 were Killed in Action (11 in 1915, 2 in 1916, 1 in 1917, 1 in 1918),

the 6 others were wounded in action at least once.

THE WAR OFFICE,
RECORDS SECTION,
ARNSIDE STREET,
WALWORTH,
S.E.17.

Reference No. *Tams Jost 1321*

SIR,

          With reference to your application dated *26th October* *12 NOV 1938*

for the replacement of your Discharge Certificate, I am directed to furnish,

from the records of the Department, the following particulars of the service

of No. *7058 L/Corporal Robert James Reed*

          The Middlesex Regiment

Enlisted *16th January 1915*

Discharged *3rd March 1920*

Cause of Discharge *Demobilization*

Para 392 (xxvi) K.R.

Service with the Colours *15.1.1915 to 26.2.1919*

Character *Very Good*

Medals, etc. *1914/15 Star*

British War + Victory Medals

Age on enlistment *24 Years 7 months*

          I am, Sir,

          Your obedient Servant,

To: *Mr R J Reed*   *L.V. Summer*

              Officer-in-Charge Records.

**War Office Record Discharge Certificate
for Robert James Reed, 12th November 1938**

Site of the cabbage patch alongside the railway embankment and ditch that was once a trench and part of the old front line visited by the author and his family more than seventy years after his Father was there.

The Burning Question

Three Tommies sat in a trench one day,

Discussing the war, in the usual way,

They talked of the mud, and they talked of the Hun,

Of what was to do, and what had been done,

They talked about rum, and - 'tis hard to believe -

They even found time to speak about leave.

But the point which they argued from post back to pillar,

Was whether Notts County could beat Aston Villa.

The night sped away, and zero drew nigh,

Equipment made ready, all lips getting dry,

And watches consulted with each passing minute

Till five more to go, then 'twould find them all in it;

The word came along down the line to "get ready!"

The sergeants admonishing all to keep steady,

But out rang a voice getting shriller and shriller:

"I tell yer Notts County can beat Aston Villa!"

The Earth shook and swayed, and the barrage was on

As they leapt o'er the top with a rush and were gone

Away into Hunland, through mud and through wire,

Stabbing and dragging themselves through the mire,

No time to heed those who are falling en route

Till, stopped by a strong point, they lay down to shoot,

Then, through the din came a voice: "Say, Jack Miller!

I tell yer Notts County can beat Aston Villa!"

The strong point has gone, and forward they press

Towards their objective, in numbers grown less

They reach it at last, and prepare to resist

The counter-attack which will come through the mist

Of the rain falling steadily; dig and hang on,

The word for support back to H.Q. has gone,

The air, charge with moment, grows stiller and stiller -

"Notts County's no earthly beside Aston Villa."

Two "Blighties", a struggle through mud to get back

To the old A.D.S. down a rough duck-board track,

A hasty field dressing, a ride in a car,

A wait in a C.C.S., then there they are:

Packed side by side in a clean Red Cross train,

Happy in hopes to see Blighty again,

Still, through the bandages, muffled, "Jack Miller,

I bet you Notts County can beat Aston Villa!"

Major Battles of the Western Front
1914 – 1918

Major Battles in which British, Empire and Commonwealth Forces were engaged on the Western Front in France and Belgium 1914-1918, and indicating the Divisions that were involved.

Date:	Name of Battle:	No of Divisions:	Type of Battle:	No. of Days The Battle Lasted:
1914.				
	Retreat from Mons.			
23-24 Aug.	Battle of Mons.	(4)1,2,3,5.+Cavalry.	Holding action.	2.
26 Aug,	Battle of Le Cateau	(3)3,4,5.+Cav:	" "	1.
	Advance to the Aisne.			
7-10 Sept.	Battle of the Marne.	(5)1,2,3,4,5.+Cav:	Defensive & Offensive.	4.
12-15 "	Battle of the Aisne	(5)1,2,3,4,5.+Cav:	Offensive & Stalemate.	4.
	1st Battles of Ypres.			
21-24 Oct.	Battle of Langemarck.	(3)1,2,7.+Cav:	Defensive	4.
29-31 "	Battle of Ghelvelt.	(3)1,2,7.+Cav:	"	3.
11 Nov.	Battle of Nonne Bosschen.	(3)1,2,3.+Cav:	"	1
1915.				
10-13 Mar.	Battle of Neuve Chapelle.	(4)7,8+Lahore & Meerut.	Offensive.	4.
	2nd Battles of Ypres.			
22-23 Apr.	Battle of Gravenstafel.	(3)27,28.+1Canadian	Defensive.	2.
24Apr-4 May.	Battle of St Julien.	(6)4,27,28,50.+Cav: +1Canadian+Lahore.	"	11
8-13 May.	Battle of Frezenberg.	(4)4,27,28,50.+2Cav:	"	6.
24-25 May.	Battle of Bellewarde.	(4)4,27,28,50.+2Cav:	"	2.
15-25 May.	Battle of Festubert.	(7)2,7,47,51+Lahore, +Meerut+1Canadian.	Offensive.	11.
25 Sep-8 Oct.	Battle of Loos.	(14)1,2,7,9,12,15,19, 21,24,28,47.+Cav: + Guards Div:+ + Meerut.	"	15.

Date:	Name of Battle:	No of Divisions:	Type of Battle:	No. of Days the Battle Lasted:
1916.				
2-13 Jun	Battle of Mount Sorrel,	(4)20.+3Canadian.	"	12.
	Battles of the Somme.			
1-13 Jul:	Battle of Albert.	(28)1,3,4,7,8,9,12,17, 18,19,20,21,23,25,29, 30,31,32,33,34,35, 36,37,38.46,48,49,56.	Offensive	13.
14-17 Jul:	Battle of Bazentin.	(13)1,3,7,9,18,21,23,25, 32,33,34,48,49.	"	4.
20-25 Jul:	Attacks on High Wood.	(5)5,7,19,33,51.	"	6.
15Jul-3Sept:	Battle of Deville Wood.	(7)2,3,7,9,14,20,24.	"	51.
23Jul-3Sep:	Battle of Pozieres.	(12)1,12,15,19,23,25,34, 48,49. +3 Australian.	"	43.
3-6Sep:	Battle of Guillemont.	(6)5,7,16,20,24,55.	"	4.
9Sep:	Battle of Ginchy.	(3)16,55,56.	"	1.
15-22 Sep:	Battle of Flers-Courcelette.	(20)1,5,6,11,14,15,20,21, 23,41,47,49,50,53,56, +Guards Div:+N.Z.Div: +3Canadian Divs:+1 Cav: +2 Indian Cav:	"	8.
25-28 Sep:	Battle of Morval.	(11)1,5,6,20,21,23,50,55, 56,+Guards Div: +N.Z.Div:	"	4.
26-28 Sep:	Battle of Thiepval.	(6)11,18,39.+3 Canadian Divs:	"	3.
1-18 Oct:	Battle of Le Transloy.	(18)4,6,9,12,15,20,21,23, 30,41,47,50,56,+N.Z.Div: +4 Canadian Divs:	"	18.
1 Oct-11 Nov:	Battle of the Ancre Heights.	(8)18,19,25,39,+4 Canadian Divs:	"	42.
13-18 Nov:	Battle of the Ancre.	(12)2,3,18,19,31,32,37,39, 48,51,63,+1 Canadian Div:	"	6

Date:	Name of Battle:	No of Divisions:	Type of Battle:	No. of Days the Battle Lasted:
1917.				
	The Battles of Arras.			

9-14 Apr:	Battle of Vimy.	(6)5,24,+4Canadian Divs:	Offensive.	6.
9-14 Apr:	1st Battle of the Scarpe.	(19)2,3,4,9,12,14,15,21, 29,30,34,37,50,51, 56,+3 Canadian Divs:	"	6.
23-24 Apr:	2nd Battle of the Scarpe.	(12)5,15,17,29,30,33,37, 50,51,63,+2 Canadian Divs:	"	2.
28-29 Apr:	Battle ofArleux.	(8)2,3,12,34,37,63, + 2 Canadian Divs:	"	2.
3-4 May.	3rd Battle of the Scarpe.	(14)2,3,4,5,9,12,14,18, 21,31,56,+ 3Canadian Divs:	"	2.
3-17 May.	Battle of Bullecourt.	(6)7,58,62,+ 3 Australian Divs:	"	15.
13-14 May.	Action at Roeux.	(4)3,12,17,51.	"	2.
28 Jun.	-------------------------- Action at Oppy Wood.	(2)5,31.	"	1.
7-14 Jun.	Battle of Messines.	(12)11,16,19,23,24,25, 36,41,47,+2 Australian Divs:+1 NZ Div:	"	8.
	Battles of Ypres, 1917. (3rd Ypres).			
	----------------			
31 Jul- 2 Aug.	Battle of Pilckem.	(12)8,15,18,24,25,30,38, 39,41,51,55,+ Guards Div:	"	3.
16-18 Aug.	Battle of Langemarck.	(14)8.11.14,15,16,20,24, 29,36,38,39,48,56,61.	"	3.
20-25 Sep.	Battle of Menin Road.	(19)3,9,19,20,23,29,33, 37,39,41,51,55,58,59, +Guards Div:+ 1 Aus, 2 Aus, 4 Aus, 5 Aus	"	6.
26Sep: -3 Oct:	Battle of Polygon Wood.	(16)3,5,7,19,21,23,33, 37,39,50,+ + NZ Div: 1 Aus, 2 Aus, 3 Aus, 4 Aus, 5 Aus	Offensive.	8.
4 Oct:	Battle of Broodseinde.	(13)4,5,7,11,19,21,29, 37,48,+ +1 NZ Div: 1 Aus, 2 Aus, 3 Aus	"	1.
9 Oct:	Battle of Poelcappelle.	(13)4,5,7,11,19,29,37, 48,49,66,+Guards Div: + 1 Aus, 2 Aus	"	1.

Date:	Name of Battle:	No of Divisions:	Type of Battle:	No. of Days the Battle Lasted:
1917 Cont'd				
12 Oct:	1st Battle of Passchendaele.	(13)4,9,14,17,18,19,23, 37,+Guards Div:+ NZ Div:+3 Aus, 4 Aus, 5 Aus	"	1.
26 Oct- 10 Nov:	2nd Battle of Passchendaele.	(23)1,5,7,14,17,18,19, 21,23,35,37,39,50,57, 58,63,+ 1 Can, 2 Can, 3 Can, 4 Can, 1 Aus, 2 Aus, 5 Aus	"	16.
20 Nov: - 7 Dec:	Battle of Cambrai.	(19)2,3,6,9,12,20,21,29, 36,40,47,51,55,56, 59, 61,62,63,+ Guards Div:+ 4 Cavalry Brigs: of Tanks.	"	18.
1918.				
	German Offensive in Picardy. ------------------			
21 Mar- 5 Apr.	First Battles of the Somme.	(45)2,3,4,6,8,9,12,14,15, 16,17,18,19,20,21,24,25, 30,31,32,34,35,36,37,39, 40,41,42,47,50,51,56,58, 59,61,62,63,66,+Guards Div:+ 1Can:Div:+4Aus: +NZ Div:+3 Cavalry Brigs:	Major Retreat & Consolidate & hold.	16.
	German Offensive in Flanders. ------------------			
9-29 Apr.	Battles of the Lys.	(24)1,3,4,5,6,9,19,21,25,29, 30,31,33,34,36,39,40,49, 50,51,55,59,61,+1Aus:Div:	"	21.
1918 Cont'd.	German Offensive in Champagne. ------------------			
27 May- 6 Jun.	Battle of the Aisne 1918.	(5)8,19,21,25,50.	Retreat & Consolidate.	11.
	The Advance to Victory. ------------------------------			
20 Jul- 2 Aug.	Battles of the Marne 1918.	(4)15,34,51,62.	Offensive.	14.
8-11 Aug.	Battle of Amiens.	(15)12,17,18,32,47,58, +4 Can:Divs:+5 Aus: +3 Cavalry Brigs:	"	4.
21 Aug- 3 Sep.	Second Battles of the Somme.	(26)2,3,5,12,17,18,21,32, 37,38,42,47,52,56,58, 59,62,63,74,+Guards Div:+5 Aus:Divs:+NZ Div:	"	14.
18 Aug- 6 Sep.	Advance in Flanders.	(15)4,6,9,19,29,30,31,34, 36,40,41,46,59,61,74.	"	20.
26 Aug- 3 Sep.	Second Battles of Arras.	(13)1,4,8,11,51,52,56,57, 63,+4 Can:Divs:	"	9.

Date:	Name of Battle:	No of Divisions:	Type of Battle:	No. of Days the Battle Lasted:
1918 Cont'd	The Advance to Victory. Cont'd			
12 Sep-9 Oct.	Battles of the Hindenburg Line.	(39)1,2,3,4,5,6,11,12,17, 18,21,24,25,32,33,37, 38,42,46,50,52,56,57, 58,62,63,66,74,+Guards, +4 Can:+5Aus:+NZ Divs: +/Cavalry Brigs:	"	29.
28 Sep-2 Oct.	Battle of Ypres,1918. (4th Ypres)	(10)9,14,29,30,31,34,35, 36,40,41.	"	5.
14-19 Oct.	Battle of Courtra.	(8)9,14,29,30,34,35,36, 41.	"	6.
17-25 Oct.	Battle of the Selle.	(24)1,2,3,4,5,6,17,18,19, 21,25,33,37,38,42,46, 49,50,51,61,62,66, +Guards Div:+NZ Div:	"	9.
1-2 Nov.	Battle of Valenciennes.	(7)4,19,24,49,61,+ 2 Can: Divs:	Offensive.	2.
4 Nov.	Battle of the Sambre.	(16)1,11,17,18,19,24,25, 32,37,38,50,56,62, +Guards,1Can:,1NZ: Divs:	"	1.

459

Summary

1. Great Britain declared war on Germany 11pm 4th August 1914.
2. British troops in action on the Western Front for the first time 23rd August1914.
3. Armistice signed 5am 11th November 1918.
4. Hostilities cease 11am 11th November 1918.
5. Peace declared at the signing of the Treaty of Versailles in Paris 28th June 1919.
6. 60 Divisions fought in the major engagements scheduled above consisting of:-

in 1914.	in 1915.	in 1916.	in 1917	in 1918.
6 British.	17 British.	44 British.	49 British.	50 British.
+ Cavalry.	+ Cavalry	+ Cavalry.	+ Cavalry.	+Cavalry.
	2 Indian.	2 Indian.	4 Canadian.	4 Canadian.
	1 Canadian.	4 Canadian.	5 Australian.	5 Australian.
		3 Australian.	1 New Zeal'd	1 New Zeal'd

Totals:

6.in 1914.	20.in 1915.	53.in 1916.	59.in 1917.	60. in 1918.

Index

Mentioned Names

Mentioned Battles

Mentioned Locations

Index

Mentioned Units